D1329577

DATE DUE

THE STORY OF THE
Initial Teaching Alphabet

Sir James Pitman, K.B.E.

THE STORY OF THE
Initial Teaching Alphabet

by
MAURICE HARRISON

Director of Education in the
County Borough of Oldham, England

PITMAN PUBLISHING CORPORATION
NEW YORK   TORONTO   LONDON

First published 1964
Reprinted with minor corrections 1965

PITMAN PUBLISHING CORPORATION
20 East 46th Street, New York 17, New York

Associated Companies
SIR ISAAC PITMAN & SONS LTD.
Pitman House, Parker Street, Kingsway, London, W.C.2
The Pitman Press, Bath
Pitman House, Bouverie Street, Carlton, Melbourne
22-25 Beckett's Buildings, President Street, Johannesburg

PITMAN MEDICAL PUBLISHING COMPANY LTD.
46 Charlotte Street, London, W.1

SIR ISAAC PITMAN & SONS (CANADA) LTD.
(Incorporating the Commercial Text Book Company)
Pitman House, 381-383 Church Street, Toronto

Printed in Great Britain by
WESTERN PRINTING SERVICES LTD., BRISTOL
F5—(G. 3570)

PREFACE

Many people from all parts of the world have written to Oldham since 1961 for information about the teaching of reading through Pitman's Initial Teaching Alphabet and thousands have visited our schools to see the children at work. I have tried to answer all the letters and now in response to many requests I have put into book form the whole story of this revolution in teaching method. Part I shows why the existing alphabet and spelling cause extreme difficulty to children (and others) in the early stages of learning. Part II tells of the efforts to develop the new approach, including earlier experiments in the U.S.A. and Britain, with reports of the teachers of those times, and compares what is known about learning to read languages in which spelling difficulties are fewer. Part III tells what has happened in Oldham schools between 1961 and 1964, with figures and statistics, teachers' reports and examples of children's written work. This part of the story covers the teaching of infant beginners and the teaching of backward readers of all ages from infancy to adulthood. It also explains how to write and read with the new alphabet.

I thank all those teachers who have supplied me with information. Only their readiness to replace much that they had long been accustomed to and to think afresh made the work in schools possible. I admire them for their vocational interest as well as express my gratitude for the reports and records which they have made available. Recognition must be made of the very important part played by the Oldham Education Committee, whose far-sighted attitude that expenditure on books was worth while if children might benefit, made possible the development of the work without financial worries. In fact, additional expenditure was not heavy but the Committee could not know this when they gave their unstinting approval for the experiment to be undertaken. Among those who helped me to find or corroborate references are Mrs. Mary Abercrombie of Edinburgh, Mr. J. Carter, Director of the Oldham Public Libraries, Dr. Godfrey Dewey of the Lake Placid Club Education Foundation, New York, Miss P. M. Downie, Chief Librarian of the Ministry of Education, Mr. K. C. Elkins of the Harvard College Library, Professor W. Haas of the Department of General Linguistics in Manchester University and Mr. R. Hall of the John Rylands Library, Manchester. To all of them I offer my grateful thanks.

I must acknowledge my particular indebtedness to Sir James Pitman who has helped me throughout and especially for his detailed advice on the use of the Initial Teaching Alphabet.

AUTHOR'S NOTE

The following abbreviations are used in the text:

i.t.a.   Initial Teaching Alphabet. This is the name of the new alphabet, the use of which is described. Sometimes when the context requires, the letters refer to the alphabet and to its associated consistent spelling system.

a.r.   Augmented Roman alphabet. This is the earlier name originally applied to i.t.a.

t.o.   Traditional orthography is the term applied to our normal everyday print and spelling.

I.Q.   Intelligence Quotient. Put in simple terms this is the ratio between the ability of a child shown by standardized tests and his chronological age. A child who possesses the general ability expected normally at his age is said to have an I.Q. of 100. An I.Q. of 90 indicates that a child of 10 years has the ability expected at 9 years of age, a child of 5 the ability expected at $4\frac{1}{2}$. An I.Q. of 110 indicates that a child is abler than average by one-tenth in terms of chronological age.

C.A.   Chronological Age. Actual age in years and months.

R.A.   Reading Age. This age shown by standardized texts is the age at which a given standard of reading skill is nowadays normally expected.

Comp. A.   Comprehension Age. This is the age at which a given power to understand reading material is normally expected. We can all read mechanically before we clearly understand, either because our reading is hesitant and occupies our minds to such a degree that the thread of the context of what we read is lost or because we do not understand the connotation or follow the argument of what we read. A Comprehension Test attempts to evaluate understanding apart from mere ability to read.

R.Q.   Reading Quotient. The ratio between the reading ability of a child and his chronological age. As with I.Q., the possession of normal ability is indicated by an R.Q. of 100.

CONTENTS

ILLUSTRATIONS

ILLUSTRATIONS IN TEXT

TABLES AND GRAPHS

ix

GRAPH

Part I

I

Introductory

In the beginning was the Word.

St. John

THE NEW METHOD of teaching reading is to start with books which are rationally spelt, that is, books in which certain definite spelling rules are used consistently throughout. The learner who has once learnt these rules is never confused. He cannot, for example, meet on one page this sentence, *They lead the way*, and on the next page, *They weigh the lead*. The beginner has enough to do in breaking a code which is absolutely simple and straightforward. The whole idea of a code of letters to be changed into sounds is new to him and the letters themselves are all new, as new as would be ἄγγελος (which is simply *angel* (*os*) as written in Greek) to most readers of English. Imagine being confronted with a book full of strange characters when you have not even developed the habit of reading and do not yet know that reading can be enjoyable and useful. Then imagine your confusion and possible ultimate frustration, if the rules for sounding the letters frequently altered, and you were only five years old.

Educationists have developed all sorts of methods in an attempt to overcome these difficulties, but the sad fact remains that many people grow up unable to read with ease and pleasure and even less able to write. In trying different methods, except for the rare experiments described in this book, nobody has hitherto simplified the spelling for the beginner, despite the fact that there is good reason to think that spelling vagaries may be the most difficult obstacle of all in the way of gaining reading confidence.

The dedicated men who first urged this approach to the teaching of reading were spelling reformers. The aim of this book is not to advocate spelling reform, although the author has long believed in its desirability. This book is about the use of consistent spelling as an initial medium intended only to introduce beginners to the reading

and writing of normally printed English. The simple spelling and the Initial Teaching Alphabet are to be cast aside as soon as skill and confidence in reading are established.

No history of the events which have culminated in the present amazing success of the Initial Teaching Alphabet in schools would, however, be complete, nor indeed would the causes of that success be fully comprehended, without knowing the story of the spelling reformers. That is why this book, particularly in its earlier part, is largely about them and relates their arguments, aims and experiments. Their story deserves to be told, if for no other reason, because, whether we sympathize with them or feel strongly antagonistic to spelling reform, we must admire their sincerity, courage and foresight in promoting a cause, which has produced from one of the main planks of their platform something of great educational value. By following their arguments we can see what difficulties have been removed from the path of the beginner and so analyse the reasons for the success of the new teaching approach. This in turn will help teachers in testing different ways of using the system in the classroom. The accounts of the school experiments of the past are particularly valuable, not only because they are not commonly known, but also because one sees similar results appearing at long intervals of time in widely different conditions and with entirely different teachers.

The spelling reformers perhaps wanted to do too much, but their main aim was always to make learning to read easier for little children. Today, the would-be reformers and the educationists who are not concerned at all with spelling reform have joined forces. Spelling reform for its own sake is no longer the aim. The one concern is to teach the ordinary reading and writing of English as we know it today.

The story from the first efforts to rationalize English spelling to the results in teaching reading today is a continuous one. Like so many great social developments it starts with the efforts of a devoted minority, meeting failure and disbelief, and ends in outstanding success in at least one particular field. The story will be read for different purposes. Most readers will be mainly concerned with what is happening in schools now, what the new alphabet is, how it is used. This is told in Part III. The writer hopes that those who are deeply interested will want to know how it all came about: it is not a bolt from the blue but a development more than a century old. The history of this development is mainly related in Part II.

The reasons for the success of the new teaching can only be properly understood if one has some knowledge of what is wrong (at least from the learner's viewpoint) with spelling as we know it. Part I discusses this and the teacher who wishes to apply the new teaching system with complete understanding of the principles which lie behind it should benefit by reading this first part. The story has been told in historical sequence because that seems the correct approach for a comprehensive understanding of the whole. References and reports are put in the appendixes at the back of the book in order not to obtrude on the text, but the attention of the serious student is directed to them and in particular to the detailed reports made by teachers who attempted a similar approach more than forty years ago.

II

The Inconsistency of English Spelling

> Our absence of any authority with such a function as the reviewing of our
> spelling, and the making of it rational, is well known. Englishmen generally
> profess to be proud of it. I am myself disposed to think that a Royal Com-
> mission might with advantage be charged with the task of reviewing our
> present spelling, of pointing out anomalies in it; of suggesting feasible
> amendments of it.
>
> Matthew Arnold (1822–1888)

FOR CENTURIES scholars and men of letters have called attention to the chaos and unnecessary confusion of English spelling.
The reign of Elizabeth I saw at least three writers on English
orthography: John Hart the herald, William Bullokar, a London
lawyer, and Sir Thomas Smith, chancellor to the Queen, whose
book, published in 1568, advocated augmentation of our Roman
alphabet in order to represent adequately the sounds of English. In
1644, Richard Hodges, a Southwark schoolmaster, published *The
English Primrose*, calling attention to the need for the "true spelling
and reading of English, as also for the True-writing thereof" and
quoting on his title page from the First Epistle to the Corinthians,
"If the trumpet give an uncertain sound, who shal prepare himself
to the battel?" Hodges, like Smith, augmented the existing alphabet
or at least employed diacritical marks (accents) with the same effect.
After Hodges' protest, there seems to have been no serious attempt
to assemble the arguments for spelling reform for a further two
centuries. Throughout this period there was, however, no suggestion
that certain forms of spelling were sacred. Men spelt largely as they
pleased and according to personal or local rules made the written
forms approximate to the sound. The trouble lay in the variety of
rules. Shakespeare spelt both his Christian name and surname in
different ways; the early Stewart kings used the combination **quh**
to represent their soft Scottish initial in words like **what (quhat)**.

The desire to bring some sort of order into spelling did, however,
appear from time to time. In America there were a number of efforts
to reform spelling. America's great philosopher-statesman, Benjamin

Franklin, embraced experiments in spelling systematization[1] within the broad compass of his many interests, and in 1793 a Dr. Thornton published his *Cadmus, or a Treatise on Written Language*, in which he recommended a wholesale reform of orthography with the introduction of several new characters. William Pelham, a bookseller of Boston, published *A System of Notation* and an edition of *Rasselas* in his system with the original on the opposite page. About 1840 Dr. Andrew Comstock published books in simplified spelling in Philadelphia. In the nineteenth century many eminent men of letters in Britain called attention to the need for some change. Lord Lytton was forthright—

> A more lying round-about, puzzle-headed delusion than that by which we confuse the clear instincts of truth in our accursed system of spelling was never concocted by the father of falsehood. . . . How can a system of education flourish that begins by so monstrous a falsehood, which the sense of hearing suffices to contradict?

These men always had in mind the effect on children's learning. Matthew Arnold, philosopher and poet, quoted at the head of this chapter, was from 1851 to 1886 one of Her Majesty's Inspectors of Schools. Like him, his fellow poet, Lord Tennyson, tried to interest the English-speaking peoples in spelling reform. Tennyson was vice-president of the English Spelling Reform Association of his day and in spite of the strong prejudice of the mid-Victorian period for "correct" spelling did not hesitate to use and demand of his printers many simplified spellings like **dropt** and **drest**. Later eminent writers, like Robert Bridges and George Bernard Shaw, have made the same sort of efforts, within limits acceptable to their publishers and readers, to break down the sense that the orthodox spelling is in any way sacred.

Statesmen who were scholars have held similar opinions. The great Victorian prime minister, William Ewart Gladstone, said: "I often think that if I had to set about learning to pronounce English I should go mad . . . when I recollect the total absence of rules, method, system," and "There is much that might be done with advantage in the reform of spelling as to the English Language." In a letter to Henry Pitman in 1888 he wrote: "If I were younger and had some things off my hands, I would gladly take hold of this

---

[1] In a letter of the twenty-sixth of September 1768, Franklin wrote in his own alphabet: "As to those who do not spell well . . . their present spelling is only bad, because contrary to the present bad rules: under the new rules it would be good."

reform." Sir Walter Trevelyan was reported in the *Daily News* in 1875 as "calling our notation a labyrinth, a chaos, and an absurdity," and Lord Brougham, eminent lawyer and one-time Lord Chancellor, expressed the view that: "The painful spelling of a passage . . . is of very little advantage to the reader; for if a person does not easily and rapidly understand the ideas expressed, he will in most cases give up reading in despair."

I often wonder how much the Education Acts from 1870 onwards are responsible in Britain for the feeling that there is a correct spelling, difficult to learn but distinguished to use. With public education many became literate in an illiterate society and, having mastered a difficult art, were proud of their new-found skill and maybe reluctant to make it more accessible and indeed so filled with a sense of superiority that they never came near to questioning its foundations, its rightness. Generally speaking, it has been the outstanding scholars, the masters of English language, the authorities on the history of the language, who have demanded spelling reform. It is those ignorant of the history and development of language, of its etymology and structure, who have raised their hands in horror at the mention of reform.

Sir George Hunter used to relate how the editor of a national newspaper once declared that to write **cough** with an F "would make Shakespeare turn in his grave". That is, of course, just how Shakespeare spelt it—"coffe," in *A Midsummer Night's Dream*. I recall how some years ago I lectured on our spelling difficulties in a northern town. A young man reported my talk in the local newspaper. Some fifty people had listened to me speak but next day 50,000 people could read in the newspaper that I was tampering with the language which Shakespeare wrote. This reporter was evidently unaware that the spellings in the school Shakespearean plays which he had read had been modernized for his convenience and that a visit to the local public library to see copies of the early folios would show that Shakespeare's spelling was often very similar to what I was advocating. The ignorant and prejudiced attitude reflected by such reporting is typical. The arrogance of some journalists, secure in the knowledge that they disseminate the "news" and can hardly be answered, is frightening. As long ago as 1880, the *Spectator* attacked the Professor of Sanskrit and Comparative Philology in the University of Oxford for his support of spelling reform in the following words: "Nothing has astonished us more than

the fact that the foremost philologist in England, Professor Max Müller, should find it in his heart to thrust the aegis of his great name and authority in front of this forgetive felony." Perhaps even the editor of the *Spectator* might have thought twice when he weighed the linguistic knowledge of "the foremost philologist in England" against his own knowledge of the bases of the English language and his ability to detect "forgeries" in its spelling.

Early man first recorded speech by picture writing. Picture writing requires concrete and picturable concepts and exceptional skill in portrayal if it is to be read and at best is limited to very factual records embodying easily represented ideas. Hieroglyphic writing followed when the earliest pictorial efforts were reduced to traditional forms and our own alphabetic characters can be traced back to such forms. Ideographic writing and syllabic writing were refinements of the hieroglyphs. Then appeared the genius—Greek legend called him Cadmus—who first saw that his spoken language could be related to his written language and the written language could be founded on a very few basic sounds and, if a sign for each was learnt, any word of the language could be represented by a combination of the signs. The alphabet was invented and is one of mankind's greatest inventions. Yet today the English-speaking peoples have to far too large an extent cast aside the use of the alphabet.

Some Oriental languages are still ideographic and a sign must be learnt for every word (or sometimes word-component). Chinese is such a language.[1] Others, such as Japanese, and unpointed Hebrew, have a syllabic writing, but even with syllabic writing the permutations on individual sounds are many and one needs either a crude relationship or hundreds of syllabic signs. The western world probably owes much of its rapid progress in many fields to the universal use of the Roman alphabet in recording its languages. Lord Bowden, the Principal of Manchester University College of Science and Technology,[2] told me that a Chinese scientist in conversation with him attributed China's falling behind in scientific

---

[1] Chinese may be described as one written language but two speeches. The symbols of the written language are so unrelated to the spoken languages, that speakers of two entirely different tongues interpret the written symbols, each into his own tongue. The two spoken languages in fact possess many dialects differing so greatly in sound as to be almost different languages.

Chinese writing may be compared to the ubiquitous western system of writing numerals. The symbol 15 is clearly understood by all, but to a Frenchman it means *quinze*, to a German *fünfzehn*, to a Welshman *pymtheg*, to an Italian *quindici*, to a Swede *femton*.

[2] Later Minister of State, Department of Education and Science.

advancement to the lack of an alphabet. He said that the mastery of a written language involving the memorization of numerous signs consumed too much time and energy, leaving too little for the application of the language. If there is any degree of truth in that statement, one can only think that we are unwise indeed to take a similar risk.

No one can write with certainty a single word of English unless he has previously seen it and memorized it. This statement is not an exaggeration. Do we spell **in** with one **n** or two **n's**? **in, inn**. Both of course with different meanings, but we must learn which to use. How must we write **of**? Or **is**? Why not **ov, iz**? We only know how to spell **the, that,** or **go, do, toe, shoe** because we have memorized them. How much of our language could we read with speed and ease if long practice had not habituated us to the appearance of the printed forms? Take the first dozen words in that last sentence and try to see them as one beginning to read. The spelling of two words only obeys clear definite rules—**much, and. Of** and **could** defy any rules. **Language** has **n** depicting **ng** (for the **g** is distinct) and both **a** and **g** with two entirely different sounds, **u** with the sound of **w** and **e** not sounded at all. **Read, speed** and **ease** like **how** and **our** use different and ambiguous forms for the same sound while **read** could in fact be either the present or past tense of the verb with entirely different sounds. I assert uncompromisingly that we English speakers are almost in the position of early civilizations which in the pre-alphabet stage used hieroglyphics and had to memorize the sign for every word which they wished to write.

These few examples are *representative of thousands—*

though, rough, bough, cough, through, thorough
stall, shall, shawl, maul, bald, water, daughter, laughter, false,
    fallacy
put, foot, could, wolf, to, mother, nut, blood (Pity the northern
    English child—and teacher!—whose local dialect helps him not at all)
sceptic, schism (Television announcers are not always sure of these!)
sceptre, schedule, schooner, scene, seen, sugar
ringer, wringer, finger, ranger, hanger (Does a singer sing or singe?)

Consonant and vowel are equally erratic—

one, gone, tone, done, swan, sewn, soul, brooch
two, too, true, drew, duty, beauty, suit, youth
three, be, sea, receive, siege, seize, sieve (Who said, i before e
    except after c?)

four, forty, door, boar, more, moor, dour (I advise consultation of
   a dictionary to get the point)
five, give, alive, live (verb or adjective?), diver, driver, river
six, sticks, accept, extra, exist, legs, exhibit, women, build, busy
seven, Devon, heaven, graven, gravel
eight, late, bait, straight, great, bay, obey, gauge
nine, lie, fly, buy, high, dye, eye, aisle, alibi, choir, rhymed, rind
   (There are more than 20 ways of writing this vowel sound)
ten, said, any, friend, leopard, heather, heater, greater

One sound change only distinguishes the following pairs of words:
the final consonant in the second word of each pair is vocalized, i.e.
t becomes d. Look at the spelling and pity the five-year-old beginning
to read. Scores of examples could be added—

plate	paint	gloat	bout	coat
played	pained	glowed	bowed	code

cute	wait	light	straight	root
queued	weighed	lied	strayed	rude

How many know that **vagary** can rhyme with **canary**? Will this
pronunciation be lost because of the spelling, as many other spoken
forms have disappeared? For example, **fault**, which Pope rhymed
with **taught**.

III

The Irrationality of English Spelling

> The etymological information supposed to be enshrined in the current
> spelling is sapped at its very foundation by the fact that it is, in sober
> fact, oftener wrong than right.
>
> Sir James Murray, first editor of the *Oxford New English Dictionary* (1888)

P ROFESSOR MAX MÜLLER said that writing was meant to indicate sound—which to the ordinary man seems virtually a
truism. He also wrote—

The great event which forms a decisive epoch in the history of spelling
is the introduction of printing.... With printed books . . . the spelling of
words became rigid and universally binding. Some languages, such as
Italian, were more fortunate than others in having a more rational
system of spelling to start with. Some, again, like German, were able
to make timely concessions, while others, such as Spanish, Dutch and
French, had Academies to help them at critical periods of their history.
The most unfortunate in all these respects was English. It started with a
Latin alphabet, the pronunciation of which was unsettled, and which
had to be applied to a Teutonic language. After this first phonetic
compromise, it had to pass through a confused system of spelling, half
Saxon, half Norman; half phonetic, half traditional. And even after
English reaches the period of printing, the confusion is by no means
terminated.... English orthography may, in the main, be traced back to
Johnson's *Dictionary*, and to the still more capricious sway exercised by
large printing-offices and publishers.[1]

One can trace present spelling further back than Johnson's
Dictionary and in the main to King James I's Authorized Version of
the Bible published in 1611. As a standard form in general circulation its influence was particularly potent. The opening verses of
the Book of Genesis are, with allowances for the change in the use of
u and **v**, quite modern in appearance.

---

[1] *Fortnightly Review*. April 1876.

IN the beginning God created the Heauen and the Earth. And the earth was without forme and voyd, and darkenesse was vpon the face of the deepe: and the Spirit of God mooued vpon the face of the waters.

Comparison with the slightly earlier spellings of Cranmer's Bible and the Geneva Bible makes the point clear—

Cranmer's Bible (1539):

IN the beginnyng God created heauen & erth. The erth was voyd and emptie, and darknesse was vpõ the face of the depe, & the sprete of God moued vpõ the face of the waters.

Geneva Bible (1560):

IN THE beginning God created Y̊ heauen and the earth. And the earth was without forme & voyde, and darkenes was vpon the depe, & the Spirit of God moued vpon the waters.

The last is the famous Breeches Bible, so called from the translation of Genesis III.7:

Then the eyes of them bothe were opened, & they knewe that they were naked, and they sewed figtre leaues together, and made them selues breeches.

Cranmer's Bible had at least dealt sensibly with the spelling of the first verb in "and they sowed figge leaues together, & made them selues aporns." Unfortunately the Authorized Version failed to follow Cranmer in this particular regard with "and they sewed figge leaues together, and made themselues aprons." The spelling "sewed" has been perpetuated.

The spelling of Alfred the Great was systematic in the sense that one symbol indicated one sound and no other. The sound might vary according to preceding or following sounds but the whole word presented no ambiguity. After the Norman conquest, English manuscripts at first preserved this sensible trait, but as Norman and Saxon became more one nation, and scribes who had been trained to write French turned to writing in English, discrepancies in the spelling forms began to appear. The amalgamation of the two nations naturally affected the speech oftener than the spelling but this in turn added to the growing discrepancies in the written forms. Among the consonants, the Anglo-Saxon guttural represented by **gh** persisted in writing even when the Latinized tongues of the invaders failed to sound it at all, e.g. **high, night,** and when they tried to

sound it but changed the sound, e.g. **rough, enough**. Their vowels went wildly astray. The broad **a** of Anglo-Saxon words like **ac** and **rad** (modern "oak, road") was confused with the **o** in words like **brocan** (modern "broke"). The distinction in sound between **ae, e, ea, eo** was lost but some spellings lingered, e.g. **east, see, sea**. Yet until the fourteenth century it is often possible to attribute manuscripts with fair assurance to their dialect source and to say in what part of England they were written. The early fifteenth century saw still more rapid changes in the spoken language, with which spelling failed to keep pace. Many of the old grammatical inflexions disappeared about this time. Spelling thus became very uncertain and by the time of the Renaissance in the sixteenth century, under the influence of students of Latin and Greek, the notion that spelling should clearly represent sound gave way more and more to the idea that it should be associated with derivation. Fantastically, the etymology was very often wrong and English spelling lost even that antiquarian interest.

In the *Advancement of Learning* Francis Bacon wrote—

> But here the question arises, whether words should be wrote as they are pronounced, or after the common manner. Certainly that reformed kind of writing, according to the pronunciation, is but a useless speculation, because pronunciation itself is continually changing, and the derivations of words, especially from the foreign languages, are very obscure; and lastly, as writing in the received manner no way obstructs the manner of pronunciation, but leaves it free, an innovation in it is to no purpose.

Benjamin Franklin answered this attitude in 1768, when he pointed out that the Italian by this argument would still be writing the Latin form *episcopus* for *vescovo* (bishop)[1]—

> Whatever the difficulties and inconveniences now are, they will be more easily surmounted now than hereafter: and *some time or other it* [spelling reform] *must be done*, or our writing will become the same with the Chinese, as to the difficulty of learning and using it: and it would already have been such, if we had continued the Saxon spelling and writing used by our forefathers.

If spelling should preserve earlier forms, how far back must we go? This is an irresolvable question.

[1] **P, b, f, v**, often interchange in the evolution of language, cf. **father**, *pater* (Latin); **pepper**, *pfeffer* (German), *poivre* (French). The word **bear** (carry) is directly related to the Latin *fero*.

ƕuatever ƕi difikƴltiz and inkanvinienſiz nau er, ƕe uil bi mor iizili ſƴrmaunted nau, ƕan hiraftƴr; and ſƴm tƴim ar ƴƕƴr, it myſt bi dƴn; ar aur rƴitiŋ uil bikƴm ƕi ſêm uiƕ ƕi Tƕƴiniiz ‡, az to ƕi difikƴlti av lƴrniŋ and iuziŋ it. And it uuld alredi hev bin ſƴtſi, if ui had kantinud ƕi Sakſƴn ſpeliŋ and rƴitiŋ, iuzed bƴi our forfaƕers.

ƴi am, mƴi diir frind,

iurs afekſƴnetli,

B. Franklin *.

Lƴndƴn,
Kreven-ſtriit,
Sept. 28, 1768.

‡ Chineſe.

* [Perhaps it would have been better to have had the new letters caſt upright, in order to have ſuited with Roman inſtead of Italic characters : But it did not occur till too late. — If any falſe ſpelling has appeared in the above, it is as fair to attribute it to the editor as to the author. E.]

1. Benjamin Franklin's Reformed Mode of Spelling (p. 478) from *Political, Miscellaneous, and Philosophical Pieces*, 1779.

Those who first used the alphabet must have set out to represent speech by written signs according to consistent rules and the acceptance of the idea that spelling should indicate derivation can only have intruded at a later date and no etymologist would accept it. The etymologist and the historian of language listen to the sound and regard the spelling of any language with extreme caution. Because of the changes in pronunciation, our present spelling in great part represents pronunciations of an earlier day, but so chaotic is our spelling now that even these spellings are useless as museum pieces. Who would now know from the spelling alone of words like **clean, deal,** that in the time of James II they were pronounced, as many Irishmen still sound them, with a vowel sound like that in **great**? Modern spelling is indicative of nothing. While the rule holds good for many words, it is completely misleading in other words like **heave, hear, reap.**

Truly enough the knowledge of a word's origin can often help to a nicer, more precise use of the word. Anyone who knows the derivation of the adjective **salutary** (from the Latin, *salus, salutis*: health) is unlikely to use the word as freely and meaninglessly as do many reporters of cases of "salutary punishment." Unfortunately, more than just a knowledge of origins is often necessary. It does not help to know the origin of **preposterous** (coming before instead of after). The spellings of **sylvan** (Latin, *silva*), **ache** (Old English, *ake*), **delight** (Middle English, *delit*), as of scores of other words, tend to hide the origin. In his *English Past and Present*, Archbishop Trench pointed out that the scholar does not need spelling indications to help him to the pedigree of words and that the ignorant is not helped by them: "The one knows without, and the other does not know with them, so that in either case they are profitable for nothing." Trench was opposed to the phonetic rationalization of our spelling and thought it was helpful in giving a word its most proper meaning to know to what other words it was related. One might argue in this vein that the l in **would** helps to recall its relation to **will**. Yet, is that really an advantage and, if it is, is it a worthwhile advantage compared with the waste of time in memorizing the spelling and the waste of ink and paper in writing five letters where three would do? Worst thought of all is that English spelling promptly smashes the argument with the analogous **could** where the l hides the relationship to **can**. Whatever argument we advance, English spelling chaos lets us down. We add an **e** to **axe**, which historically has always

been a monosyllable and we sensibly use the spelling **ox** for a word which in Old English has two syllables, *oxa* or *oxe*. William Archer wrote a pamphlet in 1909, *The Etymological Argument*,[1] in which with a host of examples he showed that English spelling obscures as much as or more than it helps an understanding of word history. Typical of many examples which he quotes are the following—

Haughty:	from French *haut*. The spelling suggests a Teutonic origin.
Island:	from Old English *iland*. The spelling wrongly suggests association with the Latin, *insula*, and **s** was inserted in the fifteenth century under French influence.
Scent:	Shakespeare wrote in the First Folio *Hamlet* "I sent the mornings ayre" and possibly was better able than we are to see that the word is directly descended from the Latin *sentio*.
Sprightly:	the spelling obscures the relationship with *sprite* and French *esprit*.
Sovereign:	spelt *soverain* by Chaucer and *sovran* by Milton correctly, for through Late Latin *sovranus* it is related to the classical *superanus*, and has nothing to do with *regno* and *reign* as the misguided scribe who introduced the **G** thought and whom untold generations of little English children have had reason to curse ever since.

Scribe and printer are responsible for many uncorrected anomalies. Chaucer never wrote an **h** in **ghost**, but Caxton's printers were Flemish and thought that initial **g** must be guttural in English as in their own language. Their mistake is perpetuated today. And worse follows: somehow **ghost** affected the spelling of **aghast** (Old English: *agast*). The scribe before the printing era, knowing that **u** followed by **m, n** or **v** in written script was confusing, closed the **u** making an **o**. In the printing age it is the opposite of helpful to put **o** for **u** in words like **come, love, ton**.

Samuel Johnson is blamed for much of our chaotic spelling because his first English dictionary crystallized so many present forms. His etymology was often pretentious: for instance, he put the **ch** in **ache** knowing nothing of Anglo-Saxon and deriving the word from the Greek ἄχος. He copied the **sylvan** which he knew and attributed it to the Greek ὕλη and so accounted for the Y. It would not be fair to Dr. Johnson to assail him too strongly for he was well aware of the muddled state of our spelling:

---

[1] Simplified Spelling Society. Pamphlet No. 3.

Even in words of which the derivation is apparent, I have been often obliged to sacrifice uniformity to custom; thus I write, in compliance with a numberless majority, "convey" and "inveigh" [and "vehicle"], "deceit" and "receipt"; "fancy" and "phantom."

Yet he has much to answer for. To him change in speech was corruption and in his own words he "endeavoured to proceed with a scholar's reverence for antiquity." Again in the Preface to his *Dictionary*, Johnson writes—

There is, in constancy and stability, a general and lasting advantage, which will always overbalance the slow improvements of gradual correction. Much less ought our written language to comply with the corruptions of oral utterance, or copy that which every variation of time or place makes different from itself, and imitate those changes which will again be changed, while imitation is employed in observing them.

Johnson could not have been aware of the laws of phonetic change. It is not easy today to realize how little was known only a few years ago about the evolution of language and about the existence of regular sound changes, much less about their history. Dr. Walter W. Skeat (1835–1912) was Professor of Anglo-Saxon at Cambridge and a fellow of the British Academy. In May 1906 he read a paper to the Academy in which he stated in relation to education that "there are few subjects of general interest and importance that are more deserving of attention than the often debated one of Phonetic Spelling." Dr. Skeat went on to say that he himself in the middle of the nineteenth century was brought up to believe "that the sounds which we employ in speaking English have *never altered!*" (The italics and exclamation marks are his own.) He remained in this belief until in 1869 Dr. Alexander J. Ellis published the first part of his book on Early English pronunciation. Dr. Sweet's *History of English Sounds* followed in 1888. Linguistic inquiry came later in this country than in some continental countries where Rask's work was known in Denmark and Grimm's in Germany much earlier in the century. This ignorance probably contributed to the separation of our spoken and written languages. Many of the biggest changes in English pronunciation have come about in comparatively recent times and the tendency to retain forms to which the eyes were accustomed can be understood, unwarrantable though it be. The more the written forms failed to retain their relationship to the

changing spoken forms, the easier it would be to overlook the disparity between writing and speech and the readier people became not to expect correspondence between the two.

There are many other good reasons why our failure to use our alphabet should arouse revolt. I recall one leader of my own education authority, Mr. Frank Tweedale, for many years chairman of the Further Education Sub-Committee, a thoughtful man who gave all his leisure to public work, who discussed English spelling with me. He said that often when speaking in public he avoided using the appropriate, cogent word, which he knew well and would certainly write, because he was afraid of mispronouncing it. Even this man, who feared little and was forthright in seeking civic progress, was imbued with that sense, inculcated by our educational system, of humiliation when he could not correlate pronunciation and spelling. Could there be any greater indictment of our spelling in the mind of the educator than that it hinders speech?

The waste of time and effort in a lifetime must be enormous. There is not one of us, be he teacher, newspaper editor, professional or business man, who does not keep somewhere on his shelves a dictionary. It is kept not only to look up the meanings of words but also the spellings, for not one of us can remember every spelling form and we dare not rely upon our alphabet. It is no guide. The time spent and the frustration arising because the thread has been lost in thinking of the correct spelling are substantial. And so accustomed to this are we English that it hardly occurs to us that the imposition need not be suffered. We do not realize that Italians, or Spaniards, or Finns, and almost all other peoples, do not have to do the same.

It is true, of course, even with a consistent spelling system, that individual pronunciations will vary and one man will still spell some words rather differently from another. But the conventional forms of the commonest words will be far more easily remembered and the spelling of the rest does not matter so long as we are more tolerant and do not view subservience to a spelling tyranny as a mark of culture and education.

It is not strictly relevant in relation to English education that our spelling misleads foreigners trying to learn our language but the point is worthy of note. Sir Gilbert Murray, O.M., Regius Professor of Greek at Oxford, who in his lifetime stood at the peak of English scholarship, wrote in 1926—

I do not think it an exaggeration when certain foreigners say to me, as they often do, "We can read English, but we do not attempt to speak it, because that is like learning another language." That is very important considering the vast world importance of the English language, and the great extent of ground over which it is spoken. We ought not to allow the path of the English language to be cumbered by such an enormous and unnecessary difficulty.

The *UNESCO Courier*, the official publication of the United Nations, in referring to the number of books translated in 1960 between European and Asian languages, reported that by far the greatest number were translated from English (1541 works, many of them American books). Japan alone received 583 English translations, compared with a total of 173 from French, 150 from German and 84 from Russian. Many of the translations into Asiatic tongues were not made from the original western language but from an English translation of the original: "The average reader in the East has no access to the majority of French, German or Russian works except through the intervention of English translators, and practically none at all to works in other languages." The *Guardian* of 18 February 1963, commented: "What a responsibility English carries in the Eastern world!" There is an important educational aspect to this responsibility, for many of these translations are of scientific and educational works intended for the student and research worker.[1]

English is already the language of the whole of the northern half of the American continent and the language or one of the languages of all member and former member states of the British Commonwealth. It is the second language taught in the schools of most European countries and is outstanding among the great international languages in its spread. Its sound system is not, by comparison with some, difficult and all over the world there are foreigners who speak English without a disturbing accent. The grammar is remarkably simple. In fact, by comparison with most languages English has virtually no grammar to be learnt. It was a German, Jacob Grimm, the founder of the modern science of comparative language, who wrote: "When we consider its richness, intellectuality and condensed adaptability no one of all other living languages may be

---

[1] As long ago as 1875, Dr. Thorell, Professor of Zoology at Uppsala, pointed out that other nations were then using English for publishing scientific research: "English, on account of its simple grammar, and as combining in nearly the same degree Teutonic and Romanic elements, is by most Europeans more easily acquired than any other language." J. H. Moore. "Address to the Leeds Shorthand Writers Association," 8 October, 1875, *The Spelling Reform*. No. 310.

placed at the side of English, not even our German language."[1]
More than half a century later another foreign scholar, Robert
Eugen Zachrisson, who became equally eminent in the study of
philology, quoted Grimm's opinion that only its "whimsical, anti-
quated orthography" stood in the way of the universal acceptance of
English.[2] Zachrisson was Professor of English in the Royal University, Uppsala, from 1921 to 1936 and in his own words: "English
must ultimately be chosen as the world international language
because it has the simplest structure and the largest circulation."
The greatest bar to the still wider spread of English lies in its spelling
which is to such degree unrelated to its pronunciation as inevitably
to mislead.

We are here, however, concerned with the education of children
and, beyond drawing attention to that point, will say no more of
English as a world language. We are, however, concerned not only
with the education of American and English children, but also with
the education of children in Africa, India, New Zealand and other
lands whose family language is not English but for whom English is
an official language and a means, often the only means, to higher
education. We are also concerned with the education of immigrant
adults, particularly to America, whose first language is not English.
For all of them, the boon of learning through a visual medium which
is adequately related to a pronunciation (which may well be more
acceptable than the sound of the speech about them) must be even
greater than to the American or British native.

It has been argued that if we changed our spelling, we should
have to reprint all our existing books. This is just not true. All books
now printed will remain as legible and acceptable as they are now.
Books printed centuries ago are legible today. Is there any difficulty
about Shakespeare's "Euen from the toonglesse cauernes of the
earth"? To go further back than Shakespeare, nobody today finds
even Chaucer difficult because of the spelling. It is only when the
language has changed that difficulty arises.

> At nyght were come into that hostelrye
> Wel nyne and twenty in a compaignye,

---

[1] "Denn an reichthum, vernunft und gedrängter fuge lässt sich keine aller noch
lebenden sprachen ihr an die seite setzen, auch unsre deutsche nicht."
    Über den Ursprung der Sprache. Berlin, 1852, p. 50.
    It is to be noted that Grimm was simplifying German script by the omission of
capital initials to his nouns.
[2] *Simplified English Spelling.* Newcastle, 1930.

Of sondry folk, by aventure yfalle
In felaweshipe, and pilgrimes were they alle.

And the meagrest knowledge of Chaucer's grammar would make "yfalle" clear.

It is indeed true that English spelling is a world problem and not merely an English one. It would be disastrous if the English language were to split into a multiplicity of mutually unintelligible languages each capable of arousing nationalistic emotions. Europe has in historical times seen the common tongue of the Roman Empire split up into Italian, Spanish, French, Portuguese, Rumanian, Romansch and so on. Widespread literacy and the printing press might have saved Latin. Yet even with these aids English speech is tending to travel the same path and but for the steadying influence of film and radio the divergences would be even greater than they are now. It may not be commonly realized that already we have to print different versions of schoolbooks for Britain and the United States, alter broadcast commentaries and so on. The natural forces of divergence are fostered by mispronunciations which are stimulated by the present erratic spelling. The impetus towards convergence, which a printed form related to the spoken form would encourage, has not been allowed to be effective because of our spelling.

IV

The Effect in Schools

As the length of time now found necessary to teach children in Elementary Schools to read and write the English language with ease and correctness is attributable in a great measure to the difficulties of the present mode of Spelling, it is advisable, for the promotion of Education, that some change should be effected, in order to remedy the evil.

Sir Charles Reed, LL.D., Chairman of the London School Board (1877)

THE PRECEDING CHAPTERS will have, I hope, dispelled any notions that there is anything sacrosanct about English spelling. A large part of our misapplication of the alphabet has no basis in history, no basis in long tradition. The existing spelling forms we see and use every day are often more recent than the educational foundations which preserve them and are too often the very mistakes of pretentious scholarship. They have no privileged claim for preservation by poet in his study or business man in his office.

> How ſweet the moone-light ſleepes vpon this banke,
> Heere will we ſit, and let the ſounds of muſicke
> Creepe in our eares, ſoft ſtilnes and the night
> Become the tutches of ſweet harmonie.

Were Shakespeare's lines less tuneful so written? What business man would not describe as idiotic any suggestion that the shorthand, in which dictation is taken down in his office, should be spelt according to the letter combinations of longhand? Any but a phonetic spelling is impossible, if it is to be efficient.

Literate adults through long habit have memorized the *appearance* of words and read with ease, even when their power to express themselves in writing is limited by spelling difficulties. It is this habituation which has led some educationists to believe that *memorization of appearance* is reading at its best and in consequence to think that children are rightly taught from the beginning by methods based on this attitude, such as the sentence method of teaching reading, instead of realizing that the methods have been invented to

meet the need enforced by the spelling.[1] Nobody has ever expected infant children to express themselves *spontaneously* in writing as they do in drawing. They have copied, and at six to seven years may write, words which they have memorized. Occasionally they try to guess the spelling of new words but the likelihood of failure has a limiting effect and they never use in writing the entire vocabulary which they use in speech.

I have asked adult audiences to learn a new code of six letters (in fact a mixture of Greek and Cyrillic characters)—$\Lambda = L$, $\Delta = D$, $\Gamma = G$, $\Omega = O$, $H = N$, $B = E$. I have then written on a blackboard in the new code the word **gone**. These adults read the word after a little mystification about the last silent letter. Then I have changed the first letter making **lone**. This was solved after a little hesitation. When the initial was again changed giving **done**, there was quite noticeable delay and some adults, in spite of their long practice in reading, failed to make the vowel adjustment. There was certainly no fluency. Even with all the foregoing practice, some still failed to read the word **one** when the initial was deleted. This is precisely the task that we expect five-year-old children to tackle with at least forty-one characters[2] plus the digraphs, and the combinations of the letters with varying phonic values are innumerable.

real, bear, tread, reap
polite, police, changed, hanged
choose, loose, lose, dose
bow (beau or bough?), bowl, howl
county, country, get, gem

How difficult a task it is for little children to convert strange signs on paper into words and mentally to translate the sequence of words into ideas, even when the rules hold good! How impossible for a long time, and for ever for some, is the feat when the rules governing the use of the signs alter again and again! It is small wonder that books become for many an image of unrewarding drudgery instead of a joy. Children's own writing shows how they try to apply non-existent rules. The following examples are taken at random from infants' school books—

[1] The views of the sentence method supporters are mentioned again on pages 75 and 87.
[2] One (and sometimes more) forms of each lower-case character plus the capitals A B D E F G H I J L M N Q R T. If we add the cursive characters for *a b F f* etc., there are ultimately more than 70 characters to be learnt.

Scool, peses of cole (pieces of coal), kold, bot, (bought), wocht (watched) plumer (plumber)

Healthy children are active children and a good teacher attempts to direct their activity towards worthwhile ends. The art of teaching lies in claiming and holding a child's interest, that is in guiding his instinctive desire to do something. A child is very logical. Effort must bring results or the child is unwilling to put forth effort. When he hits a drum he makes a noise that pleases him, so he hits the drum. He will leave the drum for a book, when the book quickly gives a return which in his estimation is better. We give infants books filled with colourful pictures in an attempt to provide early interest. Why not make printed material easier in order to accelerate the reward to the child?[1]

Thus argued the spelling reformers and this was always their foremost argument. While pointing out all the other advantages of rational spelling, the value in schools was always in the forefront of their minds. Ninety years ago Professor Max Müller asked: "Is every English child, as compared with other children, to be mulcted in two or three years of his life in order to learn it (English spelling)?" Benn Pitman described spelling reform as "for the uneducated, to help the ignorant to read, and to save children from the time-wasting perplexities of the ordinary spelling."[2] Although often aided by far-seeing men whose first interest was manufacture, commerce, journalism and politics, most of the promoters of reform were in the first place scholars. This is not surprising for the scholars dared to condemn that which they understood and were above suggestions of ignorance. Their adherence gave assurance to others, who saw the waste and foolishness of traditional spelling. Among them have been many teachers.

Those most aware of the impediments to learning imposed by our spelling are naturally teachers, who have before their eyes every day the effects. Not all teachers analyse the troubles that beset young children in their first approach to reading because they, like others, are often blinded by the habits of a lifetime to the real chaos of our spelling. Yet all teachers of infant children, and most teachers of

---

[1] If any reader doubts this argument, I suggest that he teach himself the Shaw Alphabet (Penguin Book Q29). He may then experience some of the exasperation of the infant beginner, but he can never know it all. The grown-up has the tremendous advantage of knowing the general principles underlying the interpretation of symbols. And readers of this book are likely to be better readers than most.

[2] *Life and Labors of Sir Isaac Pitman*, Krehbiel, Cincinnati, 1902.

older children too, are aware that children's mis-spellings usually arise from efforts to apply rules. The main efforts of spelling reform organizations have therefore been directed to using rationalized spelling in schools for the teaching of reading.

A personal anecdote may not be out of place here. Like many others, I had often laughed at quaint (but absolutely logical) spelling mistakes made in school. Probably I had not seen as many of them as most teachers for I never taught infants. When, however, my own children first went to school my attention became more concentrated. My elder son (now a university graduate) one day when he was just six years old brought home from school an exercise book in which among other corrected work one sentence stood out: "A hors eets gras in a feeld." In seven words he had four mistakes. He wanted to know why every word except **a** and **in** was wrong. And what explanation was there? As an intelligent little boy he had interpreted and applied correctly every rule that could possibly be known to him and he was wrong in every case. It suddenly occurred to me that it was the intelligent, inquiring children that were frustrated and dismayed by our spelling, the children with developing logical minds that dared to question and could not unthinkingly and apathetically accept what was doled out to them. In the words of the writer of one of the school reports in a later chapter: "He who reasons is lost!" I recall that that very day I began to formulate rules for a systematic spelling of English and soon afterwards, probably because my attention was alert to the subject, I saw an advertisement of the Simplified Spelling Society. A letter to the secretary of those days, Mr. T. R. Barber, brought me a supply of books and I discovered that a systematic spelling had already been evolved after careful, scholarly research by men more fitted than myself for it. Following this, I was soon after in 1942 elected to the Committee of the Society. One further story involving this same boy is worth telling. When about seven years old and now reading well, he brought to me the word **tall** and asked what it was. I explained. Then I ran through the alphabet—**all, ball, call, fall, hall, pall, stall, tall, wall.** Eureka! I was amazed. Never before had I been able to find a consistent English spelling rule and I told my son that whenever **a** was followed by two l's the sound was as in **all.** Within minutes he asked me to explain **shall.** Since we have no alphabet sign for the sound **sh,** I had missed that one.

Part II

V

Sir Isaac Pitman's Work

Future generations must look up to Isaac Pitman, the inventor of Phonetic Short Hand, as the Father of English Phonetic Spelling.

Alexander J. Ellis (1848)

ISAAC PITMAN left school in 1826 when he was 13 years old to be a counting house clerk and was later so employed in his father's own business in Trowbridge. His father was keenly interested in the movement then stirring in England for a system of general education. Six years after Isaac Pitman left school he was sent to Borough Road Training College for five months' training as a teacher in the old Lancaster monitorial system. He acquitted himself so well that Mr. Henry Dunn, Director of the Training College, wrote to his father: "You may send me as many more of your children as you can spare." In the upshot, two of Isaac's brothers and three sisters went to Borough Road Training College.

He early became interested in speed writing of which a number of systems existed although none was fast enough for verbatim reporting. Systems of shorthand before Isaac Pitman consisted of little more than substitutes for the consonants of the Roman alphabet. Pitman studied the construction of words and invented methods of indicating briefly and rapidly the frequently recurring combinations of sounds. His brother, Benn Pitman, believed that his lifelong interest in rationalizing the written and printed languages began when he was about six years old. "In reading he frequently met with words, the meaning of which he understood, but never having heard them in conversation, he was doubtful as to their correct pronunciation." Even at that early age the assiduity which characterized his later life was noticeable. He read through the whole of Webster's Pronouncing Dictionary and copied out every unfamiliar word. When in 1837 he opened a private school at Wotton-under-Edge he added shorthand to the curriculum and began to devise his own system. Thereafter he devoted his life more and more to giving free

postal tuition in his shorthand and to lecturing about it. He was a man of tremendous energy. A friend has noted that he began work at his desk at 6 in the morning, two hours before breakfast, and that he was still at his desk at 10 p.m. "His correspondence is immense ... The speed and ease with which he writes in shorthand enables him to get through an amount of work which would else seem fabulous." His free postal tuition system grew rapidly and in 1842 he published his *Phonographic Journal*, a shorthand periodical, the first issue of which ran to a thousand copies.

The demand for speed writing at that time exceeds the imagination of those of us born in the age of the typewriter, but it was huge and shorthand writers banded themselves into phonographic societies and clubs: they were enthusiasts in a new crusade. Shorthand is today a time- and labour-saving commercial device, a purely utilitarian art. The driving force behind its early spread was educational and philanthropic and was often accompanied by self-denying labour and sometimes even privation: "Where we taught one pupil for pay, we instructed five, on an average, without any thought of remuneration." Of this period Benn Pitman could write,[1] "the promulgation of Phonography in Great Britain by a band of ardent young men, moved by an enthusiasm born of the conviction of the importance of the phonetic principle as a factor in education and general progress, began in 1842." Several of Isaac Pitman's brothers became his lecturers, as well as many friends and admirers. They travelled widely, teaching and spreading enthusiasm and all for little financial recompense. "All the lecturers became, for a longer or shorter period, devoted missionaries in what they regarded as an educational and semi-philanthropic movement, teaching Phonography, more or less gratuitously, and advocating a reform in English spelling which would result in a great shortening of the time of children in learning to read, and tend to bring the elements of education within the reach of all."[2]

In 1843 Isaac Pitman met Alexander John Ellis, then of Dorking. Ellis was a wealthy man, a King's Scholar at Eton and a scholar of Trinity College, Cambridge, where he graduated 6th Wrangler in 1836. Besides mathematician he was a barrister of the Middle Temple, a musician and philologist. His writings on mathematical and linguistic subjects were extensive. Philology was his greatest

[1] B. Pitman, *Life and Labors of Sir Isaac Pitman*, Cincinnati, 1902.
[2] Ibid.

Plate I. Isaac Pitman in 1859 (aged 46)

love and when he first met Isaac Pitman, he had already for some years been working on the production of a phonetic alphabet which might be applied to the spelling of all languages and included signs for many sounds other than those required for English writing. His book *The Alphabet of Nations* was the first serious work on scientific phonetics; other works of note covered the pronunciation of Latin, Greek and Early English. Before the end of his life Cambridge University conferred upon him a Doctorate of Laws "in recognition of his great services to the history of the English tongue." Benn Pitman wrote of him: "Mr. Ellis was profoundly impressed with the importance of employing a Phonetic alphabet as a desirable, nay, necessary instrument in national education, in that it furnished the only means by which reading, spelling, and writing could become general among the great body of English people."[1]

Ellis and Pitman worked together in the production of a phonetic alphabet for English printing. Pitman devised the first alphabet, which was published in the *Phonotypic Journal* of January 1844. It consisted of upper case characters only in what are known as "caps." and "small caps.," that is, wholly in capital letters big and small. Pitman was a practical printer as well as a scholar and at the same time something of an artist, as his phonographic writing shows. He was thus the ideal practical typographer to collaborate with Ellis in their joint idea. Ellis later wrote that "the alphabet was reduced to a satisfactory working state in January 1847," and said that many persons had contributed ideas during its development. "Although it may with great justice be called the joint invention of Isaac Pitman and Alexander John Ellis, yet as great inventions take their name from those who first started and gave a practical form to the idea, even though the completion of their inventions may have been wholly or partially the work of others, *future generations must look up to Isaac Pitman, the inventor of Phonetic Short Hand, as the Father of English Phonetic Spelling.*" The italics are Ellis's.

During the first five months of 1849 the *Phonetic News* appeared, a 12-page newspaper produced in phonetic printing type and edited by Ellis. This production of a full-scale newspaper in a simplified spelling and reformed print was one of the notable events in the story of spelling reform. The paper closed down for financial reasons after some months and Ellis's type was later destroyed in a fire.

Even the 1847 alphabet, which was his fourth, did not satisfy

[1] Ibid.

Left column

No. 1, January, 1844.

ɪ E A ⊖ ,ɒ ʊ {heard} ʉ, ɪ ɪ ʌ o ʊ ɯ,
ʎ o ᴚ ɯ, W Y H, P B T D C'J C G, F V
⊖ ᴧ S Z Ƨ Ӽ, L R, M N ʊ

Specimen:

NʊƟIƲ HWOTEVER IZ MɒR Tʊ Bɪ
DEZᴧRD, OR MɒR DELᴧTFUL, ᴧᴧN ᴧᴄ
LᴧT OV TRᴚƟ : FOR IT IZ ᴧᴄ SɒRS' OV
WIZDUM   HWEN ᴧᴄ MᴧND IZ HAR-
AST WIᴧ OBSKᴚRITI, DIŚTRᴧKTᴄD Bᴧ
DᴚTS, RENDᴄRD TORPID OR SADᴄND
Bᴧ IGNORᴧNS OR FƟLSITIZ, AND TRᴚƟ
ᴄMERJᴄZ ᴧZ FROM ᴧ DᴧRK ᴧBIS, IT
ƩᴧNZ FɒRƟ INSTANTᴄNIUSLI, LᴧK ᴧᴄ
SUN DISPURSIᴚ MISTS AND VEPURZ,
OR LᴧK ᴧᴄ DƟN DISPᴄLIᴚ ᴧᴄ ƩᴄDZ OV
DᴧRKNᴄS.

No. 3, June, 1846.

ɪ ɛ a ⊖ o ɯ, i e a o u u, ɪ ơ ʊ u,
w y h, p b t d ç j c g, f v t ᵭ s z
ʃ ʒ, l r, m n ŋ.

Specimen.

Nutiŋ hwotever iz mor tu bi
dezird, or mor delitiul, ᵭan ᵭe
lit ov trut : for it iz ᵭe sors ov
wizdum. Hwen ᵭe mind iz harast wiᵭ obscuriti, distracted bi
dᵴts, renderd torpid or sadend
bi ignorans or fƟlsitiz, and trᵴt
emerjez az from a darc abís, it
ʃinz fort instantaniusli, lic ᵭe
sun dispersiŋ mists and vapurz,
or lic ᵭe dƟn dispeliŋ ᵭe ʃadz ov
darcnes.

No, 5, Proposed Jan., 1852.

ɪ ɛ a ⊖ o ơ u, i e a o u u, ɪ ʊ ɯ, w
y h, p b t d ç j c g, f v ⊖ ᵭ s z ʃ ʒ,
l r, m n ŋ.

Specimen.

NuƟiŋ hwotever iz mor tu bi
dezird, or mor delitful, ᵭan ᵭe lit
ov truƟ : for it iz ᵭe sors ov wizdum. Hwen ᵭe mind iz harast
wiᵭ obscuriti, distracted bi dᵴts,
renderd torpid or sadend bi ignorans or fƟlsitiz, and truƟ emerjez
az from a darc abís, it ʃinz forƟ

Right column

No. 2, October, 1844.

ɪ ɛ ɋ ὸ c {heard} ⊙ ⊙, i e a o u u,
ɪ ɋ ʉ ɯ, w y h, p b t d ç j k g,
f v t ᵭ s z ʃ ʒ, l r, m n ŋ.

Specimen.

Nutiŋ hwotever iz mor tu bi
dezird, or mor delitful, ᵭan ᵭe
lit ov trɒt : for it iz ᵭe sɒrs ov
wizdum. Hwen ᵭe mind iz harast wiᵭ obscuriti, distracted bi
duts; renderd torpid or sadend
bi ignorans or fòlsitiz, and trɒt
emerjez az from a dark abís, it
ʃinz fɒrt instantaniusli, ljk ᵭe
sun dispersiŋ mists and vepurs,
or ljk ᵭe dòn dispeliŋ ᵭe ʃedz ov
darknes.

No. 4, Jan., 1847.

ɛ a ɋ ⊖ o ɯ, i e a o u u, ɪ ơ ʊ ɋ,
w y h, p b t d ç j c g, f v t ᵭ s z
ʃ ʒ, l r, m n ŋ.

Specimen.

Nutiŋ hwotever iz mor tu bɛ
dezird, or mor delitful, ᵭan ᵭe lit
ov trut : for it iz ᵭe sɒrs ov wizdum. Hwen ᵭe mind iz harast
wiᵭ obscuriti, distracted bi dᵴts,
renderd torpid or sad'nd bi ignorans or fƟlsitiz, and trᵴt emerjez
az from a darc abís, it ʃinz fɒrt
instantaniusli, ljc ᵭe sun dispersiŋ
mists and vapurz, or ljc ᵭe dƟn
dispeliŋ ᵭe ʃadz ov darcnes.

No 6, Romanic Alphabet.

aa, bb, cc, dd, ee, ff, gg, hh ii, jȷ,
kc, ll, mm, nn, oo, pp, qc, rr, ss, tt,
uu, vv, ww, xcs, yy, zz.

Specimen.

Nothing whatever is more to be
desired, or more delightful, than
the light of truth: for it is the
source of wisdom. When the mind
is harassed with obscurity, distracted by doubts, rendered torpid
or saddened by ignorance or fals-
ities, and truth emerges as from a

2. Isaac Pitman's Alphabets (from *Life and Labors of Sir Isaac Pitman*).

Pitman and he devised a fifth printed alphabet in 1852.[1] He also devised a script alphabet which he called Phonetic Longhand. In addition he devised new symbols for the numbers 10 and 11 and kept his business accounts by a duodecimal system of numeration.

Pitman had discontinued his school in order to devote his whole time to the production of books and other papers about writing and spelling reform. In his own words: "The immediate cause of the extended practice of shorthand was the diffusion of the middle classes of society. It has yet to be extended to the lowest classes and this will be the mission of Phonography combined with Phonetic Printing." Shorthand and phonetic printing were to Isaac Pitman two aspects of the same theme: writing and printing reform were one. As his shorthand won enthusiastic approval and was adopted on all sides, while he maintained his great output of work with it, he tended more and more to make the less successful project, phonetic spelling, his real love. And as they were phases of the same process so the successful one had to pay for the less successful: "If it were not that Phonotypy needs the profits of Phonography, I should directly throw the system up to the booksellers and earn my living by teaching: but I can do nothing for Phonetic Printing if I do not preserve to myself the profits of my three Shorthand teaching books."

In 1843 he divided his journal into two sections and the second section dealt with spelling reform and was known as the *Phonotypic Journal*. "As Phonography becomes the general medium of written communication Phonotypic printing must follow." From this time forward he regarded his system of shorthand chiefly as an introduction to spelling reform to which he virtually devoted his life and his income. Another contemporary wrote: "He has no love for money save for its use in promoting his ends. His personal wants are few and simple and every penny beyond what is required for them is devoted to the phonetic propaganda." He himself wrote: "I was twice assessed for the income tax. I appealed and proved that my income was under £100. The commissioners appeared surprised that I should carry on an extensive business for the benefit of posterity."

[1] "The alphabet which Mr. Ellis and myself had employed until 1851 was so defective that type-founders and printers would not look at it as a possible alphabet for representing the English language in books. Mr. Besley, the eminent type-founder, remonstrated somewhat sharply with me for thinking to overturn good-looking printing by bad. 'Your page,' said he, 'is covered with little hooks, and tails, and triangles.' I spared no labour and no expense in removing this obstacle to the general introduction of phonetic printing." A. Baker, *The Life of Sir Isaac Pitman*. London, 1913.

The writing reform continued to grow but Isaac Pitman would never for one moment permit it to be severed from its association with English spelling. He always reminded his shorthand teachers when they went out on their tours: "Do not fail, after your pay classes are formed, to give a lecture on the phonetic reform." Through this constant striving, classes were established in many places. They were to be found in Sunday Schools, mechanics' institutes, ragged schools and other institutions where young and old gathered to seek some educational outlet. The information about these efforts is not always complete and much of it is to be gleaned only from references in Ellis's and Pitman's publications.[1] In a letter to Benn Pitman of the 3rd January 1852, A. J. Ellis writes of Benn Pitman's efforts "crowned with the most brilliant and deserved success." He refers to "the experiment which you instituted at the Pauper Schools, at Swinton, near Manchester, upon a class of fifty of their dullest children; upon the criminals at the Preston House of Correction; and the Glasgow Bridewell; your foundation of the Manchester, Preston and Sheffield Phonetic Schools for adults."

A few examples will serve to indicate the philanthropic approach, the difficulties encountered and the successes which made the efforts seem worth while. In 1848 a Mr. McGowan established an evening class in Manchester; his students were of a wide age-range, from the mid-teens to the mid-forties. After nine lessons eleven of these students were able to read phonetic print and were beginning to read the New Testament in traditional spelling. After eighteen lessons all members of his "first division" could read in traditional print, while his "second division" were making great progress in phonotypy. Leo Grindon's Manchester Phonetic School ran successfully for ten years and was later absorbed in the educational service of the Manchester and Salford Co-operative Society. In 1849 Benn Pitman taught fifty persons in Swinton to read phonetic print in one month and his brother, Henry, thirty persons in the workhouse at Liverpool in "a few lessons." We hear, too, of sixty adults being taught to read at Lancaster. A teacher at Haddington Ragged School started a first-year class with Phonotypy and alongside had a second-year class which had been traditionally taught: he found the former's progress far swifter and that he could teach these bereft children to read with Phonotypy as quickly as it was possible to teach children from good homes with ordinary print. The poor children's speech also notice-

[1] See note on p. 41.

Characters.	Names of Letters as expressed in the formed Sounds pure	*Sounded* [respectively] as in [the Words in the Column below.]	[*Manner of pronouncing* the Sounds.]
o	o	Old.	The first Vowel, naturally, and deepest sound; requires only to open the mouth, and breathe through it.
a	a	John, Folly; Awl, Ball.	The next requiring the mouth opened a little, or hollower.
a	a	Man, can.	The next, a little more.
e	e	Men, lend, Name, Lane.	The next requires the *Tongue* to be a little more elevated.
i	i	Did, Sin, Deed, feen.	The next still more.
u	u	Tool, Fool, Rule.	The next requires the *Lips* to be gathered up, leaving a small opening.
ʌ	ʌ	um, un; as in umbrage, unto, &c. and as in *er*.	The next a very ſhort Vowel, the Sound of which we ſhould expreſs in our preſent Letters thus, *uh*; a ſhort, and not very ſtrong *expreſſion*.
	huh	hunter, happy, high.	A ſtronger or more forcible aſpiration.
gi	gi	give, gather.	The firſt CONSONANT; being formed by the *Root of the Tongue*; this is the guttural hard *g*.
ki	ki	keep, kick.	A kindred found; a little more acute; to be uſed inſtead of the hard *c*.
iſh	iſh	(ſh) Ship, wiſh.	A new letter, wanted in our language; our *ſh*, ſeparately taken, not being proper elements of the ſound.
iŋ	ing	(ng) ing, repeating, among.	A new letter, wanted for the ſame reaſon.---Theſe are formed *back in the mouth*.
en	en	end.	Formed *more forward* in the mouth; the *Tip of the Tongue to the Roof* of the mouth.
r	r	Art.	The ſame, the tip of the tongue a little looſe or ſeparate from the roof of the mouth, and vibrating.
ti	ti	Teeth.	The tip of the tongue more *forward*; touching, and then *leaving*, the roof.
di	di	Deed.	The ſame; touching a little fuller.
el	el	ell, tell.	The ſame; touching juſt about the *gums of the upper teeth*.
es	es	Effence.	This found is formed, by the breath paſſing *between* the mouth end of the tongue and the *upper teeth*.
ez	ez	(ez) Wages.	The ſame; a little denſer and duller.
eth	e'ɥ	(th) think.	The tongue under, and a little *behind*, the upper teeth; touching them, but ſo as to let the breath paſs between.
edh	e'ɥ	(dh) thy.	The ſame; a little fuller.
ef	ef	Effect.	Formed by the *lower lip* againſt the upper teeth.
ev	ev	ever.	The ſame; fuller and duller.
b	b	Bees.	The *lips put together*, and *opened* as the air paſſes out.
pi	pi	peep.	The ſame; but a thinner ſound.
em	em	ember.	The *cloſing of the lips*, while the *e* [there annexed] is ſounding.

* [N.B. Theſe new letters are marked with an aſteriſk * to diſtinguiſh them, and ſhew how few new ſounds are propoſed. E.]

3. Table of the Reformed Alphabet of Benjamin Franklin.

ably improved. This work went on in the school for six years until the teacher left.

In 1850 a Mr. Williams of the Secular School, Edinburgh, taught an experimental group with Phonotypy and a control group traditionally. The transition to normal spelling was made by the experimental children after nine months. These were all the children "of thrifty parents." At an examination held in public it was found that the experimental group were in advance of the others. In the Ragged School in Dumfries a group of very poor children, half clothed and often ill, had to be bribed to go to school at 8 a.m. in the month of December. There was no fire. Six months later they could read the New Testament in phonetic print. It was remarked of these children that they developed an English accent. While one does not wish to disturb national accent, this bears out the relationship, often noted, between the seeing of consistent spelling and speech habits.

It was always being reported that, after learning to read well in phonetic print, the reading of ordinary print caused no difficulty. Alexander Ellis taught his own infant daughter to read phonetics and reports that she passed effortlessly from phonetic to standard print. There are several reports of the introduction of Phonotypy into private fee-receiving schools in order to improve speech.

We hear of experiments in the United States. The Boston Phonetic School was founded in 1850 to exhibit the use of Phonotypy in teaching reading. A cross-section of a dozen children were taken out of a group of fifty. Three were non-English-speaking German children and the remaining nine were the children of immigrant Irish labourers. In three months they had reached the standard usually reached in eight months. Spelling competitions were common in America and these children took part in these public exhibitions and won such public fame that they were examined by a committee of the Massachusetts State Legislature. The committee reported of their reading of phonography, phonotypy and normal type that they performed "in a style rarely equalled by adults, never by children of their age." The system of teaching reading was recommended for introduction into all primary schools in the state of Massachusetts, and was introduced into 153 public and ten private schools. More is said of these experiments in American schools in the next chapter.

A testimonial fund had been raised in the United States but Isaac Pitman refused to accept personally the sum contributed and asked

that it be set aside as the nucleus of a fund to aid spelling reform. In 1862 a similar testimonial fund was subscribed from all over Britain as the result of an appeal by Sir Walter Trevelyan. Again, Isaac Pitman dealt with the money raised in similar fashion as before: "I feel that I have no right to receive such a sum of money and appropriate it to my own purposes." He admitted that he had to borrow heavily at times in his work and the sum subscribed was later used, together with other moneys donated, for the establishment of a new Phonetic Institute, as he called the office from which he did his work. Hitherto he had for years carried out his work from an office and workshop in a poor back street of Bath.

During the period 1844–1851 the Phonetic Councils of America and of England were very active. In his constant seeking for improvement Isaac Pitman several times changed letters in his Phonotype Alphabet (and in his shorthand). These changes often caused friction. The harshest criticism that has been levelled against him, apart from the fact that he drove those who helped him as he drove himself, was his unyieldingness where his spelling was concerned. He would listen graciously and pleasantly to every argument and then serenely go his own way. He had many arguments with the Councils, his advisory bodies, and with his great helpers like A. J. Ellis. Benn Pitman believed that his brother's "mania for change and improvement . . . did more to check the spread of Phonetic Reform, stop practical teaching, and dampen the ardour of those friendly to orthographic consistence, than all other causes combined." Despite such possible repercussions of his never-ceasing search for perfection, Isaac Pitman's own altruism and wholehearted enthusiasm prevailed over difficulties and his friends continued in his support.

In one great essential Isaac Pitman was very farsighted. Unlike many other spelling reformers he did not seek to represent sound in precise phonetic form, but to do so on a broad basis which sufficed only to discard anomalies in spelling and leave no doubt in the mind of the reader as to what was intended and how it should be sounded. Professor Max Müller wrote in *The Fortnightly Review* in 1876—

> What I like in Mr. Pitman's system of spelling is exactly what I know has been found fault with by others, namely that he does not attempt to require and to express in writing those endless shades of pronunciations which may be of greatest interest to the students of acoustics or of phonetics. Writing was never intended to photograph spoken lan-

JON.

ꞒAPTER 1.

IN ꓷe begíniꞃ woz ꓷe Wꙅrd, and ꓷe Wꙅrd woz
2 wiꓕ God, and ꓷe Wꙅrd woz God. ꓷe sɛm woz in
3 ꓷe begíniꞃ wiꓕ God. Ɵl ꓕiꞃz wer mɛd ꓕr꙲ him; and
4 wiꓕout him woz not eniꓕiꞃ mɛd. ꓷát whiꞒ haꓕ bįn mɛd
5 woz leif in him; and ꓷe leif woz ꓷe leit ov men. And ꓷe
   leit ʃeineꓕ in ꓷe darknes; and ꓷe darknes aprehended
6 it not. ꓷer kɛm a man, sent from God, h꙲z nɛm woz
7 Jon. ꓷe sɛm kɛm for witnes, ꓸat hį meit bɛr witnes
8 ov ꓷe leit, ꓸat ol meit beljv ꓕr꙲ him. Hį woz not ꓷe
9 leit, bꙅt kɛm ꓸat hį meit bɛr witnes ov ꓷe leit. ꓷe
   tr꙲ leit, whiꞒ leiteꓕ everi man, woz kꙅmiꞃ intu ꓷe
10 wꙅrld. Hį woz in ꓷe wꙅrld, and ꓷe wꙅrld woz mɛd
11 ꓕr꙲ him, and ꓷe wꙅrld niú him not. Hį kɛm ꙅntu
12 hiz ơn, and ꓸɛ ꓸat wer hiz ơn resjvd him not. Bꙅt az
   meni az ·resjvd him, tu ꓸem gɛv hį ꓷe reit tu bekꙅ́m
13 Ꞓildren ov God, įven tu ꓸem ꓸat beljv on hiz nɛm: h꙲
   wer born, not ov blꙅd, nor ov ꓷe wíl ov ꓷe fleʃ, nor
14 ov ꓷe wíl ov man, bꙅt ov God. And ꓷe Wꙅrd bekɛm
   fleʃ, and dwelt amꙅꞃ ꙅs (and wį beheld hiz glơri, glơri
   az ov ꓷe ơnli begoten from ꓷe FꙠꓸer), ful ov grɛs and
15 tr꙲ꓕ. Jon bɛreꓕ witnes ov him, and kreieꓕ, seiꞃ, ꓷis
   woz hį ov h꙲m ei sed, Hį ꓸat kꙅmeꓕ after mį iz bekꙅ́m
16 befơr mį: for hį woz befơr mį. For ov hiz fulnes wį
17 ol resjvd, and grɛs for grɛs. For ꓷe lọ woz given ꓕr꙲
18 Mơzes; grɛs and tr꙲ꓕ kɛm ꓕr꙲ Jįzꙅs Kreist. Nơ. man
   haꓕ sįn God at eni teim; ꓷe ơnli begoten Sꙅn, ꓸat iz
   in ꓷe b꙲zom ov ꓷe FꙠꓸer, hį haꓕ deklɛrd him.
19   And ꓸis iz ꓷe witnes ov Jon, when ꓷe Jiuz sent ꙅntu
   him from Jer꙲salem prįsts and Ljveits tu ask him, H꙲
20 art ꓸou? And hį konfest, and deneid not; and hį
21 konfest, Ei am not ꓷe Kreist. And ꓸɛ askt him, Whot
   ꓸen? Art ꓸou Eleija? And hį seꓕ, Ei am not. Art ꓸou
22 ꓷe profet? And hį anserd, Nơ. ꓷɛ sed ꓸerfor ꙅntu
   him, H꙲ art ꓸou? ꓸat wį mɛ giv an anser tu ꓸem ꓸat
23 sent ꙅs. Whot sɛest ꓸou ov ꓸeiself? Hį sed, Ei am
   ꓷe vois ov wꙅn kreiiꞃ in ꓷe wildernes, Mɛk strɛt ꓷe wɛ

4. The Gospel According to John. Page from the Authorized
Version of the Bible, in the Phonotypic Alphabet, published in 1850.

1 IN ƌe begíniꞑ woz ƌe Wurd, and ƌe Wurd woz wiƌ God, and ƌe Wurd woz God.
2 ƌe sam woz in ƌe begíniꞑ wiƌ God. (3) Ɵl tiꞑz wer mad bj him; and wiƌƨt him woz
4 not eni tiꞑ mad ƌat woz mad. In him woz
5 ljf; and ƌe ljf woz ƌe ljt ov men. And ƌe ljt ƒjnet in dqrcnes; and ƌe dqrcnes comprehénded it not.
6 ᛫ ƌar woz a man sent from God, huuz nam
7 [woz] Jon. ƌe sam cam for a witnes, tuu bar witnes ov ƌe Ljt, ƌat ol [men] truu him
8 mjt belév. He woz not ƌát Ljt, but [woz sent] tuu bar witnes ov ƌát Ljt.
9 [ƌát] woz ƌe truu Ljt, hwiꞑ ljtet everi
10 man ƌat cumet intuu ƌe wurld. He woz in
11 ƌe wurld, and ƌe wurld woz mad bj him, and ƌe wurld nꞷ him not. He cam untuu
12 hiz ɷn, and hiz ɷn resévd him not. But az meni az resévd him, tuu ƌém gav he pᵹer tuu becúm ƌe sunz ov God, [ev'n] tuu ƌém
13 ƌat belév on hiz nam : hwiꞡ wer born, not ov blud, nor ov ƌe wíl ov ƌe fleƒ, nor ov ƌe
14 wíl ov man, but ov God. And ƌe Wurd woz mad fleƒ, and dwelt amúꞑ us, (and we behéld hiz glori, ƌe glori az ov ƌe ɷnli begót'n ov ƌe Fqƌer,) ful ov gras and truuƌ.
15 Jon bar witnes ov him, and crjd, saiꞑ, ƌiz woz hé ov huum j spac, Hé ƌat cumet qfter me iz preférd befór me : for he wóz
16 befór me. And ov hiz fulnes hav el we
17 resévd, and gras for gras. For ƌe Lᴑ woz giv'n bj Mᴑzez, [but] gras and truuƌ cam
18 bj Jezus Crjst. Nᴑ man hat sen God at eni tjm ; ƌe ɷnli-begót'n Sun, hwiꞡ iz in ƌe buzum ov ƌe Fqƌer, [hé] hat declárd him.
19 AND ƌis iz ƌe record ov Jon, hwen ƌe Juz sent prests and Levjts from Jeruz-
20 alem tuu qsc him, ꝗ Húu qrt ƌᵹ. And he confést, and denjd not ; but confést, Ⱶ am
21 not ƌe Crjst. And ƌa qsct him, ꝗ Hwot den. ꝗ Árt ƌᵹ Ɛljas. And he set, Ⱶ am
22 not. ꝗ Nᴑ. ƌen sed ƌa untuu him, ꝗ Húu qrt ƌᵹ ; ƌat we ma giv an qnser tuu ƌém ƌat sent
23 us. ꝗ Hwot saest ƌᵹ ov ƌjsélf. ᛫He sed, Ⱶ [am] ƌe vᴑs ov wun crjiꞑ in ƌe wildernes, Mac strat ƌe wa ov ƌe Lord, az sed ƌe
24 profet Ɛzaas. And ƌá hwiꞡ wer sent wer
25 ov ƌe farisez. And ƌa qsct him, and sed untuu him, ꝗ Hwj baptjzest ƌᵹ den, if ƌᵹ be not ƌát Crjst, nor Ɛljas, neƌer ƌát profet.
26 Jon qnserd dem, saiꞑ, Ⱶ baptjz wiƌ woter : but ƌar standet wun amúꞑ ꞷ, huum ye nᴑ

1 tacet awá ƌe sin ov ƌe wurld ! (30) ƌis iz hé ov huum j sed, After me cumet a man hwiꞡ iz preférd befór me : for he wóz befór me.
31 And j nꞷ him not : but ƌat he ƒud be mad manifest tuu 'Izrael, ƌarfor am j cum bap-
32 tjziꞑ wiƌ woter. And Jon bar record, saiꞑ, Ⱶ sᴑ ƌe Spirit deséndiꞑ from hev'n ljc a
33 duv, and it abód upón him. And j nꞷ him not : but hé ƌat sent me tuu baptjz wiƌ woter, ƌe sam sed untuu me, Upón húum ƌᵹ ƒalt se ƌe Spirit deséndiꞑ, and remaniꞑ on
34 him, ƌe sam iz hé hwiꞡ baptjzet wiƌ ƌe Hᴑli Gost. And j sᴑ, and bar record ƌat ƌis iz ƌe Sun ov God.
35 Agén ƌe necst da qfter Jon stud, and túu
36 ov hiz disjp'lz ; and luciꞑ upón Jezus az he woct, he set, Behóld ƌe Lam ov God !
37 And ƌe túu disjp'lz herd him spec, and ƌa folᴑd Jezus.
38 ƌen Jezus turnd, and sᴑ ƌem fólᴑiꞑ, and set untuu ƌem, ꝗ Hwot sec ye. ƌa sed untuu him, Rabj, (hwiꞡ iz tuu sa, beiꞑ inter-
39 preted, Mqster,) ꝗ hwar dwelest ƌᵹ. He set untuu ƌem, Cum and se. ƌa cam and sᴑ hwar he dwelt, and abód wiƌ him ƌát
40 da : for it woz abᵹt ƌe tent ᵹr. Wun ov ƌe túu hwiꞡ herd Jon [spec], and folᴑd' him,
41 woz Andru, Sjmun Peterz bruƌer. He ferst fjndet hiz ɷn bruƌer Sjmun, and set untuu him, We hav fᵹnd ƌe Mesjas, hwiꞡ
42 iz, beiꞑ interpreted, ƌe Crjst. And he brot him tuu Jezus. And hwen Jezus behéld him, he sed, ƌᵹ qrt Sjmun ƌe sun ov Jᴑna : ƌᵹ ƒalt be cold Sefas, hwiꞡ iz bj interpret-
43 aƒun, Ꞁ ston. ƌe da fólᴑiꞑ Jezus wúd gᴑ fort intuu Galile, and fjndet Filip, and set untuu him,
44 Folᴑ me. Nᵹ Filip woz ov Betsada, ƌe
45 siti ov Andru and Peter. Filip fjndet Natánael, and set untuu him, We hav fᵹnd him, ov huum Mᴑzez in ƌe Lᴑ, and ƌe Profets, did rjt, Jezus ov Nazaret, ƌe sun
46 ov Jᴑzef. And Natánael sed untuu him, ꝗ Can ƌar eni gud tiꞑ cum ᵹt ov Nazaret.
47 Filip set untuu him, Cum and se. Jezus sᴑ Natánael cumiꞑ tuu him, and set ov him, Behóld an 'Izraeljt indéd, in huum iz nᴑ
48 gjl ! Natánael set untuu him, ꝗ Hwens noest ƌᵹ me. Jezus qnserd and sed untuu him, Befór ƌat Filip cold ƌé, hwen ƌᵹ wost
49 under ƌe fig tre, j sᴑ ƌé. Natánael qnserd and set untuu him, Rabj, ƌᵹ qrt ƌe Sun ov
50 God ; ƌᵹ qrt ƌe Ciꞑ ov 'Izrael. Jezus qnserd and sed untuu him, Becóz j sed untuu

5. The Gospel according to S. John. Page from the Phonotypic Edition of the
Revised Version of the New Testament, published in 1892.

guages; it was meant to indicate, not to paint sounds. . . . Language deals in broad colours, and writing ought to follow the example of language, which, though it allows an endless variety of pronunciation, restricts itself for its own purpose . . . to a very limited number of typical vowels and consonants.

The tide of spelling reform has ebbed and flowed often in the last hundred years and has never flowed fast, but the current has continued. The spelling reform movement, with the interests of children learning to read as its main aim, began with Isaac Pitman and has endured ever since. It has often lain dormant but it has never died. His work led to the earliest school experiments, to the first approaches to the Government. He went some way towards compromise with traditional spelling and advocated a simplified spelling with an initial teaching alphabet leading to ordinary reading.

His grandson, Sir James Pitman, has profited by Sir Isaac's experience. New letters closer to the letters of ordinary print are now being used and compromise with ordinary spelling goes to the very limit compatible with the admission of no ambiguity. Sir James Pitman is the first to proclaim that the Initial Teaching Alphabet (Augmented Roman) now being used is tremendously indebted in its basic concepts to Phonotypy.

In 1894 Isaac Pitman, then in his eighty-second year, said: "Phonography has reached the top of the hill and may now be left to run alone. Phonotypy has still the height before it and requires all the help to the patient that I can give it during the few remaining years of my life." In the summer of that year the honour of knighthood was conferred upon him and soon after Sir Isaac retired from the business which he had in so unusual and disinterested a manner established and his two sons, father and uncle of the present Sir James Pitman, took over control and expanded it to the great teaching and publishing undertaking that it has since become. Sir Isaac Pitman continued his crusading work and it is recorded that his last appearance on a public platform in advocacy of spelling reform was at a meeting of the Bath branch of the National Union of Teachers on the 20th June 1896. He died on the 22nd January 1897, in full possession of his amazing faculties and shortly before the end passed on this message: "To those who ask how Isaac Pitman passed away say, 'Peacefully, and with no more concern than in passing from one room into another to take up some further employment'." One of his biographers wrote—

What is said of the British Empire may be said of Pitman's Phonography—the sun never sets upon it. To an age which appreciates time- and labour-saving inventions, Isaac Pitman's shorthand appeals with especial force. But to his strenuous advocacy of the much needed reform in our spelling it has been comparatively indifferent. Some day, and possibly sooner than anticipated, the reform of our orthography will become a practical question. When that time arrives the lifelong labours of Isaac Pitman in this direction will not have been in vain.

Note. For references to this early work see the collected volumes of the *Phonotypic Journal* and the *Phonetic Journal* for the years 1849 to 1859 published in London by Fred Pitman. Also Fred Pitman's collection of pamphlets entitled *The Reading Reform* (London, 1854).

VI

Nineteenth-century Experiments with Phonetic Spelling

I hope there may come a time, before the twentieth century closes, when the claims of a phonetic spelling will be fairly considered, impartially and logically. . . . It is no small disgrace to us that its claims are now met only with sneers and scoffs, cautiousness and prejudice, and by objections that have been exposed over and over again.

Walter W. Skeat, Professor of Anglo-Saxon, Cambridge (1902)

IN THE NINETEENTH CENTURY the demand for a simpler and more consistent spelling gathered force, largely through the labours of Sir Isaac Pitman, in Britain and in the United States. The influx of non-English-speaking immigrants to America and the attitudes to academic learning of a pioneering community have together seemed, by contrast with the conservative traditions of English society, to preserve a freer approach to spelling in America, just as they have often livened the spoken language with pithy phrases and constructions, often unscholarly in origin, but ultimately winning approval in England as elsewhere. That the United States should, therefore, have played a large part in the educational experiments with consistent spelling is to be expected.

Towards the middle of the last century, Dr. A. J. Ellis had brought the weight of his scholarship to support his proposals for reform. In his *A Plea for Phonetic Spelling*,[1] he carefully compiled tables, showing the extent of the perversity of English orthography. With examples, he proved that the letters of the alphabet are used in at least 642 different ways, and that the forty or so sounds of the English language are represented by not fewer than 615 signs (letters or combinations of letters). He claimed that of the "200,000 words which may be said to constitute the language" not more than one hundred simple ones, such as be, so, no, post, mild, are pronounced as the vowels are known. The rest have to be separately

[1] A. J. Ellis, *A Plea for Phonetic Spelling*. London, 1848.

memorized. Phonotypy which evolved from his collaboration with Isaac Pitman was taken to America by Benn Pitman.

There appears to have been an early school experiment using A. J. Ellis's Glossic alphabet but the first reports of experiments in teaching children to read through systematic spelling come from Massachusetts, where the *First Phonetic Reader* published in Cincinnati by Benn Pitman was used. Although little is known of the teachers concerned and their work, we have references to their reports that in reading and speech their pupils were "years in advance of most children who had been taught in the old way." The first extensive experiment was undertaken at Waltham, Massachusetts, between 1852 and 1860. Dr. Thomas Hill was a former President of Harvard University and at this period was chairman of the School Committee in Waltham, Massachusetts. There he inaugurated a series of experiments in the schools of Waltham using Isaac Pitman's Phonotypy to introduce children to reading during the first six to eight months at school. The children later went on to read traditional print. In 1899 a report of the American Philosophical Society set out the results—

> We tested it thoroughly for six and seven years in the town of Waltham, Massachusetts, which then had about 800 children in the public schools. The effect upon the school life of the town was very marked. The saving of time in teaching the children to read and to spell enabled us to introduce exercises for the eye and the hand, thus cultivating habits of observation, skill in drawing and writing, and geometrical ability. The fonetic print corrected the brogue of the Irish children and the Yankee dialect of the American in a surprising manner. An improvement in the moral and intellectual tone of the schools was also noticeable, arising certainly in part from giving the children interesting reading instead of such absurd falsehoods as that of saying that "sea," "you," "pea," spells "cup."
>
> Fears were expressed that this method should injure the pupils' spelling. In order to test that question, I took pains to procure, several times, lists of words which had actually been used in Boston, Roxbury, and other places, with the percentage of failures on each list. Springing these lists, without warning, upon classes of the same grade in Waltham, we always found our percentage of errors very much smaller than in other towns, sometimes I think only one third as large. We also questioned each pupil in our high-school as to the amount of time which he or she had devoted in his or her whole school life to fonotypy and fonography. Comparing these times with the percentage of errors in

spelling, by the same scholars, we found that those who had read the most fonotypy made the fewest mistakes.

Another similar experiment was tried out in 1866 by Mr. William T. Harris, the School Superintendent of St. Louis. The system used was devised by Dr. Edwin Leigh, who spent twenty-five years in perfecting it. According to Sir Charles Reed, in an address to the Social Congress at Brighton in 1875—

> It is really "Pronouncing Orthography." It shows the exact pronunciation of every word and a special form of letter is used for each sound of it. Letters which have no sound are printed in a hair-line, or light-faced type. It thus shows the pronunciation without changing the spelling, and even preserves the familiar form or face of the words, as we are accustomed to see them.

Teachers everywhere testified to the saving of time, and those who began with reluctance had almost invariably come to advocate the system. This evidence followed years of experience in a very large number of schools—

> I myself watched neglected children learning to read, noting particularly the facility with which they learned the phonic letters and sounds; they took evident interest in it, and progress was clearly seen; in fact, though I remember in my earlier days to have been familiar with a book called *Reading Made Easy*, I never saw the thing till I saw the instruction under this method. Beyond this, they take interest in practising the sounds, all of which they learn; they spell correctly by sound, they pronounce distinctly and accurately and they read fluently and naturally.

In 1867 the School Board of St. Louis after a number of experiments reported in favour of introducing Leigh's method into all the primary schools. Harris later became U.S. Commissioner for Education to the Federal Government in Washington. A U.S. Bureau of Education circular of 1893 carries his report that from eighteen to twenty-four months could be saved in learning to read through systematic spelling and for the first time we hear of attendant gains in the development of personal factors, such as the love of books.

The school experiments spread to other parts of the United States as the following extracts from reports indicate.

Under the St. Louis School Board experiments were conducted in 1868 in the Clay School. The Superintendent reported: "Its

[Simplified Spelling's] introduction has been followed by far greater results than were at first anticipated; not only has it tended to the eradication of defects in enunciation, but there has been a saving of time to the extent of a whole quarter in the course of the first half year." In 1869 the School Board officially reported: "A given standard of good reading can always be reached in about one half the time. . . . They make better arithmetic and grammar scholars, and are more wide awake, attentive and discriminating." In 1870 the Superintendent wrote: "Each year increases our admiration of the work. Gain in time—quite one half—distinct articulation, and better spelling represent the undoubted advantages." Again in 1871, "Sounds are not to be used only to spell with, but to read with."

The Report of the Illinois Board of Education of 1871 testified: "Pupils are found in their second year of schooling who have read many books. They learn to read so quickly and by comparatively so little effort, that reading is a pleasure, which could not be said under the old system."

In the 1871 Report of Washington University on its primary schools, one reads the view of the Superintendent that never had he heard boys after so short a time under instruction read with such good expression and spell so well. Professor Stone of the University said: "We have very many scholars who have finished the whole primary course in two years, three being the time usually allowed. We have no difficulty in the transition to common print," and Professor Waterhouse commented: "It is a shame that children lost so much precious time when I was a boy. This system is unrivalled for theoretic simplicity and practical success. A thorough trial in the primary schools of the University has fully established its success."

In Iowa, again in 1871, a class of children averaging six years of age, in five months accomplished what on the part of a class averaging eight years of age, but using the ordinary type, had required fifteen months.

Boston teachers reported similar experiments in their city—

> The system was introduced in February 1873. The results were immediate, and to me wonderful; none of us entertains the slightest doubt about the advantage of the system. The children learn to read in half the time it formerly took and do not contract that old habit, so hard to eradicate, of reading one word at a time, as though they were pronouncing a column of words from the speller. The teachers find no difficulty about spelling.

After four years' trial another teacher said: "Pupils do four times as much reading: they read more intelligently." The Superintendent of the Boston School Board, Mr. Philbrick, wrote—

> When the experiment was commenced, I had no bias in its favour or prejudice against it. The inventor, who spent many years in perfecting the system and in bringing it to the notice of educators, asked to have it tried, and it has had a long and fair trial on a large scale. The result has been eminently successful. It seems to me, therefore, that the time has come when the Board should adopt the system, and make it obligatory in all the Primary Schools.

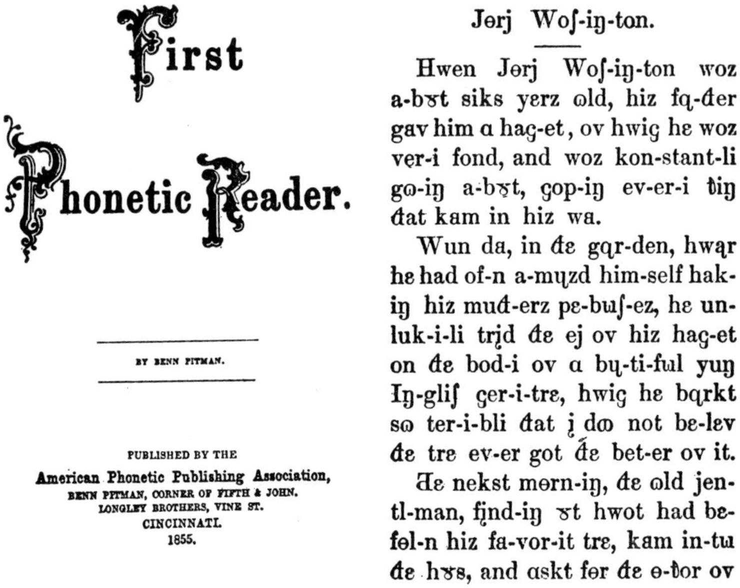

First Phonetic Reader.

BY BENN PITMAN.

PUBLISHED BY THE
American Phonetic Publishing Association,
BENN PITMAN, CORNER OF FIFTH & JOHN.
LONGLEY BROTHERS, VINE ST.
CINCINNATI.
1855.

Jərj Woʃ-iŋ-ton.

Hwen Jərj Woʃ-iŋ-ton woz a-bɤt siks yerz old, hiz fą-đer gav him a haç-et, ov hwiç he woz ver-i fond, and woz kon-stant-li go-iŋ a-bɤt, çop-iŋ ev-er-i ŧiŋ đat kam in hiz wa.

Wun da, in đe gąr-den, hwąr he had of-n a-mųzd him-self hak-iŋ hiz mud-erz pe-buʃ-ez, he un-luk-i-li trįd đe ej ov hiz haç-et on đe bod-i ov a bų-ti-ful yuŋ Iŋ-gliʃ çer-i-tre, hwiç he bąrkt so ter-i-bli đat į do not be-lev đe tre ev-er got đe bet-er ov it.

Đe nekst mərn-iŋ, đe old jen-tl-man, fįnd-iŋ ɤt hwot had be-fəl-n hiz fa-vor-it tre, kam in-tu đe hɤs, and askt fər đe o-ŧor ov

6. "First Phonetic Reader" by Benn Pitman, 1855

The Board of Public Instruction of New York reported in 1871: "Much time is saved in teaching to read by this method, and the children are better trained by it for other instruction. It is, therefore, recommended to all the schools."[1]

[1] These accounts of Dr. Leigh's system and of the American experiments are taken from the reported address of Sir Charles Reed, Chairman of the London School Board, to the Society of Arts in London on the 29th May 1877. The report of the meeting at Adelphi, London, is printed in detail in *A Plea for Phonetic Reform*, edited by Isaac Pitman. London, 1878.

We have a record of one school experiment from about the same time on this side of the Atlantic, which was conducted at Portland Infant School, Ireland. The following account comes from Pitman's *The Spelling Reform* of 1875[1]—

Of the children who have learned phonetically, and are now in the Second Book of the ordinary National School series, and who will have completed a two years' course of instruction by May next, there are thirty-two, all making satisfactory progress; a large percentage being expected to pass the Inspector next examination. They are more than half-way through the book, and are even better spellers than they are readers. . . . The importance of this statement as to the number of children in the Second Book can only be properly estimated when taken in connection with the fact that, for the seventeen years . . . before the introduction of Phonotypy, there never was a class of more than three or four in the Second Book, and then only laboring through it often having spent three or four years at school. . . . Of children . . . whose attendance will only be a year next May, there are over twenty. Their progress is also of the most satisfactory description, more especially in romanic (i.e. traditional) writing. . . . It would have been impossible for teachers, no matter however hard they might labor, to have attained such results under the old system.

The references to books and examinations may sound amusing to teachers today. They were deadly serious matters in 1875. This was the period when standards of reading assessed book by book and examined by visiting inspectors at regular intervals determined the amount of government grant which school managers would be paid and ages at which children could leave school and take up employment. He was indeed a daring teacher who risked experiment outside well-known methods.

These old experiments were uncontrolled and objective testing was unknown, but the reports of all these teachers and educational administrators taken together have value. Not the least of their importance lies in the fact that the reports, like those of the 1920s, parallel in a remarkable degree the findings of the 1960s. One can only guess at the cause which underlay the cessation of such successful work and it must have lain in the poor supply of books. The experiments seem to have lost impetus when they lost the guiding force of the experimenter of the moment.

The first Elementary Education Act reached Britain's Statute

[1] No. 314.

Book in 1870. This and succeeding acts established School Boards to administer education throughout England and Wales. When introducing the Bill into the House of Commons, Mr. W. E. Forster had said: "We ought not to rest until, in this island of ours, every English child has an elementary education. That means reading so that it can understand what it reads; writing so that it can be read; and cyphering. These are necessities." The Education Report presented to Parliament five years later by the Duke of Richmond and Gordon contained the following figures. Out of half a million school-leavers each year—

> It appears that only about 100,000 of the children in any year even get beyond the reading of monosyllables, or an easy story-book, or about one in five of the children growing up into manhood year by year. Only about 75,000, or about one in six, satisfy the Inspector on any subject beyond the 3 R's, and only about 20,000, or one in twenty-five, are able to read a short paragraph from the newspaper with a fair degree of accuracy.

Educationists the length and breadth of the country were alarmed by the failure of the new Act to achieve its basic purposes, of which reading came first. The anomalies of English spelling were often seen to be a prime cause of this failure and the evil effects of irrational spelling on other subjects was noted. Mr. J. M. D. Meiklejohn, Professor of History and the Art of Education at St. Andrews University and formerly Assistant Commissioner of the Endowed Schools Mission for Scotland, writing in the *Daily News*, compared the difficulties confronting English teachers with those of teachers in Germany and France. He referred to the "two-fold disease" of English spelling: that printed signs indicate different sounds and that the same sound is shown by different symbols. He said that while French suffered from one of these diseases, German was wholly consistent. He added that this did not complete the list of the comparative difficulties of the English teacher for, instead of forming steady and consistent habits, the English child's "experience is so conflicting that it almost goes to prevent him forming any habits whatsoever." The fact that consistency of spelling rules appears to lead to confidence in the logical consistency of rules in other subjects has been noted in the most recent schoolwork.

Some years before at a meeting of the Philological Society, Mr. Russell Martineau suggested that a Royal Commission should be

formed to consider how English spelling could be rationalized to make reading easier. This suggestion was supported by the Rev. J. Ryce Byrne, one of Her Majesty's Inspectors of Schools, in his official report in the Educational Blue Book, 1869.

In official reports evidence of the difficulties of teaching reading accumulated. Attention was directed to these reports at various meetings of the London School Board and, in 1876, a proposal was made for the appointment of a Royal Commission and a circular was sent to 277 school boards in England and Wales asking for views on the proposal. At its Liverpool conference the National Union of Elementary Teachers supported the scheme. In January, Isaac Pitman, indefatigable as ever, sent out a manifesto to all the school boards stating the case for simplified spelling as a help in teaching reading. One hundred school boards gave their support to the London proposal.

On the fourteenth of March 1877, the London School Board set up a committee to draw up a memorial seeking the appointment of a Royal Commission. Meetings of support were held and newspaper comment for and against was rife. *The Times*, traditionally cautious of proposed change, went so far as to recommend that children should be taught to read and write in the first three standards on "the easy phonetic plan." There was a public conference on Spelling Reform at the headquarters of the Society of Arts on the twenty-ninth of May, under the chairmanship of Dr. A. H. Sayce, Professor of Philology at Oxford, and among many eminent speakers was Isaac Pitman. On the twenty-fifth of July the London School Board adopted its memorial, which asked the Committee of the Privy Council on Education "to move the Government for a Royal Commission to inquire whether it would be possible to reform spelling in the interests of primary education, and of thus making the arts of reading and writing accessible to the bulk of their children." It asked for investigation into the best method of reforming and simplifying English spelling. It pointed to the unsatisfactory results in the new board schools which several inspectors of schools attributed largely to the difficulties of the existing spelling. It called attention to the support of eminent men in all walks in England and America, of scholars and teachers. (The Spelling Reform Association was founded in the United States in 1876 and included in its membership many of the leading phoneticians, philologists and lexicographers of America. Most prominent in its establishment was Dr. Melvil Dewey,

who later was from 1889 to 1899 secretary to the Regents of the University of the State of New York, by which office he was in charge of higher education throughout the state. The office of Education Commissioner had not then been created.)[1]

On the eighteenth of January 1878, the Duke of Richmond and Gordon, who as Lord President of the Privy Council was the minister responsible for educational affairs,[2] received a deputation from the London and many supporting School Boards[3] and another from the Society of Arts. The Lord President heard the deputation and promised to lay its views before the cabinet. Nothing further came of the matter.

While the official approach was unsuccessful, it had not been in vain. Following the example of reformers in America, a Spelling Reform Association was established here and for the first time we read in connection with the organized reform movement the names of two men, Professor W. W. Skeat and Dr. G. B. (later Sir George) Hunter, who were to play a major part in carrying the movement forward into the next century. The career of the Spelling Reform Association was brief. It published a number of pamphlets and organized meetings, but there were great differences of opinion about the precise manner of reform, and energy was frittered away in arguing these details.

[1] Until 1905 Dr. Melvil Dewey was Director of the State Library of New York, the State Library School and the Home Education (today called Adult Education) Department.

[2] Until the Board of Education Act of 1899, the Lord President of the Privy Council was the minister responsible to parliament for educational affairs. From 1899 to the Education Act of 1944, educational affairs in England and Wales were in the hands of the President of the Board of Education. From 1944 to 1964 responsibility for educational matters has lain with the Minister of Education.

[3] School Boards preceded County and County Borough and (till 1944) certain Borough Councils as the authorities charged with the local administration of education in Britain. The Elementary Education Act, 1902, established the Councils as Local Education Authorities in England and Wales and they act through Local Education Committees. Practice in Scotland and Northern Ireland is similar.

VII

Approaches to the Government

Spelling reforms have been passed in Germany and Sweden, systems of phonetic spelling have been designed for Turkish, Russian, and for Chinese—but England still prides herself upon an orthography which rather represents King Alfred's pronunciation than that of His Majesty King George the Fifth.

Professor R. E. Zachrisson of the Royal University, Uppsala (1930)

SIR ISAAC PITMAN was dead and the Spelling Reform Association moribund. The topic of spelling reform receded from the public stage, but in scholastic circles it was not forgotten. In 1881, Dr. Henry Sweet of Oxford, President of the Philological Society, suggested in his *Partial Corrections of English Spelling* a limited scheme of spelling reform. Many thought this limited goal more realist than to seek a truly rational system. A scheme of the sort was carried out in the United States during the presidency of Theodore Roosevelt. Roosevelt gave instructions to the U.S. Stationery Office that certain simplified spellings should be used. Among these were the reversal of **r** and **e** in words like **theatre**, the spelling of **program, thru,** and many others. They were particular rationalizations and not based on rules of general application. Unfortunately, the lists ended when Roosevelt ceased to be president. This incident strengthened the arguments of those who stood for the enunciation of rules to be universally applied and this has been the attitude adopted by the Simplified Spelling Society in England. Professor Skeat tells us that, when Sweet published his cautious proposals, there was scarcely a newspaper or periodical in Britain which did not denounce them: "The indignant writers were discussing a subject which they had never studied, and which they did not understand; and they did so with perfect honesty, because they were not in the least aware of their own ignorance."[1]

At a meeting in the Holborn Restaurant, London, on the tenth of September 1908, the Simplified Spelling Society was founded.

[1] *Problem of Spelling Reform*, p. 14.

Those present were Mr. William Archer (London), Dr. F. J. Furnivall (London), Mr. E. P. Gaston (London), Professor I. Gollancz (London), Professor H. Stanley Jevons (Cardiff), Mr. J. J. Munro (London), Mr. A. W. Pollard (London), Professor W. W. Skeat (Cambridge), and two visitors from the United States, Professor James W. Bright (Baltimore) and Dr. C. P. G. Scott (New York). Speaking from the chair, Professor Skeat referred to "the difficulties that had been encountered in former years by the scholars who had urged a simplification of English spelling. It was proposed to make a renewed effort to overcome these difficulties by means of a Society which should co-operate with the Simplified Spelling Board of New York." In its constitution the aim of the Society was stated to be to recommend simpler spellings of English words than those now in use, and to further the general use of such simpler spellings by every means in its power, and to co-operate with the Simplified Spelling Board of America.

The Simplified Spelling Board had been incorporated in New York in 1906. Dr. Melvil Dewey again (see pp. 49–50) played a big part and was particularly influential in winning the support of Andrew Carnegie, whose financial gifts made its foundation possible. Professor Skeat was the first president of the Simplified Spelling Society in Britain and on his resignation in 1910, he was succeeded by Professor (later Sir Gilbert) Murray who was president of the Society until 1946. The early minutes mention many contributions to the Society's funds. The most outstanding benefactor was Mr. Andrew Carnegie who several times donated sums of £1,000; other outstanding contributors were Dr. G. B. Hunter and Mr. W. Morrison. An appeal for membership was made in 1913 in the following terms—

> The Association invites all persons interested in improvement of English orthography of any kind whatsoever, whether mainly for elementary school instruction or for national adoption, however much they may differ in opinion as to the mode, character, or extent of such improvement, to become members of the Association.

In 1910 the Society had published its *Proposals for Simplifying the Spelling of English* for private circulation among its members. The proposals were based on the assumption that no simplification could be of much practical value unless it were systematic. At the same time the need to win popular support was regarded as of first im-

portance and it was decided to make no startling departures from current usage. Accordingly no new characters were to be introduced and there were to be no new diacritics (detached marks in the form of accents and so on), and normal spelling was to be retained as much as possible. This principle of least disturbance necessitated an exhaustive and scholarly survey of current spelling usages in order to give to each sound the symbol in commonest use. The whole purpose was to evolve a system which while wholly consistent would be easily readable by those habituated to present spelling.

A monthly periodical, *The Pioneer*, was until late in the 1914–18 war regularly published and circulated among the members, the numbers of whom fluctuated but often exceeded a thousand. From the beginning interest was concentrated on schoolchildren. The Society was for many years represented at educational conferences and often rented a stall at the exhibitions organized in conjunction with the annual conferences of the National Union of Teachers.

A number of infant readers were printed in "Simplifyd Speling" and experiments were arranged in a number of schools in Scotland, largely through the efforts of Mr. R. Jackson, Lecturer in Phonetics at Dundee Training College. There were ultimately five readers and rhyme books illustrated with line drawings, but they were far from being the attractive, spaciously printed, colourful books supplied in infant schools today. After the First World War, encouraged by the remarkable success of these experiments, the introduction of simplified spelling into schools was extended and reports of what happened in schools from London and Herefordshire to the north of England and in Scotland are given at some length in the next chapter.

As early as 1913, a petition to the Board of Education was being discussed. The First World War forced a postponement of this project, but in 1916 the Society approached Mr. Arthur Henderson, a former President of the Board of Education, about the "inclusion of Spelling reform in the Bill which is in preparation for the reconstruction of education after the war," and at a meeting in March 1917, the minutes refer to sanction by the Board of Education for "the conducting of experiments with simplified spelling in several elementary schools in England and the secretary was instructed to arrange these as soon as possible." What form the sanction took is not made clear in the minutes, but there was clearly some administrative encouragement. A minute of 1924 reports that "the officials

[of the Board of Education] have shown very considerable sympathy with our Movement and have helped in several ways."

The never-failing success of the experiments of the 1920s prompted renewed approaches to the government. The members of the Simplified Spelling Society were well aware that antagonists of reform were wont to use the variety of schemes put forward as though their variety were an argument against reform. It is true that too many ardent reformers have been so sensitive about their pet theories that at times it has seemed as though they would forgo reform rather than see it carried through by a method different from that of their own choice. The Society, therefore, put forward no claims for its own method: it was decided only to ask for the appointment of a committee to consider the need for spelling simplification and, if the evidence favoured this, then for the committee to make recommendations. In July 1923 a deputation from the Simplified Spelling Society waited upon Sir Charles Trevelyan, the President of the Board of Education. Sir Charles admitted the difficulties which accompanied traditional spelling but expressed the view that "the appointment of a Commission or Committee could not be expected to result in any scientific solution, unless the supporters of Spelling Reform were able as a preliminary to decide upon an agreed and definite scheme."

The members had sincerely felt that only a nationally based body should decide upon a scheme. They had been hoping to solidify agreement upon the need for reform without acrimony among reformers. However, since Sir Charles Trevelyan's official view was that a system of spelling should be produced in order to show that the job was practicable and to provide a scheme for discussion, Simplifyd Speling as used in the infant reading books during the experiments of the preceding years was the Society's answer. In 1926 a proposal to this effect was addressed to Lord Eustace Percy, who was then President of the Board. No action seems to have been forthcoming in spite of a parliamentary question by Commander Bellairs, M.P., asking whether the petition had been received and what action had been taken. In the words of Mr. Harold Cox, Editor of the *Edinburgh Review*, writing in 1930: "Nothing has yet been done. The matter unfortunately is one that would win no votes for any political party." Efforts were made to secure broadcasting time from the British Broadcasting Corporation.

During the 1930s Sir George Hunter, the shipbuilder of Wallsend-

on-Tyne, devoted a great deal of time to the cause of spelling reform and appointed his personal secretary, Mr. T. R. Barber, to organize this one of his many activities. During this period the work of the Simplified Spelling Society was virtually carried on by Sir George and Mr. Barber. They were tireless in their efforts to win public support.[1]

The next President of the Board of Education was Viscount Irwin,[2] and in 1933 a memorial was addressed to him in the following terms—

> The undersigned, who are interested in Education, and in the question of simplifying English spelling; in view of the growing need of an international language for use in international Conferences and Meetings and in publications of world-wide interest; and in view of the increasing conviction in Sweden, Germany, and other countries, that the English language, which is already used by nearly two hundred million of our world's population, can best supply that need, but that its inconsistent and difficult spelling is a hindrance; respectfully submit, for your consideration, the request that you will appoint a representative Committee, to consider whether English spelling can be and should be simplified, and if so, what improvements should be recommended, for optional or general use.

The memorial was signed by the representatives of eighteen British and two overseas universities. Three hundred and twelve university signatories included vice-chancellors, heads of colleges or holders of professorial chairs. The professorial signatories alone covered every branch of learning from astronomy and engineering to mathematics, chemistry, economics, commerce, modern languages, Hebrew and Sanskrit. There were names of those in the forefront of British scholarship and the names of many to become renowned later. In addition a similar memorial was signed by 125 members of the House of Commons and other memorials came from the National Union of Teachers, the National Union of Women Teachers, the National Association of Schoolmasters, the Incorporated Association of Assistant Masters in Secondary Schools, the Modern Language Association, the Association of Women University Teachers. The Bishops of Coventry, Leicester, Sheffield, Bristol, Monmouth and Salisbury gave their written support.

Lord Irwin agreed in principle that it was reasonable and fitting

---

[1] Mr. Barber was secretary of the Society for twenty-five years until his retirement in 1954, when Dr. Horace King, Member of Parliament for Southampton Itchen, took over the office. Dr. King's part in this educational reform with i.t.a. has been an important and an onerous one.   [2] Later the Earl of Halifax.

for Spelling Reform to be considered and dealt with by the Board of Education but beyond that the President would not go, although the setting up of a committee to consider whether English spelling could be improved and simplified hardly of itself committed anybody to anything. Lord Irwin's letter of the seventeenth of March 1933, to Mr. W. G. Pearson, M.P., who had asked for the reception of a delegation, seemed to suggest that he wanted a scheme agreed by all the reformers, although it was understood that his predecessor wanted only a scheme. The reformers acted quickly and, in a letter of the sixteenth of May 1933, Sir George Hunter again asked Lord Irwin to receive a deputation and put forward the system of the Simplified Spelling Society as a scheme agreed by a very representative group. He reminded the President of the Board of Education of the school experiments and expressed the hope that a Departmental Committee would take a comprehensive view of the case for spelling reform, and would consider its bearing on education in the schools, its economy in printing, and its value to the many speakers of different languages in the British Empire: both in the use of English as an auxiliary world language and in preserving the purity of the English language and pronunciation. The promoters foresaw no special expenditure; the system used existing traditional type. While it was not expected that spelling could be changed by duress, it was felt that any changes recommended would be voluntarily and gradually adopted.

The reformers expected that a Committee would be set up and were extremely disappointed when this was not done. They had done all those things which they had been asked to do by successive ministerial heads of the education service. Lord Irwin, however, while admitting the great importance of those supporting the request to him and that the agreement on a scheme "goes some way to meet a difficulty experienced by my predecessors," expressed the opinion that reform could not "enter the region of practical affairs until it has secured a large backing not only of learned, but of popular opinion." The President of the Board of Education was asking the well-nigh impossible in requiring a wide public demand for a reform. The value of reform could hardly be impressed upon the general public in such manner as to rouse an enthusiastic demand. This was not because the case could not be proved, but because the public could not be brought to listen. George Bernard Shaw once said that a financial profit must be shown before the public will stop to

listen. This may be a Shavian exaggeration but it is historically true that reforms follow often from the work of the few rather than from the demands of the many who ultimately benefit.

Sir George Hunter wrote to Lord Irwin in June and again in July expressing the great disappointment of the reformers, who felt that they had carried out adequately all that had been asked of them: "We have complied with the only stipulation laid down by the President of the Board." He said that at least a committee of inquiry could do no harm and could possibly be of value. Lord Irwin was adamant. He could not "recommend the expenditure of time and money which the proposed inquiry would involve, particularly at a time of universal preoccupation with national and international problems touching the livelihood of millions." The time was not opportune! In his last letter on the eighth of July, which concluded the correspondence, Sir George Hunter said that the reformers would endeavour to comply with the further stipulation, to arouse and demonstrate support for spelling reform. Sir George died in 1937 and he showed his own resolve in this undertaking by leaving to the Simplified Spelling Society a large bequest to aid their work. Even this led to further demonstration of unsympathetic official attitudes. The Society's work was not regarded as educational by the Commissioners of Income Tax and in spite of the Society's plea that they were engaged in work of an educational character, they had to meet tax demands on their income from this and other sources as though they were a profit-making association.

VIII

Early Twentieth-century Experiments

> This Executive is of the opinion that the Board of Education should insti-
> tute an inquiry into the advisability of introducing some practical measure
> of spelling reform.
>
> Resolution of the National Union of Teachers (1927)

IN AN ARTICLE on Spelling Reform, the editor of *The Edinburgh
Review* recorded that: "At the Conference of Educational Associations in January 1926, it was stated that in a number of
schools experiments had been made in teaching children to read
and write first of all through a simple phonetic scheme of spelling,
and that these experiments had been invariably and conspicuously
successful." This was the last large-scale experiment in using
simplified spelling in schools before that of today. The reports,
which came from schools in England and Scotland, were the
reports not only of teachers and headteachers, but also of His
Majesty's inspectors of schools and of outside observers. They are
often detailed, giving dates, class numbers and the names of assistant
teaching staff. They were collected and published by the Simplified
Spelling Society in 1924.[1]

Three of the reports come from Dundee. At Clepington School
some twelve children were chosen at random from the new entrants
and were taught to read from a simplified spelling reader, *A Ferst
Reeder in Simplifyd Speling*, published by the Simplified Spelling
Society: additional reading material consisted entirely of extracts
from the books ordinarily used in the school, which were written on
the blackboard in simplified spelling. After ten months the children
were introduced to normal spelling. They received throughout the
same amount of instruction as other children would receive during
their first school year. After fourteen months at school these children
read as well as children admitted earlier who had been five months

---

[1] Simplified Spelling Society, Pamphlet No. 7 (Pitman). See also R. Jackson, "Phonetics and Phonetic Texts in the Teaching of Reading," in *Miscellanea Phonetica* (International Phonetic Association) 1914.

longer at school. The speech of the experimental children was freer and clearer than that of the others. This judgment is confirmed by Mr. Robert Jackson, Lecturer in Phonetics at Dundee Training College (A),[1] by the headmaster of the school, and by the infant mistress. The results of the experiment were reported by Mr. (later Professor) Daniel Jones to the Simplified Spelling Society.[2] A few months later the infant mistress read a paper on the experiment to the annual meeting of the Society, in the course of which she singled out as particular benefits arising from the use of consistent spelling, the saving of time and increased fluency in reading and expansion of vocabulary (B). It will be noted that beyond one book, the experimental children's reading consisted for ten months of extracts transcribed from other books and written on the blackboard, which of itself created a burden for the teachers and must have been to the disadvantage of the children.

At the beginning of the school year in August 1916, the infant mistress of Dens Road School, Dundee, used simplified spelling as an introduction to reading. By the end of the school year she was able to report that in six months most of the children were reading books usually only read after a year in school (C).

At the same time as at Dens Road School, two teachers at the Morgan Academy, Dundee, began a similar experiment. At the end of six months the simplified primer had been read through and children were given a traditionally spelt book, not normally read until after eight to nine months' schooling. The teachers remarked on the avoidance of drudgery, the pleasure taken in reading and the greater fluency in speech (D). In the following year it was reported that the Dundee Education Authority was "delighted, enthusiastic in fact" over the results.

A little earlier than these Dundee experiments, before the publication of the Simplified Spelling Society's *Ferst Reeder*, there is recorded a similar piece of work at Lumphinnans School in Fifeshire. Miss McCullam, a teacher of infant children in the school, used a modified form of the International Phonetic Alphabet to give children their first steps in reading. Mr. Jackson, as a member of the staff of the training college at Dundee, had exceptional opportunities of watching the work in these four schools and he wrote of the Lumphinnans School experiment: "Within a comparatively short time

---

[1] The lettered references in this chapter refer to Appendix III.
[2] Simplified Spelling Society's Minutes, 22nd September 1915.

the pupils learnt to read anything that described facts within their own experience, and to write and spell any such words as come within their natural diction with almost perfect accuracy." In all the schools he noted improvement in diction and in extent of vocabulary. He drew the conclusion that forty signs to represent the sounds of English speech can be learnt in a few weeks and "that thereafter only a little practice is needed until the pupil can decipher any word whatever that forms part of his daily diction, or that, keeping in mind the stage of his mental growth, can legitimately be introduced in teaching."

Mr. Jackson noted that in none of the four schools had there been any difficulty for a child in changing from the simplified spelling to traditional orthography. Writing soon after a visit to Dens Road School at a time when the children from the experimental class were in the process of making the transition, he said that he had listened to hitherto unseen reading from ordinary spelling. It was apparent that training in reading with a consistent relationship of sound and symbol had provided a basis from which the children tackled and easily read normal spellings with ease. Two and a half years after the beginning of the experiment at Clepington School, Mr. Jackson tested the children there and found the experimental children still ahead of the others in reading and in purity of speech, and equal in spelling.

The headmaster of the Intermediate School at Bridge of Allan in Stirlingshire, prompted by accounts of some of this work which had been reported in the *Scottish Educational Journal*, began an experiment in his school in August 1919. By this time the Simplified Spelling Society had published three school books, having added to the *Ferst Reeder* a *Sekond Reeder* and *Jinglz and Storiz*. These were supplied free to interested schools. He quickly discovered that progress in reading was confident and much quicker: "In six weeks' time the pupils were reading 'Little Boy Blue, come blow up your horn,' whereas, at the same time in the previous year, they had been reading (from Chambers' *Effective Readers*, First Primer)—

My fat cat has a kit.
Sam hit the kit on his leg.
Can the mit fit on the rag?

and other equally 'classical' literature." We have in 1963 improved on this sort of cacophonous nonsense in our early school books,

Gon Out.

A man went too hiz nai-borz hous and rang the bel. The maidservant oepnd the dor. "I wish too speek too eur maaster," hee sed. "Hee'z gon out," shee aanserd. "Then I wil speek too eur mis-tris," hee sed. "Shee'z gon out, too." "That's a piti; but per-haps thai'l soon kum bak. I wil kum in and sit by the fyer and wait for them." "I m sori, ser," the maid sed, "but the fyer'z gon out too."

7. A page from Book I of *A Reeder in Simplifyd Spelling*

but we have improved only in one aspect: equally uninteresting,
although less hideous, material can still be found in reading books
for the very young. His Majesty's Inspector, Mr. W. G. Fraser,
kept in touch with the work at Bridge of Allan and ten months after
the experiment began made special reference to it in a report following a general inspection of the school. The report was embodied
in the General Report for 1920 of Mr. F. R. Jamieson, His Majesty's
Chief Inspector of Schools in the Southern Division of Scotland:

> At one school the attempt is being made to teach the initiatory stages
> of reading by means of Simplified Spelling, the text book used being
> that published by the Simplified Spelling Society. The plan adopted
> is to use this book for the first six months of school life, and then to pass
> on to books in the ordinary spelling. This transition is clearly the
> critical stage, and it may be said, as the result of experience, that it
> has caused no loss of time. For, though no extra time has been given to
> reading, *the children at the end of the year are much better readers than
> they used to be under the old system, both of their text books and of unseen
> matter.* The confusion that might have been apprehended had not been
> produced.[1]

Of the transition to traditional spelling the headteacher himself
wrote: "This transition—dreaded as a period of difficulty—really
occurred naturally, and with no special difficulty. The teacher
hurried into my room to say that she found the pupils reading from
one of Chambers' Effective Reading Sheets (illustrated), which
hung in a corner, their idea being to get some explanation of the
picture." The headmaster, as his report shows, realized that the
children wanted to read, they were seeking an explanation of the
illustrations, reading for the sake of the content and not to complete
a task. They accepted the change in spelling without question when
their teacher told them that they had hitherto spelt in an easy way
but were now going to spell like grown-ups. "That alike flattered
and pleased them." Every word of that account could have been
written about the children of today: indeed the parallelism with
today's reports is remarkable. After seven months in school these
children were "a full term ahead" and were reading a school book
never before attempted till the second year in school.

The General Report of the Chief Inspector of Schools, quoted
above, went on to say—

[1] General Report for the Year 1920. Edinburgh, December 31st, 1920.

At first sight it would seem that the facts constitute strong evidence of the superiority of the new method. But when it is noted that the improvement in reading has been accompanied by improvement in spelling, writing and arithmetic, it becomes evident that we must use caution in forming a judgment. It is hard to see how a method of teaching reading can of itself help arithmetic. Is it not possible that the interest of a new experiment has had a stimulating effect on the teachers, which is reflected in the results in all subjects? And if this be so, how much of the improvement in reading is due to this stimulus, and how much to the method itself?

This paragraph is a fine example of official caution. The children's work has improved in all ways, not only in reading. Therefore, can it not be that there are causes at work other than an improved method of teaching reading? The inspector's caution makes what he has to say all the more reliable: there can be no question of over-statement. The same general improvement is noted today but modern psychology provides an answer which may not have been as clear forty years ago.

The headmaster of the Bridge of Allan Intermediate School, writing four years later, referred to this general overall improvement, which had continued. The children's faith in the consistency of logical rules was never upset and self-reliance grew and was never discouraged by anomalies. He was sure that the inspector's query was fully answered by this reasoning and referred to the dictum of the surgeon, Sir William Macewen, at a meeting of the British Association: "Scientific study in any branch of knowledge prepared the way for rapid advance in any other branch of knowledge." The headmaster was right, of course; the same phenomenon of increased skill in other subjects is seen today to be an accompaniment of consistently spelt and happily learnt reading. Another comment of this headmaster was: "Our children now spell better than ever before, and they are eager readers." After five years the consistent spelling approach was still being used and the teachers declared that they would not willingly go back to the older methods. When the "Geddes Axe" economies of 1924 forced education authorities to cut down their expenditure, the Stirlingshire Education Committee issued a list of text-books to be used in their schools. Simplified spelling books were naturally enough not in the list but those in the school were dilapidated and needed to be replaced. The headmaster suggested to his staff that they must now order only listed books. The

teachers at once offered to buy new simplified spelling books out of their own pockets. In the end the Simplified Spelling Society came to the rescue and provided replacements free of charge. The headmaster summarized the results after five years' work in the following words—

> In the first two years it saves from three to six months of school time, and calls for no special skill in teaching. It makes work easier and happier for teacher and taught. It encourages reasoning power and fosters self-help because from the first it presents interesting matter told in language natural to a child and not distorted or twisted to suit the difficulties of spelling, as must be the case with the best of phonic readers. It increases keenness and creates a taste for reading. In five months' time the children will "burst into writing" as naturally as Italian children would do. It gives confident and clear articulation and enunciation, owing to the complete absence of anomalies and exceptions, and therefore tends to improve speech. The children read in a natural, happy, and interested tone, quite different from the conventional school shout or drawl. The experiment "consumes its own smoke," as it is all over in from seven to nine months. It affects the Infant Room only. It does *not* affect spelling adversely—rather the reverse—and can call for no criticism from anyone. Parents can be told that the method has been reported on officially, and has proved successful in other schools. If adopted throughout the school it would save from one to two years of school life, and would provide a release of time and energy for other things (E).

These experiments were not confined to Scotland nor to the area where Mr. Jackson's zealous encouragement might be expected to extend. The two following reports come from London. In January 1919 the headmistress of Honeywell Road School, Battersea, spoke at a meeting in University College, London, about the teaching of reading and writing "on phonetic principles" in her school and gave demonstration lessons with a group of twenty-four children. She had been impressed by the results of the work in Scottish schools and decided to make a controlled experiment in her own school, where she established two classes of similar age and experience, one taught to read on orthodox lines and the other through simplified spelling. "In this way we hoped to arrive at as fair and true a comparison as could possibly be obtained—the classes being composed of children of the same type, taught by the same teachers, under similar circumstances, and in the same surroundings." The

headmistress was very careful in her assessments of the results. She refused to talk about time saved until the children were older but she was already convinced that learning to read was made "a happier experience for a little child." Some years later when the Simplified Spelling Society was compiling its reports in 1924, the headmistress, by that time retired, told the compilers of the rapid progress of children in reading because they were never confused by variations in spelling rules, that children delighted in exercising their power to build words because they were never disappointed in the result, and they were never afraid to attempt the pronunciation of an unfamiliar word. Transition to ordinary spelling caused little difficulty. Slight changes were not noticed at all and only complete anomalies in spelling nonplussed the children. Nevertheless, children who had learnt to handle books were "much better fitted to grapple with the inconsistencies of our language than they were when they began school life." This headmistress said that she had never seen little children so keen on any lesson as were her experimental classes on their reading (F).

At the end of two years the classes referred to above were tested by an impartial and experienced judge, and the results obtained in spelling and the mechanical art of reading proved that these children (average age seven years eight months) were considerably in advance of their age in those two subjects, and that they could read and spell better than classes of children of the same age and in the same school, instructed by the same teachers under similar conditions—but taught entirely on the usual methods.

The teachers of the classes and I had convincing evidence that learning to read on the Simplified Spelling plan was far the happier experience for the little child beginning its school career, and that the children taught on the Simplified Spelling Method, being able to read intelligently nine months earlier than those trained on orthodox lines, had extra time for silent reading, and their use of the Classroom Library showed that the power to read created a love of reading even in young minds.

The headmistress of St. Katherine's Infant School, Tottenham, reported similar successful work after some five years' observation of the children concerned.

The success attending the experiment was a great surprise to all concerned. In six months, not only were twenty-two out of the twenty-five children reading fluently from the conventional spelling, but they

had attained a clearness of speech and a fluency and originality of expression in written composition hitherto unapproached by children of the same age in the school. It was suggested at the time that the evil effects of the Simplified Spelling might re-assert themselves as the children progressed through the Senior Schools and writing was made more use of. I am now in a position to say that such is not the case, and those responsible for the same children, now in Standard IV, are not only delighted with the ease with which they make use of the conventional spelling, but are among the most ardent supporters of the method.

This headmistress, like some of the Scottish teachers, thought the vital factor to be that the children were "always reading for meaning and sense." When transferring to conventional spelling this habit stood the child in good stead: the context helped him exactly as it helps expert readers: "Our experience has been that no child who has been allowed sufficient time to become fluent when reading from Simplified Spelling has failed to transfer that fluency when reading from the orthodox." Concerning writing, it was noted that the children wrote exactly what they wished to say and that there was no need to alter phraseology so as to include words the spelling of which was known: "Natural and childlike compositions are possible."

The fact that the children reproduced in their writing their own speech was of great help to the teachers in detecting unsuspected speech defects and inaccuracies. The headmistress lists a number of these and they are precisely the sort of speech inaccuracies that are discovered through children's writing today (G). Such would often go undetected, for the average teacher cannot possess the trained ear of the phonetician. Presenting the correct sound to the child in simplified spelling often of itself enables him to make the correction: the eye teaches what the ear has failed to indicate.

Children whose speech is in any way defective, derive great benefit from the method of reading by Simplified Spelling. The longer time devoted to the sounds of words, instead of to the variety of their forms, enables many of these defects to be overcome. We have had many instances in which children's speech has been entirely transformed. At present we have under observation a little girl of six, whose ordinary conversational speech is practically unintelligible, but she reads from the *Jinglz and Storiz*, enunciating perfectly. Her compositions, which are quite fluent, reveal the many inaccuracies of her ordinary speech,

and enable us to deal with them; while her reading encourages us, by revealing what it may eventually become.

York Road School in Leeds was in 1918 a school typical of a poor district in the heart of a large industrial city. The headmaster (H) described his children as sturdy and charming but "obscured and handicapped by a sordid environment." Their speech was a hybrid, a Yorkshire dialect coarsened and spoilt by slovenly diction. Very few possessed a book and the only books most of them ever looked at were school books. In May 1917 one of two classes of children, who had already seen some normal print in the reception class, were given simplified spelling readers. The other half of the age group were taught by the traditional method. After six weeks the experimental children were reading easy sentences, which would not ordinarily have been expected for another two to three months. Then the illness of the teacher caused a break in the work until the following October. The substitute teacher was unsympathetic and it was only through the intervention of His Majesty's inspector that the work was resumed. By the end of the following month the brighter children were reading and needed little help with the stories in their first book. The headmaster reports—

> This self-help feature of the Simplified Spelling, by which the child of its own initiative discovers the words and, unaided, reads and understands sentences, did more to convince the class teacher of the immense advantages of Simplified Spelling than any amount of theorizing could have done. Here was practical proof, and both the headmistress and the class teacher expressed surprise at the amount of work accomplished beyond anything they had expected or hoped for. When once the children have overcome the initial difficulties of associating sounds with signs there is nothing more to learn. The children can proceed on their own initiative to decipher any and every word.

The headmaster condemned the "sinful waste of childhood and of teachers' time" caused by dictation and spelling exercises, and foresaw that the confidence inspired by logical word-construction might make such soul-destroying exercises unnecessary. The inspector who watched this work and who encouraged it when it seemed likely to lapse was H.M.I. Mr. P. L. Gray, who in reporting the work by (in his words) "two similar classes of very ignorant children, aged about five, one taught on ordinary lines; the other on Simplified Spelling" said: "It certainly appeared at the end of a year that the

Simplified Spelling class could read more fluently and more advanced reading matter, than the ordinary class." This was a school beset by severe difficulties and where head and class teachers were ready to give in. Even amid all these circumstances of staffing difficulty within and poverty-stricken antagonistic environment outside the school these children showed that learning to read need not be "a long and tedious process, extending more or less throughout the whole of school life."

The speed with which newcomers to letters start out to read comes out often in these reports. At Lyons Council School, Hetton-le-Hole, Co. Durham, a class of fifty children began working on the simplified spelling approach on the fifth of November 1917. Seventeen days later the class began reading from the first book. Many teachers today make no attempt at formal reading for the first term in school and there are many reasons for this attitude. Maybe that cautious approach was not so prominent forty years ago, but I have noticed that teachers today are generally speeding up the beginning of formal reading. Whether earlier reading is desirable or not, these reports show that it is possible, if one wishes to do it. By the beginning of the second term, the Hetton-le-Hole class finished the first book and were ready for the second. Apparently the children moved at a class speed rather than at individual speeds as is common today. The teacher commented: "The brighter children of the class needed no help in their reading. This is one of the great advantages of a Simplified System, the child can discover for himself, can read unaided; the dullest child of all being able to do this to some extent. A new world of interest is opened out to the child as soon as he can read unaided . . ." There was no difficulty in transferring to ordinary spelling. They at once read fluently on being given traditionally printed books: some were already reading traditional print at home before their teacher gave them the books in school: "The children have learnt to read in eight months, from November 1918 to June 1919, by first reading fluently from the Simplified Method, then transferring to the ordinary spelling, and being allowed to proceed on their own with the latter." Besides the great saving of time, this teacher was impressed by the decrease in drudgery in teaching and the increase in interesting reading for the children (J).

There were several other reports. The headmistress of a Manchester private school was "delighted" with the new approach which

brought interest and increased enjoyment to children. Many parents of these children opposed the idea at first and because of this some children at this fee-paying school had to be left out of the experiment. By 1924 all were satisfied that the method had been proved worth while (K).

The good effect on children's conduct, noted today, was brought out in a report from Hull (L). Here the headmistress talks of the increased development of character and capacity shown in greater self-reliance and wider reasoning power. Not only would her teachers regret a return to the older system but His Majesty's Inspector, who had been doubtful about the results when the experiment began, found them "eminently satisfactory." The headmaster of a Hereford school (M) reported that his inspector said "that he had never in the whole of his experience seen children so advanced in reading." Children of seven years were reading books intended for children of nine. Until the headmaster could find a method which could show greater progress he asserted that the method would be taught in any school under his control. One of his staff was not enthusiastic when the work began; he changed his attitude when he "saw what a delight the children took in the subject" of reading. This man was particularly impressed when he found that dull children developed interest in books. Every report marks this interest: at another Manchester school the children were "reading fairy tales at a time when other children are trying to memorize words" (N). There are other reports in similar vein. Simplified spelling was tried in at least one special school for educationally subnormal children. A minute of the Simplified Spelling Society of the twenty-fifth May 1923, recorded the receipt of a letter "from Mr. Walsh of the McMillan School for Mentally Defective Children, Bradford, testifying to the splendid success of Simplified Spelling in his school."

The reports became almost monotonously repetitive. The same things are referred to again and again—greater joy in learning to read, unexpected power of expression in writing, tremendous gains in time and always surprise because the transition to ordinary print is easy and natural and scarcely noted. All these things are said today, exactly the same things. Clearly for teachers forty years ago and teachers now, the pre-eminent difficulty in reading is the memorizing of the chaos: all expected that memory of consistent spelling would have no "transfer value" in memorizing traditional spelling. In the

proof it is clear that the spelling reformers were right. Confidence with a book and not memorization of spelling forms is the important factor. Given that confidence, the child turns from one form of print to another (and back again if need be) and is no more worried by difficulties than the adult who for the first time sees i.t.a. print and reads it. Teachers tried then and try now to explain this by talking about memorization of word-patterns and so forth. To be sure, these things help and that is why Sir James Pitman has been at great pains to make the Initial Teaching Alphabet of today look as nearly as possible like traditional print, but the root of the ease of transition is confidence and interest.

When we adults read we do not consciously look at single letters, possibly not at each individual word. Having learnt to read i.t.a. equally fluently, young children transfer the same fluency to traditional print and, for the most part, do not consider the form of the print. That is why they hardly notice the differences between one alphabet and the other.

IX

New Spelling

A man's culture is largely judged of by the extent to which he is able correctly to handle these hard words. . . . No literature in the world abounds
as English does in characters made ridiculous to the reader by the manner
in which they misapply or distort "big" words. Shakespeare's Dogberry
and Mrs. Quickly, Fielding's Mrs. Slipslop, Smollett's Winifred Jenkins,
Sheridan's Mrs. Malaprop, Dickens's Weller senior, Shillaber's Mrs.
Partington, and footmen and labourers innumerable made fun of in novels
and comedies might all of them appear in court as witnesses for the plain-
tiff in a law-suit brought against the educated classes of England for
wilfully making the language more complicated than necessary and
thereby hindering the spread of education among all classes of the
population.

Dr. O. Jespersen: *Growth and Structure of the English Language*

DURING THE 1930s Sir George Hunter was until his death the
mainspring behind the Simplified Spelling Society. Even the
office of the Society had been transferred from London to his
home town of Wallsend-on-Tyne. The disappointment of 1933 had
naturally a depressing effect after the great hopes which had been
held. There had in fact been no committee meetings between
January 1931 and July 1935. An accidental meeting on board a ship
in mid-Atlantic between Professor Lloyd James and Mr. I. J. (now
Sir James) Pitman in 1935 may be said to mark the starting point of
the modern phase of the movement. Together they decided that the
brilliant school successes of the 1920s should be followed up and a
new effort made. At a meeting in 1935 Professor Lloyd James had
been elected to the committee and in May 1936 Mr. Pitman was
elected. Following Sir George Hunter's death, the committee was
re-formed and a study of the next appropriate stage of the work
begun.

The committee decided that its first task should be to produce a
new edition of the *Proposals for Simplifying the Spelling of English*.
There had been four editions since the first edition of 1910 and
modifications and improvements had been made. The fifth edition
was to be completely revised, rewritten and made available to the

general public, and Mr. Pitman undertook to be responsible for the
publication. The committee supervising the work consisted of Mr.
Peter Hadley, Professor A. Lloyd James, Professor Daniel Jones,
Mr. Harold Orton, Mr. I. J. Pitman, Mr. Walter Ripman, with
Professor Gilbert Murray as chairman and Mr. T. R. Barber as
secretary. The work of rewriting was entrusted to Mr. H. Orton
(now Professor of English Language in the University of Leeds).
In the preface to the book, Professor Lloyd James said that it sought
to present the considerations involved in a scientific approach to
the problem of spelling reform.

> Scores of schemes of simplified spelling have been invented: how
> many of the inventors have studied the facts of the problem as minutely
> as the authors of this booklet I should not care to estimate. But now
> that the facts are available, there is no excuse for future inventors to
> rush in. This booklet is the Spelling Reformer's *Vade Mecum*: it is
> one of the most remarkable statistical investigations into English
> spelling ever undertaken.

Professor Lloyd James did not exaggerate. The book analysed the
spelling of English thoroughly, clarifying existing spellings, their
frequency absolutely and their frequency in ordinary continuous
English speech, that is in terms of word frequency. The arduous task,
first begun by Mr. Walter Ripman and Mr. William Archer, was
evaluated afresh and careful consideration was given to the statistical
investigations of Dr. Godfrey Dewey, New York, into the recurrence
in speech of English words.[1] The compilers set themselves the
following aims—

(1) To avoid the introduction of new characters. (This would
permit the use of existing typewriting and printing machines. It
would also allow telephone dialling, the use of the Morse Code,
Braille, and so on.)

(2) To introduce no new diacritics.

(3) As far as possible to avoid combinations of letters not already
familiar.

(4) To depart as little as possible from the current spelling. (The
retention of the familiar whenever possible could only be beneficial
and the careful study referred to was of particular value here.)

(5) To arrange that the significance of each letter—other than
paired letters, e.g. ch, ie—should not depend on any other letter

---

[1] *Relativ Frequency of English Speech Sounds*, Harvard Studies in Education, 1923.
Dr. Godfrey Dewey is the son of Dr. Melvil Dewey. See pages 49, 52.

(e.g. the lengthening of the vowel sound in **hope** by the addition after the consonant of final **e**).

(6) To economize in the use of letters wherever inconsistency or ambiguity could be avoided at the same time.

(7) To make allowance for existing divergences of pronunciation. (If Southern or Northern English had been considered alone more economies of presentation could have been offered.)

The eminent European philologist, Professor R. E. Zachrisson of Uppsala, had evolved his Anglic for use in teaching English in Sweden since the last revision of the *Proposals*. This is an example of Anglic.

My system ofrs a numbr ov lodgical and consistent, thoe not aulwiz nue, spelings ov evry English sound. For this very reezn sum ov its forms may apeer strandge to the jeneral reeder, but with the exeption ov a fue diegrafs . . . Anglic has fue spelings which ar not met with in manuescripts ov urly literery wurks or in the aensient correspondens ov roialty and noebelmen. Thus to giv oenly a fue illustrations King Henry VIII repeetidly rote WON for ONE . . . and his dautr Queen Elizabeth went in for such spelings as STAUKE for STALK and CLARK, HART, for CLERK, HEART.

Anglic aimed at bringing order into the present confusion by using to represent a sound that one of the existing spelling variants which is most common, e.g. **ee** for the vowel sound in **chief**, **i** (sometimes **ie**) for that in **sign**. Trial courses in teaching English by the new medium were first tried out at Uppsala in 1930. The lessons were attended by many of Sweden's foremost educationists, including the rector of the university, various professors and phoneticians and members of the Swedish ministry of education. Judgments on the results were outstandingly favourable and the leading Swedish newspapers described them in such terms as "astonishing" and "splendid." In June an Anglic Association with a capital of £4,000 was set up to further the establishment of Anglic as an international language for facilitating co-operation and peaceful intercourse between nations.

Naturally, there was a strong bond of interest between the English reformers and Professor Zachrisson. At an international conference in London, held in June 1930, Professor Zachrisson made some simple alterations in his own original proposals on the advice of the English and American representatives present and in preparing the fifth edition of their new proposals the Simplified

Spelling Society took careful note of Zachrisson's work. In Professor Orton's own words of tribute and acknowledgment in a recent letter to me: "Of course, Zachrisson's Anglic had a very great effect upon our deliberations, perhaps all the more so because I am an old pupil and colleague of that great man." The scheme of the Simplified Spelling Society was called New Spelling (or Nue Speling). It was published in 1940 and approximated closely to Anglic.

Some compromises with the five aims described above were unavoidable but they were few: **dh** was used for the initial consonant sound in **that** contrasted with **th** for the first consonant in **thin**. It seemed logical, since **d** represents the vocalized form of **t**, that **dh** should similarly relate to **th** and Welsh readers would not find the sign unfamiliar, viz. the sound of **dd** in Welsh. **zh, aa, uu** were also used, e.g. **vizhon** (vision), **saam** (psalm), **fuud** (food).

Opportunities were seized to publicize the new spelling and members of the society gave talks to groups in all parts of Britain, in universities and teacher training colleges, to Rotary clubs and to any groups who would listen. Full approval of the desirability of reform was virtually always expressed, for when people come to think about the subject, there is indeed no other answer. The addresses to training college groups were regarded as particularly important for it was always believed that the breakthrough, when it came, would be made in the schools, in teaching children to read.

The Second World War did not stop the activities of the spelling reformers. In fact the committee of the Simplified Spelling Society was very active with plans but there were serious difficulties in the way of publishing material, arising mainly from the acute paper shortage. The paper shortage continued long after the end of the war in 1945 and it is hard to realize today how much difficulty it caused. It was decided to print in Nue Speling, with attractive illustrations, a number of infant books. The first of these was *Dhe Litl Red Hen*, a well-known infants' story which is printed in many forms by a host of publishers. I wrote the story afresh in Nue Speling and in its 34 pages there were 17 full page five-colour illustrations. The attractive lay-out made the actual cost of production much exceed the possible selling price, but it was felt that the Society's funds were being well spent in making this sort of appeal to children and teachers. The book was published by Messrs. W. Heffer & Sons Ltd.

Several other books were prepared for publication, *Dhe Raelwae*

"Huu wil help to miks mie flour and to maek sum bred?" sed dhe Litl Red Hen.

"Not I," sed dhe poosy

"Not I," sed dhe pupy

"Not I," sed dhe pigy

FRED YOUNG.

Plate II. A page from *Dhe Litl Red Hen*

Enjin, Dhe Three Baerz, Dhe Enchanted Hors, Sinbad dhe Saelor, Aladin, Sinderela, Dhe Sleeping Buety. A leader writer in the London *Evening News* of those days who got hold of *Dhe Litl Red Hen* criticized us severely for wastage of paper. It was pointed out in reply that infants were not expected to read small type and twenty words or fewer to a page were very reasonable. The leader writer tilted at us again and the correspondence went on for some time, providing quite an amount of free advertisement. The paper shortage forced the Society to hold up the printing of the books, other than *Dhe Litl Red Hen.* They were retained, with illustrations prepared, ready for printing as soon as that could be undertaken. It was realized that the earlier school work had been so successful that it would have continued if an abundant supply of books had been available. The Society was determined that this time the books would be supplied and that Sir George Hunter's bequest should be utilized to this end. Wartime activities delayed the work in several ways. A request for the inclusion of the projected school experiment in the agenda of the Association of Directors and Secretaries of Education[1] was made. The executive committee wished to include the subject but asked that it be deferred because of urgent wartime business.

The Society's efforts were now definitely concentrated on the use of Nue Speling as an introduction to reading in schools. In 1946 two pamphlets of mine were published: *The Use of Simplified Spelling in Teaching Infants to Read and Write,* and *A Teachers' Manual to Accompany the S.S.S. Series of Readers and Story Books for Infants.* The former referred to the earlier experiments in schools and attempted to answer the arguments advanced by some educationists of standing against the view that phonetic spelling would help "word-building." One inspector of schools who was a staunch supporter of the sentence method of teaching reading, contended that the simplification of English spelling could not materially aid the young learner, because it was wrong to teach reading by analysis of words into sounds and that the only good method was to teach words, and indeed phrases and complete sentences.[2] There is so much good sense in the assertion that children should learn to read whole phrases, as fluent readers naturally do, that it is easy to overlook two important points. First, that the child must learn to recognize words new to him by reference to the component letters, and

[1] Now the Association of Education Officers.
[2] See page 87 for more of Dr. Jagger's argument.

secondly that simplified spelling would make fluency in reading complete sentences as wholes much easier to acquire, by generating quick confidence and making new and interesting books accessible early. This sentence-method enthusiast went further, however, and made the claims, in my view untenable by anyone not hopelessly biased against change, that English spelling had now become ideographic and that this was accepted; that the phonetic principle had practically disappeared from the language; and that this was an advantageous position in the development of a language. There was much more which, as a complete disbeliever, I could not attempt to state fairly.

This was an attack on spelling reform, not from an untutored person who objected to changing his habits, but from a leading educationist, an inspector of schools for one of the biggest local education authorities in the country, arguing about pedagogic principle.[1] It has always been my belief that, if English teachers had not been confronted by the chaotic spelling which they had to teach, none would ever have felt impelled to invent the sentence method (or several other non-phonic methods), far less to make their extreme claims for the natural rightness of these methods and in fine, that such arguments were made *post hoc ergo propter hoc*.

Inquiry into school methods of teaching reading in countries with a phonetically spelt language, such as Finland, Italy, Spain or Turkey, was not practicable in wartime Europe and inquiries to various professional educational organizations suggested that there was in this country little or no information on the point. This lack of information was surprising at the time. In a later chapter which deals with post-war inquiries I suggest that maybe in these countries there exists no sense of a reading problem of the sort we have.

It was, however, possible to seek out information in Wales with its bilingual schools and the phonetic spelling of the Welsh language. The principal of a women's training college told me that she knew of no school in Wales where the reading of Welsh was taught by the sentence method nor had she been able to discover any such after careful inquiry. In her opinion there was "not the same need for this method in the teaching of Welsh, as Welsh is a phonetic language, and the same difficulties do not arise as in the teaching of English." I asked whether she knew of Welsh schools where English is taught by the sentence method alongside the teaching of Welsh

[1] Cf. page 87.

by the phonic method. It seemed important to prove, if proof existed, that the same teachers who supported the sentence method where English was the subject, put their faith in the phonic method when the peculiar difficulties of the English language had not to be faced. I was commended to one of His Majesty's Inspectors of Schools who had a special official responsibility for language problems in Welsh schools and had wide experience over a large area, which included industrial and rural districts and parts of Wales where English predominated and parts where the spoken tongue is essentially Welsh. This inspector knew well, therefore, English-speaking schools and schools where English had to be taught as a foreign language. He was quite definite on the following points—

(1) Spelling caused more trouble than anything else in the teaching of English to Welsh children, and it was not unknown for Welsh teachers to simplify English spelling in the first stages of teaching it to Welsh children. It is only fair to add that instances of this practice, known to him, were rare.

(2) He knew no school whatever in Wales where any method other than the purely phonic method was used in teaching the Welsh language to Welsh children, but he knew a number where the sentence method or the look-and-say method in some form or in some combination with the phonic method was used for the teaching of English. Since all Welsh state schools are bilingual, it followed that Welsh teachers who used such methods where English is concerned never used them where the phonetically spelt Welsh language is concerned. He mentioned in particular a Swansea school where the pure unadulterated sentence method was used for the teaching of English. It is not often that one finds the sentence method completely relied upon in this way in England. It had, however, never occurred to any teacher in that school that the same method should be used in the teaching of Welsh.[1]

(3) I mentioned the claims of sentence-method enthusiasts that their method was the correct way of teaching spelling of any form, whether phonic, ideographic or chaotic. In his view there was no reason whatsoever to depart from the phonic method where a language was spelt phonetically, and he was clearly of the opinion that anyone using and teaching a phonetically spelt language would

[1] This was confirmed by Mr. T. J. Rees, Director of Education for Swansea, who in his letter to me said: "After hearing our spelling rules, any Englishman can read a page of Welsh to me and I shall know what he is reading. No foreigner who does not know English can do the same with a page of English."

never for a moment think it necessary to invent any method approximating to the sentence method.

It seemed unlikely that one could find a more experienced and impartial judge than such a one, whose work took him into schools of every type and whose particular interests bore upon this problem of learning to read the English language, with its unsystematic spelling, and the Welsh language, with its consistent spelling rules. A woman colleague of this inspector bore out what I had learned from him. She did not know of a single Welsh school where the phonic method "does not form the basis and mainstay in the reading of Welsh." She added that Welsh children who can read Welsh have little difficulty in learning to read English, but that "writing is a different matter. It is here that chaos sets in." The promoters of the new way of learning to read through simplified spelling would expect that the bilingual Welsh children, having learnt to read Welsh would learn to read their second language fairly readily. They would have acquired confidence and an interest in books.

The argument that word-building by phonics is the natural way to learn to read seems to be supported in the actual work of Welsh teachers. The fact that this support found in Welsh practice is unconscious is not the least of its merits.

I would myself put the whole argument simply as follows. Psychologists may investigate and produce a host of reports and statistics (and it is well that they do) but the argument remains the same and the observations of tens of thousands of teachers over the years and the generations are only reinforced. Children are extremely logical and their interest can be aroused only in an activity which has purpose and value, and by that I mean purpose and value from the child's point of view. Babies develop speech when it becomes evident to them that speech has a value and is helpful in obtaining things which they want. A baby soon forgets a new word if no notice is taken of him when he uses it. In the same way infants develop skill in reading when it becomes clear to them that by reading they are able to get pleasure from the books which are put in their hands. Children, whose interest in books has been excited by colourful pictures and by hearing stories read, are zealous to possess themselves of the skill to read, but their zeal can soon dwindle if at best their reading is uninteresting or at worst if irksome drudgery is associated in their minds with books. What should be a happy activity becomes a task and the first spontaneous desire to read is,

especially where dull children are concerned, not seldom quenched for ever. Often that first desire and excitement, which could have grown into a love of books and creative self-expression, is not easily aroused again. When a child shows a desire to make things with tools, the wise teacher does not give him tools difficult to use nor a difficult medium in which to work. The child is given simple tools and material with which he can achieve early success. So his self-confidence grows. He early reaches a goal and his interest is stimulated; his progress toward more difficult goals is accelerated.

Ability to read and write is of such vast importance to the full development of the child, since through it alone can he hope to gain access on a wide scale to the thoughts and ideals of his fellow men, that it is not too much to say that to put any unnecessary deterrent or hindrance in the way of learning to read and write is a highly culpable act.

The simplification of English spelling may be regarded as the provision of a simple tool appropriate to the child. We are accustomed to provide simple tools throughout the school curriculum, tools graded to the stage of achievement reached by children. We see this quite clearly where painting, handwork, physical training, mathematics and all other subjects except reading and writing are concerned. We have, however, become so habituated to the chaotic spelling of the English language, and we have become so accustomed to regarding ability to use this ridiculous and chaotic system as a mark of learning and culture, that we have been blinded to the need for simplifying it, even to the possibility of simplifying it. Research workers have for years inquired into this and that method of teaching reading, have invented different approaches, evolved special vocabularies, apparatus, varicoloured letters. None of them has seen that one of the variables is the spelling itself and that the spelling equally with the form and the illustrations and the apparatus can be changed. It is only through changing the spelling that all the words normally used in speech can be put in a beginner's book. This makes the book realistic and therefore truly interesting. Simplified spelling avoids simplification of language. We must avoid language simplified to a level below the child's requirements, language which condescends to him. The child already has command of language: he possesses speech. What he reads should be as rich as his speech, and should extend it. The readiness of children to write in i.t.a. at a very tender age—under five years—shows this.

Mr. Ronald Morris of the Durham University Institute of Education in his *Success and Failure in Learning to Read*[1] has well said—

> It is instructive to compare a representative sample of "sentence-method" primers and first-readers commonly produced for schools with a representative sample of books sold to parents for reading to children under five years of age. The comparison can be quite startling. The book for the under-five is typically far richer in plot, characterization and use of language than the material offered to the older child in his first years at school.

[1] Published by the Oldbourne Press, London, 1963.

X

The Parliamentary Bills

Of 152 would-be policemen who applied for membership of the Rochdale force in 1952, only twelve were accepted. Chief Constable Mr. S. J. Harvey comments: "The spelling of some of the candidates was atrocious, and in the worst case a man made thirty-one spelling mistakes in his short dictated paper, and, of ten selected words, spelled all of them incorrectly."

Extract from the *Sunday Express*

Of the 141 men and women who applied in 1962 to join the Oldham Police Force, sixty-nine were rejected on educational grounds. The Chief Constable, Mr. Fred Berry, said: "The education test is not stiff by any stretch of the imagination. A boy who goes to school until he is fifteen or sixteen should get through easily, but we find that spelling is atrocious."

Extract from the *Oldham Evening Chronicle*[1]

ATTENTION HAD BEEN directed to the comparative illiteracy of the population during the war, when educational reports on men enlisted in the armed forces received public notice. The Ministry of Education in an official report[2] stated that more than 30 per cent of recent school leavers were backward in reading. The time was ripe for sympathetic consideration when, on the eleventh of March 1949, Mr. Mont Follick, M.P. for Loughborough, presented his Private Member's Spelling Reform Bill to the House of Commons. Part I of the Bill asked for the establishment of a Committee to produce a scheme for the simplified and consistent spelling of the English language on a rational basis and Part II required that

[1] I would not criticize the police examination candidates. The *Sunday Express* quoted the ten selected words and no doubt the readers of the paper, seeing the words spelt for them, were as complacent as the examiners in their belief that they could spell. Sir James Pitman has a list of nine ordinary English words and is prepared to give ten shillings to anybody spelling them correctly on forfeit of one shilling for each word misspelt. Two of the ten words quoted by the *Sunday Express* are in the list. I recently dictated the list to a gathering of seventy teachers: nobody spelt them all correctly. Let all who criticize anybody else's spelling beware.

[2] *Reading Ability*. Ministry of Education Pamphlet No. 18 (1951). Pamphlet No. 32, *Standards of Reading*, published in 1957, showed only slight improvement. The latest Ministry report of all says: "Roughly a quarter of the modern school population aged fifteen have a reading age of thirteen years or less." *Half Our Future*. Report of the Central Advisory Committee for Education (England). H.M.S.O. 1963.

rational spelling should be used first in schools, later in government publications and so on. Mr. Follick let it be understood that he desired only to proceed with Part I of the Bill with a view to making English a world language and to eliminate unnecessary drudgery and waste of time at school. Despite this concession and the reduction of the effect of the Bill to a request for an inquiry, it was officially opposed and the government opposition, as the Minister's speech showed, was not even directed against the aims of the Bill: the opposing arguments consisted of irrelevances. On second reading on the eleventh of March 1949, the Bill was debated for five hours and lost by 87 votes to 84. The Minister of Education on behalf of the Government said that the whole of his argument in resisting the Bill was that we had not arrived at the stage at which one could begin to apply compulsion, even if the Bill was accepted. At present there were at least five systems of new spelling being advocated. It was completely impracticable to try to deal with this matter by legislation. Progress in these matters was made by evolution rather than by revolution or formal legalistic measures.[1]

The Minister appears to have overlooked—

(1) that other countries had reformed spelling by legal enactment,

(2) that all that was being sought was a Committee to consider a rational spelling system,

(3) that evolution in language leads naturally to diversity. In spite of Front Bench opposition and a mass of ill-argued opposition to the "cranks," as a glance at Hansard will show, this defeat by three votes was indeed a moral victory.

The Minister of Education was Mr. George Tomlinson, a great educationist, who had spent a lifetime of struggle for the education of poor children as local borough and county councillor and as Vice-President of the Association of Education Committees. Even he was shackled by past precedents. In a letter of the tenth of March to me, he wrote—

> I do not rule out the possibility that in due time there might be a case for setting up some Committee to investigate the matter, but to set up a Committee before there is any substantial body of public opinion in favour of a reform would be futile. As I see it therefore the onus is on the advocates of a reformed spelling to secure some reasonable measure of public support for their views. When this has been done it would then be reasonable to set up an official inquiry to consider

[1] *Daily Telegraph*, twelfth March 1949.

how far the desires of those interested could and should be met. The plain fact at the moment is that in spite of many years—I might almost say centuries—of propaganda by a small number of enthusiasts, the public at large remain quite unconvinced of the merits of their case. In these circumstances I see no point in an official inquiry, and therefore even less point in any proposal for legislation. Another aspect of the matter which should not, I think, be overlooked, is that the Americans have made some fairly significant changes in the spelling which they took across the Atlantic with them without any legislation. I should imagine that any generally accepted changes in spelling which commend themselves to people in this country would similarly be effected without the necessity of legislation. I wish the advocates of reform would also remember that in this country we are but a small part of the English speaking and English writing world. Any proposal for the reform of our spelling should therefore, if it is to have any chance of achieving permanent validity, be concerted with at any rate the Dominions and the United States.

Why these issues should make it in any way undesirable to inquire into the subject is not explained any more than it was in 1933.

Press comment on the Bill was mixed. Mr. Mont Follick had invented a simplified spelling of his own and it was more difficult to decipher than Nue Speling: it was in this regard unfortunate that Mr. Pitman was seconder and not promoter of the bill, for Nue Speling, which he favoured, would by its appearance have appealed more than did Mr. Follick's system and this the newspapers published exclusively as samples of what reformed spelling would look like. The old arguments came back here and there to welcome the Bill's rejection as, for example, this statement in the *Head Teachers Review*[1] of April 1949: "We do not think our nation generally would welcome another piece of legislation to bring us into line with a language that might be extremely logical on paper, but would rob us of the heritage of the beauties of our prose and poetry through the centuries." While impatient of his ill-based argument, I respect this editor who published in full in his June issue a letter of mine in which, *inter alia*, I asked: "Were Shakespeare and Milton not as beautiful in the seventeenth century as now, or have we added to the beauties of both by re-spelling them?"

Generally the narrow majority against the Bill and its being debated in parliament won prestige for the cause of simplified spelling. As Mr. F. Fairhurst, M.P. for Oldham East, wrote: "There

---

[1] Publication of the National Association of Head Teachers.

was no doubt who carried the 'oners' of the day" (fifteenth March 1949). Mr. Follick himself wrote: "This is not the end. I think we have done a great deal to stir up a lot of interest, not only in Parliament, but in the whole country, judging from my mail. It is now up to influential people . . . to go out and preach the doctrine so that next time we shall be more successful." There is no doubt that at long last Spelling Reform had become in the view of the general public a topic worthy of serious thought.

George Bernard Shaw wished to systematize English spelling and at the same time replace the Roman alphabet by an entirely different set of symbols more economical of space and time: his sympathies were with the supporters of the Bill. He wrote to Mr. Pitman on the twenty-second of March, congratulating him on the results: "Virtually you broke even with the Government, which was enormously beyond the best that could be hoped." He added: "It is now clear that these Private Members' Bills are waste of time. A letter from me to that effect was printed in *The Times* of the nineteenth. You must go ahead with a primer with the type every printer has in stock."

An illuminating sidelight on the attitudes of the House of Commons springs from the background of this story. The next Private Member's Bill down for hearing was the Fox Hunting Bill and many members with a greater interest in the preservation of foxhunters' privileges than in spelling reform were present. The near success of the Spelling Reform Bill doubtless owed something to the fact that the longer it was kept alive, the less would be the opportunity offered to the promoters of the Fox Hunting Bill which was next in the list for hearing.

In the parliamentary session of Autumn 1952, Mr. Mont Follick was again successful in the ballot for Private Members' Bills, being drawn Number 5. The second Simplified Spelling Bill, which he promoted in 1953, marks the beginning of the last stage in the long crusade for an officially backed school experiment. Mr. I. J. Pitman again seconded the bill, but in fact Mr. Follick allowed Mr. Pitman full responsibility for the printing of the Bill and for its conduct in the House of Commons.

The Explanatory Memorandum to this Bill, in at first sight rather puzzling language,[1] required the Government to institute research into the improvement of reading standards in the country. The organization ("association" was the word used) appointed to under-

[1] See Appendix IV, p. 204

take the research must among other methods inquire into the use of a consistent spelling system as an approach to learning to use traditional spelling. If the research proved the value of a consistent spelling approach the research organization should recommend to Parliament a spelling system to be used, which might be accepted or varied. The adoption in schools of any new method would still remain a matter for decision by the local education authorities concerned.

Mr. Pitman in presenting the Bill to the House of Commons summed it up as requiring the National Foundation for Educational Research in England and Wales and the Scottish Council for Research in Education to seek these main objectives. First they were to conduct research into the reasons for the failure in teaching reading ability, shown by the Ministry of Education's own publication *Reading Ability*, which showed that some 20 per cent of the school population leave school to become adult illiterates; secondly to determine for purposes of an investigation the most suitable form of simplified spelling; and thirdly to report on the benefits, if any, of its use, both in reducing the high proportion of illiteracy and in quicker teaching of literacy.

Mr. Pitman moved the Second Reading of the Bill on the twenty-seventh of February 1953. He emphasized that investigation was the aim of the Bill and that only after a favourable report approved in turn by the Minister and both Houses of Parliament could anything else happen. Nothing would be forced on anyone: all depended on free will and proven success. He referred to existing experience: "The present results are so deplorable that this House and the Minister must take notice of them," and he pointed out that every year 400,000 to 500,000 five-year-olds began their schooling, of whom some 129,000 to 150,000 were destined to leave school unable to read properly. They could not read long or complicated sentences because the technique of reading absorbed so much of their faculties that, by the end of the sentence, they had forgotten the beginning and could not understand it. He added: "We know that the same sort of figures happen in Australia and America, and it seems to be particularly connected with the English-speaking world." Since it was known that something was wrong, then something should be done. In support of him Mr. R. Morley, M.P. for Itchen, said: "As a class teacher for nearly fifty years I know it is our ridiculous and illogical spelling which is the chief handicap in teaching children to read."

The report of the debate in *Education* (sixth of March 1953) quotes four opponents of the bill. They were reported as saying—

(1) This is an attempt to step down our educational standards because reading is a little difficult and requires concentration and thought. . . . This is a Bill to make things easier for bad spellers.

(2) The adoption of simplified spelling would debase and impoverish the character of the language. . . . Simplified Spelling would violently impair the delicate fabric of our language, and tend to put the language out of the poet's reach.

(3) The Bill proposed a system of spelling which was to be printed and read, but never written, . . . it would confuse the less intelligent pupil by making him learn two systems of spelling. Children who find difficulty in reading should be taught intensively in small groups.

With the last sentence teachers might agree: they will still agree about small classes with the new method. This with the Government spokesman's words was *Education*'s selection of the opposition speeches and it makes clear the impoverishment of their argument. The official spokesman of the Government in opposition to the Bill was the Parliamentary Secretary to the Ministry of Education, Mr. K. W. M. (now Sir Kenneth) Pickthorne. He suggested that the position nationally was improving and was being exaggerated in relation to the position in other countries, that the Association of Education Committees was opposed to the Bill, and that the Bill sought "to impose financial implications and specific assurances about administrative decisions." The House of Commons must have noted where the strength of argument lay and possibly thought it high time that financial obligations in connection with so important a matter should be undertaken. The Second Reading was carried by 65 votes to 53 and went to Committee where it was again approved in the face of Government opposition. Government opposition had been exceptionally fierce and even in committee efforts to prevent acceptance of the Bill by procedural tactics had been employed; as for instance, when many opposition members left the committee in an attempt to put further discussion out of order for lack of a quorum. This move was defeated by the rapid assembly of some who, while not actively supporting the Bill, felt at least that a Bill sent to committee by the House was worthy of debate and should not be killed by procedural methods when those who disliked it could not gain their way by argument.

Happily, the foolish irrelevances of most of the opposition re-

marks in the House of Commons were not repeated in the educational press, but the following extract from a letter written by Dr. J. H. Jagger, Divisional Inspector of Schools to the London County Council, in the *Journal of Education* (April 1953) shows that there were nevertheless some educationists who had little hope of success from any research: "English writing today is an ideographic system —or, as those who regard it as a system intended to represent sounds would say, it is perfectly irregular. As a means of representing ideas it is unequalled: as a means of representing sounds, as a phonographic system, it is useless." Dr. Jagger went on to say that since English pronunciation varies from place to place the language if spelt according to one group's pronunciation would still be "aphonographic and therefore ideographic, to any speaker in proportion as the sounds of his speech differ from those of the speech chosen."

This argument overlooks completely the answers rendered by Professor Max Müller in the last century and by Sir James Pitman today. Every group interprets written symbols according to its own use of the language: the symbols represent what the reader would as a speaker and listener expect. The southerner reads "saw" and "sore" alike, the northerner reads them differently, as he speaks.

Of the debate on the Bill Dr. Jagger said that none of those who spoke "evinced any awareness that the ability of children of five to seven years of age to learn to read by any means or any spelling system, consistent or inconsistent, might be an assumption; and that, if this assumption be conceded, it draws with it the remarkable conclusion that in the process of learning to read the ordinary direction of acquiring knowledge and skill is reversed. Ordinarily, the mind proceeds from the known to the unknown, from the whole to the part, from the concrete to the abstract. Reading is getting the meaning of written and printed symbols . . . For him [the little child] significant words and sentences are the only realities." This assertion assumes that the child's comprehension is static in relation to his age. The truth as shown by experience is that the child's comprehension expands alongside his reading.[1]

[1] Dr. Jagger, whose views are quoted here and on page 75, was always opposed to spelling reform and an advocate of the sentence method of teaching reading, in connection with which he has edited a number of school books. His arguments are set out at some length in Chapter VIII of his *English in the Future* (published by Thomas Nelson & Sons, Ltd.). He concludes there that simplified spelling has been killed by "total lack of interest on the part of the public, a lack of interest founded on sound practical sense, on an instinctive recognition of the fact that the proposals, if applied, would confer no advantage." Dr. Jagger quotes from the publications of the Simplified Spelling Society, so presumably had read about the school experiments of 1870 and 1920!

The Parliamentary Secretary's statement during the debate on Second Reading that the Association of Education Committees was opposed to the Bill was true but the implications of his statement were misleading. In an editorial in the Association's official journal *Education*, the secretary of the Association, Dr. W. P. (now Sir William) Alexander, said that the Association agreed with the Minister of Education, Miss Florence Horsbrugh, in objecting to compulsion on the Minister to interfere in a matter which was normally not her concern but that of the education authorities and the research bodies, but he pointed out that the Association was in no way opposed to the purpose of the Bill, which was to secure research into the teaching of reading, and to find out whether simplified spelling would be a contribution to the improved teaching of reading. He suggested that the Minister should provide money for such research: "If the Minister is not prepared to make a grant for the purpose of research, then the sponsors of the Bill are left with no alternative but to seek the approval of the House of Commons itself to the terms of their Bill in order that the duty to do this shall be placed with the Minister." He asked why the Minister had not offered a grant since it was generally recognized that there was a problem worthy of research: "It may be that those who sponsor the Bill will be proved to be wrong in their belief . . . but in order to prove that they are wrong research is necessary. The Minister seems to be taking the view that, without any research being undertaken, she can just decide that they are wrong . . . We may have grave doubts about the virtues of a system of simplified spelling but at least we are prepared to find out the right answer."

On the seventh of May Mr. Follick's question: "To ask the Minister of Education if she will state her policy towards proposals by a competent research organization to investigate possible improvements in the teaching of reading by means of a system of simplified spelling," received the following answer from the Minister of Education—

Any such organization could rely on my interest and goodwill for their proposal as for any proposal designed to investigate possible improvements in this field of education. Such interest and goodwill would not imply any prospect of additional grant. It would be for the organization concerned to secure the willing co-operation of local education authorities, teachers and parents, and these must in my view remain free to decide with what particular forms of research they wish

to associate themselves. All concerned in any such researches could rest assured of my good wishes for their work.

Mr. Follick and Mr. Pitman both appreciated that the Bill's next hurdle, the House of Lords, was likely to be formidable. It was clear that the Minister was severely embarrassed by the Bill's success in the Commons in face of her opposition. On receiving this answer, they agreed to withdraw the Bill. They had no financial aid from the Government but at least they were now assured of co-operation.

Just before this, Dr. Alexander wrote to me in a letter dated the twentieth of April 1953—

> We believe that the Minister should indicate her preparedness to facilitate research and we are wholly in favour of such research. . . . We have therefore been seeking to use our good offices to influence the Minister to give such assurances as would enable research to be undertaken and the Bill as such to be withdrawn. . . . Unfortunately the National Foundation for Educational Research seems very hesitant about indicating their preparedness to tackle the job, but I am still hoping the necessary assurances can be given and the problem resolved. . . . Would you think it a good idea to table a resolution for the Annual General Meeting, phrased appropriately, calling on the Minister to secure that research is undertaken on the teaching of reading and, in particular, the use of a simplified method of spelling?

It was essential that the local education authorities should be ready to provide schools for any future experiment and it was also necessary to show the Minister that they supported wholeheartedly the contemplated research. Sir Graham Savage was a former Education Officer to the London County Council and before that Chief Inspector to the Ministry of Education: he was now chairman of the Simplified Spelling Society. Already in February he and I together had taken steps to inform the Association of Education Officers of the aims and argument of the Bill and a full exposition of the Simplified Spelling Society's position was sent officially to all education officers.

Following Dr. Alexander's suggestion, the Oldham Education Committee was very pleased to table the following resolution: "That this Association is of the opinion that research should be undertaken on methods of teaching reading, including inquiry whether the use of simplified spelling would be an aid to the teaching of reading," which the Bootle Education Committee agreed to second.

The readiness of my own education committee is not surprising. It was in Oldham that simplified spelling had been most recently put to use in schools. In the summer of 1947, Miss P. O. Bennett, then headmistress of Hathershaw Infants' School, reported to me that she had in her school ten children, who because of their age would leave in a few weeks' time for the junior school and who could not read. She had never before had so large a number of complete "non-starters" and she was very unhappy about them. Every method of intensive teaching had failed to have effect. She suggested that she might try simplified spelling. *Dhe Litl Red Hen* (see page 74) was the only printed book available. Over the weekend she constructed what apparatus she could by hand. In less than a fortnight she was able to report that all the children were reading. The Education Committee knew of this small-scale and effective effort. Their interest in furthering any work in this direction had never abated and I must pay a particular tribute in this connection to my chairman, Mr. J. T. Hilton, J.P., himself by profession a teacher, whose encouragement and support have never failed. In their minutes of June, the Oldham Education Committee recorded—

> It was felt that while there should be no compulsion from the Ministry on anyone to adopt any particular methods, recent criticisms of the reading ability of children made it desirable that there should be as full an inquiry as possible into possible improvements in school methods and that all bodies interested in education should welcome any form of research which would promote educational efficiency in this field.

The motion went forward to the Annual Conference of the Association of Education Committees, where it was carried without opposition. *Education*, of the tenth of July, reported the proceedings as follows—

Mr. Maurice Harrison (Oldham) moved the following resolution—
Simplified Spelling

"That this Association is of opinion that research should be undertaken on methods of teaching reading, including inquiry whether the use of simplified spelling would be an aid to the teaching of reading."

He commented first of all that he regretted the title given to the resolution because he did not want to talk about simplified spelling but about educational research. Mr. Harrison did not support the charges which had been levelled against the standard of reading in the country;

he thought it was as good as it had ever been since public education was begun, but that did not deter him from wanting to explore every possible method of improving the standard. When a Bill had come before the House and was accorded a second reading, recommending research into the teaching of reading and suggesting the use of simplified spelling, some suspicion had arisen that the Association was not only opposed to the Bill, but opposed to research. "The real purpose of this motion before you," he said, "is to make it clear that this Association is composed of real educationists who are not opposed to research in any form."

On the twenty-eighth of October a deputation from the Association of Education Committees waited on the Minister. In presenting the resolution, they stated that "the Association were neither for nor against simplified spelling."[1] They merely thought that a sufficiently good case had been made out by its exponents for the whole question to be examined by an impartial body, and hoped that the Minister would encourage such a process. In reply the Minister said that while no proposal for research had been submitted to her, she was not opposed to any form of research that was proposed by responsible bodies, but that it was not for her to initiate such research. The Minister's assurances to the proposers of the Bill and to the Association of Education Committees were clearly based on the undertaking of a controlled experiment by a reputable research body.

The failure to obtain any financial aid from the Ministry was a very serious matter for the reformers. It is not easy for the general reader to grasp the tremendous cost involved in the production of books on the scale needed and this is surely the explanation why the successful experiments of the past were abandoned. To make the production of school readers profitable, commercial publishers must look to a sale of forty or fifty thousand copies. Subsidizing the printing of books from which publishers see no sure profit, the expense of research covering the salaries for a period of years of a large and highly trained staff, with all the heavy administrative charges involved, is a costly business, running into scores of thousands of pounds. The funds of the Simplified Spelling Society alone were not sufficient. The Society was not dismayed, however. It had already offered to pay the expenses of promoting the Bill: it now set out to get the experiment afoot.

[1] Association of Education Committees, Executive Minutes, twenty-sixth November 1953.

XI

Learning to Read in other Languages

The Italian language has a sensible spelling, and it has been calculated that the Italian child takes a year less than the English child to learn the spelling of its mother tongue.

Walter Ripman, Chief Inspector in the University of London (1930)

THE SIMPLIFIED SPELLING SOCIETY had made three important decisions. The first was that spelling reform as a general issue was to be relegated into the background, and that the Society's efforts were to be concentrated on the educational aim of teaching children to read. Secondly, that the next experiment in schools should not collapse for want of books. They felt that the successful work of the 1870s and the 1920s could not have been allowed to languish and end if the supply of books in the new spelling had been adequate. It was obvious that the need for writing out so much of what the children had to read asked too much even of enthusiasts, and that children with only five or six books, and those necessarily of the "primer" variety, never had access to a library where interest and skill might develop until reading in any medium had virtually no difficulties, and when such difficulties as it had faded before confidence and love of books. This decision faced the Society with a very difficult problem of finance. Its own funds were limited and would be wholly consumed: there was no leeway for making good mistakes. The Committee received an estimate in July 1949 that it would cost some £5,000 for the printing only of necessary school books for the minimum number of children which would be sufficient for a conclusive experiment. They commented, "Our previous experiments were carried out with very little expenditure." The third decision was that the experiment should be undertaken by a body of national repute, not directly interested in the results, as a problem of scientific research to be proved or disproved beyond question, with appropriate scientific controls and comparisons among children of similar type and from the same backgrounds taught by traditional methods.

As early as 1947 the Society's officers approached London University's Institute of Education about undertaking the research. Professor G. B. Jeffery, then Director of the Institute, expressed "provisional and non-committal interest in the idea of the school experiments." Professor Jeffery went so far as to ask Ginn & Co. Ltd. for permission to print their first three Beacon Readers in Nue Speling. It was hoped to receive this permission and to be able to make a start "as soon as the crisis in the printing trade admits of the publication of the necessary books."[1] A year later the printing difficulty was still as great as ever and staff changes at the Institute had slowed down activity.

Progress was made, however, in 1949 when the Institute of Education decided to look for a suitable research worker and to give him experience in teaching reading in infant schools. In the meantime Professor Bruce Pattison, who was head of the Division of Language Teaching, was asked to prepare the ground. This it was thought at the time would involve the preparation of infant reading books.

In July 1954 Professor Pattison approached the Oldham Local Education Authority concerning the organization of a pilot experiment in one school, and the authority, in conjunction with the headmistress who had used Nue Speling in 1947, at once responded.[2] This tentative approach was not, however, followed up. For its part the Society agreed to make available to the Institute a sum of £5,000 and a covenant for an annual payment to make good this undertaking was signed with the University of London in April 1951. The University agreed to keep the money in a separate fund to be applied to the educational purposes intended by the Society. It was hoped that similar financial assistance would be forthcoming from interested bodies in the United States, among them the Simpler Spelling Association of America and Columbia University, New York. Professor Pattison was in touch with Teachers College, Columbia University and "hoped to be able to report agreement in principle and agreement also on the main details of the projected research, and in particular on the system of alphabet to be used and the types and numbers of titles of books to be prepared in order that the time-consuming work entailed may be begun as soon as possible."

In January 1952 it was reported to the Society that the Institute

[1] Simplified Spelling Society Committee minutes, July 1947
[2] See p. 90.

of Education had appointed a small committee to set up a research association. In order that the research should be convincingly dis-interested the Simplified Spelling Society had now completely withdrawn from the arrangements. The only member of the Society on this committee was its treasurer, Mr. I. J. Pitman. The committee in due course appointed Dr. W. R. Lee to supervise the inquiry.

It was felt in the first instance desirable to establish, if possible, whether irregular spelling was a proven contributory cause of reading difficulty. For many years, there has been much inquiry into teach-ing methods and their appropriateness to various stages of children's personal growth. Out of such studies in the field of learning to read, controversies have arisen, mainly in the English-speaking world, about the relative benefits of the phonic, the look-and-say and the sentence methods of teaching and various combinations of them. The two latter methods have no doubt been stimulated by the comparative failure of the first, which was once general. Various factors affecting the development of children have been analysed: their mental and emotional growth, their physical abilities, and their psychological difficulties at different stages. Theories, stoutly pro-claimed, have been enunciated about ages of readiness to read and write, about optical ability to distinguish printed signs and about manual dexterity to imitate them. One factor which always seems to have been overlooked was the spelling itself. Nobody (for the pedagogues had forgotten or ignored the work of the spelling reformers) had questioned the anomalies of English spelling nor (so far as I have been able to discover) the inadequacies of the Roman alphabet either here or in countries where English is not used. In June 1957 the Institute of Education published the results of an inquiry into the question: "Is the irregularity with which English is spelt an important cause of reading difficulty?"

The inquiry was directed to finding out—

(1) The experience of teachers in countries where the language is more regularly spelt than in English;

(2) How far English children's reading errors are related to spelling; and

(3) Whether children in this country form any association between the sounds of English and the frequent ways in which these sounds are spelt.

Inquiries were made with reference to the first aspect in more than thirty countries from Peru to India and it soon became clear

why my own inquiries during the war years had been fruitless. Apparently "spelling regularity has never been the subject of reading research." Since there was barely any agreement about what constitutes good or bad reading and methods have a variety of often conflicting names, it was very difficult to draw conclusions from the replies. Spelling is generally far more representative of sound, and orthographic rules are far more generally consistent in other languages than in English, and it had not occurred to educationists in other lands to question these correlations in an approach to the teaching of reading.

It was found that in virtually all countries the first aim is to analyse sentences, words or syllables into more fundamental units and ultimately into sounds represented by letters of the alphabet. A list of common words sometimes serves as the starting point, as is usual in Holland and Poland, or the children's own sentences are written on the blackboard as in Belgium, or children's stories may be used as in Luxembourg. Analysis is then followed by synthesis. When the sounds are recognized and associated with printed forms, syllables or words are built up from the sounds. This can broadly be likened to the phonic method with a preceding look-and-say stage.

The difference between practice in England and elsewhere seems in general to be that the look-and-say stage in other lands is only a step towards sound recognition. The synthetic stage is often very short. For instance, we are told that Greek children analyse words into syllables and then letters, but that a month later "the youngsters are able to read quite easily any book that is printed with the words divided into syllables." (Greek is, of course, a highly polysyllabic language.) This is admittedly a simplification of the report but essentially correct. Clearly, with a language like French, where the endings of words are indistinct and there is often liaison with following words, the analytic approach begins from the sentence, for the young child will be less aware of the beginnings and endings of words than in languages like German or Italian which tend to have clearly defined endings. "The initial approach in France is generally by means of a 'sentence' method but this is quickly followed by analysis and synthesis." From Yugoslavia comes the report: "It is most important to make the pupils feel and understand that the words are composed of sounds." A phonic method is general in Denmark and Sweden and is prescribed officially in Russia and Turkey, although

there is a point at which certain Russian syllable formations must be taught as wholes. In some countries, notably in South America, e.g. Chile, Ecuador, Mexico, a syllable or sentence method appears to be gaining official favour. The syllable method also predominates in Spain. It is, however, not by any means always clear whether "syllable method" means the recognition of syllabic wholes by look-and-say or the building up of syllables from sound elements. It may be that, since most research in this field is American, educationists have accepted conclusions which apply rather to English ortho-graphy. This is quite possible, as English-speaking research workers have never suggested that their conclusions are a consequence of English spelling difficulties. Finland depends upon a synthetic method "suited better to be used by us than in England." In India "the methods most commonly used are variations of the syllable approach or of word approach in which the words are taught as wholes first and then retaught in relation to the constituent syllables." Norway talks of a "sound-blending" method, but it seems that the blends are first reached through analysis into sounds.

This section of the report shows that there are very few countries in which one method only is employed, and when teachers are free to choose there is a variety of practice. It is in fact almost impossible to compare, for languages vary in so many ways, in syllabic con-struction, in grammatical variety, and in ways some of which are not, without lengthy exposition, easily described in another language with different semantic attitudes or syntactic and other constructions. One fact stands out: that where an alphabet is used rarely if ever are words taught as ideographs, to be memorized as wholes with the spelling only a rough guide, even though in some countries non-phonic initial approaches win approval. "Non-phonic," however, in the context of these other languages does not mean what it may mean in English: word-building seems always to be an expected end. Very cautiously the report draws the conclusion that in England: "There is perhaps a general tendency to abjure analysis and synthesis at the beginning and to postpone it to a later stage than, on the whole, non-English countries do."

The supporter of simplified spelling could readily claim that what can be sifted from this mass of not easily comparable evidence reinforces his argument! Dr. Lee drew the cautious conclusion—

A close association between methods and languages, viewed from an orthographical standpoint, does not exist. This does not mean, of course,

that orthography has had no influence on teaching methods. . . . It does mean, however, that we cannot draw much support from the experience of teachers in the 'regular spelling' countries, taken as a whole, for a view that controversy over method is confined to English-speaking countries, and that if English spelling were regularized these controversies would disappear.

This is true enough and there is no evidence that this or that method will achieve the best results with a regular spelling. There will always be room for experiment on method. The speed of learning to read claimed in some reports, e.g. from Greece and Belgium, is remarkable by English standards. The absence of reference to the spelling difficulties we regard as natural may be very enlightening. The very general assumption that, having learnt elements, one builds syllables, words and sentences is clear. Brought up in a free-falling space we should be unaware of the effects of gravity: maybe those brought up with consistent spelling are unaware of the effects of orthographic chaos.

Inquiries where English and another language are both taught brought some interesting replies. From South Africa, we are told that English-speaking children used a longer look-and-say stage than Afrikaans speakers, that from twelve years of age the latter have a larger vocabulary in Afrikaans than the former in English and "Afrikaans children can learn to read Afrikaans far more quickly than English children can learn to read English." A phonic method appears to be more generally used in the teaching of Afrikaans than in the teaching of English.

The value of comparison between learning to read two languages in bilingual schools is doubtful because one of the languages may be preferred. It may be the language of the home, or the language leading to a career, or preferred for political or social reasons and so on. A Welsh inspector said that Welsh-speaking children do not experience less difficulty in learning to read Welsh than English-speaking children in learning to read English, but at once added that there was a shortage of books and aids for the teaching of Welsh and "if there were not the position might be different." A teacher in Mexico said that American children with all the advantages of living in a literate society learnt to read English far more slowly than American Indians and Mexicans learnt to read their regularly spelt languages. She added that the Indian children had a special incentive: the art of reading was a new and precious possession.

Interest, of course, must play a huge part and this is a main plank in the spelling reformer's claims, that he would provide quick success and lively interest at an early stage. An English teacher in Peru said that her infant daughter learnt to read Spanish far quicker than English.

Inquiry into the frequency of reading errors was attempted but in only one instance was the Institute's research officer able to report. In a Serbo-Croat school he found the ability of pupils to correct their own errors "most striking." "Not a single child was unable to do so immediately after the teacher had said, 'Look at it again.'" The Yugoslavian teachers said that the mistakes usually resulted from words which were not part of the children's vocabulary. This is understandable for the children's knowledge of the sounds in such cases would not always be clear and definite.

Again, the report draws the conclusion that this study hardly helped with the problem of whether a child learns to read more easily a regularly spelt language—

We can only guess that fuller advantage can be taken of a "phonetic" stage . . . and that if the "phonetic" stage is in practice given more attention in regular spelling countries, as on the whole it appears to be, progress there must be more rapid for this very reason. Yet the fact is not demonstrable. There are many interwoven factors besides spelling that exert their influence on reading success.

Because of the complete lack of objective reading tests in most countries and the different ages at which children begin school, it was felt that no comparisons of value could be made. Again, the supporter of reform may ask whether the omission in the majority of countries to worry about tests of reading age is not of itself significant.

The repeated references to the teaching of syllables and division into syllables suggests another possible easement of learning to read English when rationally spelt. English is unique among the languages of Europe and indeed, with rare exceptions such as Chinese, among all languages, in that it is largely monosyllabic. Synthesis, word-building, becomes by that very reason a much easier process in English than in nearly all other languages. Consider any modern English writing. I take a book haphazard, open it at random and read—

And think this heart, all evil shed away,
A pulse in the eternal mind, no less
Gives somewhere back the thoughts by England given;
Her sights and sounds, dreams happy as her day;
And laughter learnt of friends; and gentleness,
In hearts at peace, under an English heaven.

Thirty-six monosyllables, ten disyllables and two trisyllables in forty-eight words (and three of the disyllables, "evil," "given" and "heaven," may be monosyllables). That is fairly typical. If one considers any paragraph in this book the preponderance of monosyllables must be striking and in ordinary everyday speech the proportion would be bigger still.

If progress in reading is hindered by spelling irregularity then it should be more difficult to read irregularly spelt English words than those spelt regularly. An inquiry to find out whether this happened was launched by the Institute of Education in a number of schools in London and Ireland. It was soon found that such an inquiry is by no means so simple as it may at first sight look. What is irregularity? Which of the many ways of representing sound by signs are the regular ones? Is conversion into sound the test and, if so, where stands silent reading? In his *The Analysis of Written Middle English*, Professor A. McIntosh says that there is room for a study of written English as a manifestation of language worthy of separate regard, and not merely considered as "dependent upon its spoken equivalent."[1] It was decided that a regularly spelt word meant a spoken word each phoneme (separable sound) of which is spelt as it is most often spelt. If one includes the various letter forms, A a a etc., there are more than 2,000 ways of representing the forty to fifty sounds of English! There are distinctions in pronunciation shading off one into another. At what point should one draw the line and specify that the main sounds of English number a hundred or sixty or fifty or forty? What is even within broad limits the correct pronunciation? Dr. Godfrey Dewey's *Relativ Frequency of English Speech Sounds*[2] was broadly drawn upon for word and spelling frequency, Professor Daniel Jones's *Outline of English Phonetics* and *An English Pronouncing Dictionary* for pronunciation. Dewey's word lists, being American-English, could be used only as a basis in

---

[1] Transactions of the Philological Society.
[2] Harvard University Press and Pitman, 1923.

English schools. Even Professor Jones's dictionary could not be as rigidly accepted in the Irish as in the London schools.[1]

It would be superflous to pursue all the difficulties, many of which are logically insuperable. Enough has been said to show a few of them and to indicate how wide are the tolerances within which any conclusions must be stated. Further, the answers to many psychological problems have yet to be established. What evidence, for instance, is there that children establish a mental link between letters and sounds? Is what the child sees influenced by what he expects in the context?

The inquiry was in many ways misdirected. It was fundamentally wrong in that it was based upon the reading behaviour of children who could already read rather than on those who were learning from the beginning. Irregularly spelt words such as "the," "was," "of," had become known and familiar before the children were tested to find out whether the irregular spellings were or were not "a major cause of reading difficulty." In spite of this and other defects (which tended to cancel out difficulties arising from spelling) the compilers of the report felt able to state—

> On the whole children in the junior schools had slightly greater difficulty with the more irregularly than with the less irregularly spelt words in the passages, as the analysis of errors showed. In the reading of isolated words too there was a slightly stronger tendency to fail at those more irregularly spelt. . . . About one-fifth of the misreadings of isolated words appeared to involve the attribution to letters of sound-values they possessed in other words. The burden of all this is that "irregularity" was a cause, but evidently by no means a major cause,[2] of reading difficulty. . . . Children in these schools have, by and large, not formed a mental association between the sounds of English and the most frequent spelling of these sounds . . .

[1] Dr. Daniel Jones, Professor Emeritus of Phonetics in the University of London, joined the committee of the Simplified Spelling Society in 1910. Reference to the work of the Society would be woefully incomplete without reference to his outstanding services for more than fifty years. Apart from a heavy correspondence conducted by him, the Society is indebted to him for many works from his pen. All compilers of standard works on Nue Speling have expressed their gratitude for his help and guidance, and his *English Pronouncing Dictionary* and *Outline of English Phonetics* have always been the accepted basis for the Society's standards. When Sir Gilbert Murray resigned from the presidency of the Society in 1946, Professor Jones was unanimously elected in his stead. When in 1950 Professor Jones himself wished to retire, the Society pressed him to remain as president although Sir Graham Savage took over the duties of Chairman of Committee.

[2] I personally cannot trace the basis for this reservation, "by no means a major cause." It seems to me an unwarranted assumption.

Enough had been discovered for the report to be concluded with the hope that further thought might be devoted to the problems of relationships "between features of the written language and reading success."

The causes of reading difficulty are evidently manifold and complex. That spelling irregularity should be found as at least a part cause of different hindrances and since most or all of the several hindrances are interdependent, one must ask whether the removal of the spelling difficulty could not profoundly affect the whole complex picture. With regularized spelling the association of visual patterns with comprehension would be accelerated in several ways. First, because the reader would experience no doubt on the score of sound; secondly, because there need not arise confusion between one word and another word differently sounded but similarly spelt. Confidence would grow because rational order would be expected by the child. Interest might be early established and all the evidence emphasizes the importance of quick interest. The cumulative effect of rational spelling clearly might be great. Learning to read is too complex in its ramifications for a particular aspect to be studied in isolation. The only way to test the effect of spelling consistency on learning to read is to use consistent spelling for the purpose and to compare the results with those of learning to read with traditional spelling. The University department had at least shown academically and apart from any pressure from the Simplified Spelling Society that there were clear scientific grounds for experiment in a neglected field.

Part III

a spesimen ov i.t.a. printiŋ

ie hav just cum from a scœl whær ʃhe nue reediŋ iʃ taut. ie met ʃhær a littl girl ov siks. ʃhee iʃ ʃhe œldest ov a larj family liviŋ on an œldham houʃiŋ estæt. tœ yeerʃ agœ ʃhee woʃ a ʃhie nervus ᴄhield, tœ frietend tœ tauk. ʃhee haʃ wun priezd personal poʃʃeʃhon—a dog-eerd anᴛholojy ov verʃ, given tœ her bie an œlder ᴄhield. ᴛhat littl girl ov siks haʃ just red tœ mee very buetifœlly wurdʃwurᴛh's daffodilʃ. ie askt her whie ʃhee ᴄhœʃ ᴛhat pœem. ʃhee replied ᴛhat ʃhee luvd daffodilʃ.

tœdæ ʃhee speeks wiᴛh ᴄharm and confidens. ᴛhe œnly critisiʃm ov her reediŋ ov ᴛhe pœem miet bee ᴛhat ʃhee red it raᴛher kwickly, tœ neerly at ᴛhe speed ov sielent reediŋ. ʃhee found ᴛhe pæj in ᴛhe bœk bie lœkiŋ up ᴛhe pœet's næm in ᴛhe alfabetical indeks.

œnly ᴛhe sircumstanseʃ ov ᴛhat story ar novel. ᴛhe aᴄheevment ov ᴛhat littl girl ov siks yeerʃ iʃ ov itself færly commonplæs in œldham nouadæʃ.

octœber, 1963

XII

The Initial Teaching Alphabet

The Board's decision to impose a more appropriate test in English than Ordinary level English Language was taken only after it had received strong evidence that many university students left school woefully lacking in the ability to use and to understand their mother tongue.

Northern Universities Joint Matriculation Board. June 1963

IN ORDER TO carry out a satisfactory experiment large numbers of books would have to be specially printed; it was therefore inevitable that the retention of the existing alphabet or its replacement by another should be discussed. The Simplified Spelling Society was well aware of the invention of many proposed alphabets and, as we saw in Chapter IX, in promulgating Nue Speling had, after careful consideration of the problems involved, avoided the creation of new letters. The arguments which guided the Society to that decision were not wholly applicable in the new circumstances of the 1950s. At a meeting of the Committee of the Simplified Spelling Society in April 1954, it is recorded that "Discussion followed on whether the Society should indicate to the University of London Institute of Education its approval of a system of reformed spelling in which varying shapes of letters are used to indicate different sounds. Finally it was agreed that the Society does not and cannot dictate to the University nor to its research-workers any method of reformed spelling." The Society very properly decided that it must not interfere in the conduct of the experiment.

Mr. Pitman had naturally a complete knowledge of his grandfather's work and aims concerning a new alphabet and he was a member of the committee of the Institute of Education controlling the research. In 1959, Sir James Pitman (he had recently been knighted) invented the Augmented Roman Alphabet. He described its aim in this way—

The alphabet here put forward is a "reformed" Roman one. It is new. It is, however, an augmentation of the existing lower-case Ehr-

hardt alphabet of the Monotype Corporation, and its augmentations have been designed for the purpose of providing a consistently alphabetic representation of the English language, suitable primarily for teaching reading to English-speaking children (and adults), and secondarily for teaching English speech and reading to adults (and children) who already speak some other language and may also read it in Roman characters.

Sir James was at pains to make clear that the alphabet is not a design for reforming spelling but a device for teaching reading to be used in the initial stages only. It was "a teacher's tool, a grading of the material for the early stages of teaching, one to be left behind and forgotten, when it achieved its teaching purpose."

With this clearly defined purpose in view, two basic changes are made in the written forms. First, there is one fixed form for each character. The learner is never confused by variant letter forms, and so real repetition, the value of which Infant Teachers have always recognized, is greatly increased. This means that capital letter forms different from 'small' or 'lower-case' forms are banished and that the small letters are themselves always of the same shape. Thus there is the single form g and not G, g and g. When capital letters are required, they are simply the small letters written large: the word "and" is always so written and the forms AND, And and &[1] cannot occur. A lifetime's habituation has made us adults slow to see that all those forms must appear very different things to the infant beginner. Secondly, the digraphs are printed as one letter both in their spacing and in their shaping. In mishap the s and h clearly have their normal values, and in biʃhop the middle consonant is clearly a single sound. The child who sees leꞇher (leather) cannot misread the word as **let her**. The forty-five characters of the Augmented Roman Alphabet or (as it has later been renamed) the Initial Teaching Alphabet- (i.t.a.) are far fewer than those the beginner must master in order to read traditional orthography. With A, a, *a*, G, g, g, B, b, D, d, and the rest, more than seventy characters must be learnt for reading our customary spelling.

The new alphabet is not intended to be spelt phonetically but, subject to the strict rule that one sign should always represent one sound and one sound only, its appearance in use is kept as close as possible to the appearance of traditional print. With this in mind,

---

[1] All these forms are found in many infant books: the ampersand is usually in the name of the publishers. The curious child puzzles over it with the rest of the print.

there are two characters for the consonantal sound which occurs twice in the word **oozes**. The normal z (zed) is used when that letter traditionally occurs, while ƨ (zess), an *s* in z shape, i.e. a reversed z (this letter was used in Anglo-Saxon times for this sound) is used whenever traditional orthography (t.o.) uses s for the voiced sibilant z sound. ƨ has always the unvoiced sound as in yes.

Some of the inconsistencies of t.o. are retained, as to remove all these inconsistencies would enhance the difficulty of the transfer. c and k both give the sound k and they are used as they occur in t.o. Both c and k are used when they are both present in a t.o. word such as kick. Double letters are written when they occur traditionally as in littl. y is used both as a consonant and as a vowel, according to its normal use, thus: yes and penny; i, of course, also gives the sound i as in pin:—

Thus: cracks appeerd in ſhe sæfty zœnƨ
      cracks appeared in the safety zones

The unstressed neutral vowel is written as it is in t.o.: ſhe; cubord (cupboard); instant; pœlar (polar); constabl; tæpiɾ; abbot; onor (honour); octopus; muɾmuɾ. This form is expected to afford a sufficient clue to reading the unstressed neutral vowel.

Rules and examples are a guide to writing i.t.a. but there is no wrong spelling, provided that the spelling offers no possibility of misreading that could result in misunderstanding. Subject to this proviso, the spelling is rendered as like to the traditional orthography as possible. All spelling is a compromise, for speech varies from person to person, from district to district, from year to year. Teachers when writing should try to follow the rules, and reading will accustom them to the usually accepted forms, but it would be folly to waste time and to worry over minor distinctions. Conformity to a standardized convention is for the mass productions of the printer and publisher, not for the individual teacher, much less individual child. The southerner hears no distinction between *paw* and *pore*, the Yorkshireman is certainly aware of a difference and the Scotsman makes a very clear distinction and none is more correct than the others and all may learn to read both. The traditional spelling is thus a guide. Teachers ought, of course, at any time to be reasonably conformist in their spellings, but no teacher should be afraid to spell with the Initial Teaching Alphabet for there is no absolute right or wrong, provided always that the signs

represent broadly the expected word. For example, jud3 is suggested for **judge** and ḍitꞔ for **ditch** because the ḍ and t are found conventionally but juj and ḍiꞔ are not incorrect. The present writer, possibly because of his Yorkshire origin, writes blꙍ for **blue** and blue for **blew**, but southerners cannot hear the distinction and use blꙍ for both words. It does not matter. Representation of the expected sound alone is important. The printed form will represent different sounds to the southern Englishman and to the Scot. But neither of them is in reality listening and both are silently comprehending. Thus each will read the sound he expects and comprehension for either is no less easy (indeed even easier) than comprehension between them when they speak to one another. Finally, and again to facilitate transition to reading normal print, the shapes of the letters themselves reflect the care and genius of their inventor. Sir James Pitman took into consideration the fact, not so commonly realized, that when we read fluently and quickly we look only at the upper part of a line of print. If we cover the bottom half of any line, we can still read the text quite easily but if the upper half is covered very great difficulty is experienced in reading.

When masked at the bottom the result
is easy to read·when masked at the
top it is seen to be harder to read.

(*When masked at the bottom the result is easy to read : when masked at the top it is seen to be harder to read.*)

In i.t.a. the upper appearance of the characters remains almost unchanged: virtually all the distinguishing features of the new characters are located in the lower half.

this is printed in an augmented roeman alfabet the purpos
ov which is not, as miet bee suppoesd, too reform our spellin
but too improov the lernin ov reedin

ᚦhis is printeḍ in an augmenteḍ rꙍeman alfabet, ᚦe purpos ov whiꞔ is not, as miet bee suppoꙍsḍ, tꙍ reform our spelliŋ, but tꙍ imprꙍv ᚦe lerniŋ ov reeḍiŋ.

When children have read 200 or more books (and as will be seen, a very substantial proportion of five-year-olds using i.t.a. do read as many within a few months) they are already apparently skimming

along the tops in the manner of proficient readers. Consequently they readily recognize words in normal print and indeed they seem unaware of any difference.

Sir Isaac Pitman blazed the trail a century ago and one can see traces of his alphabet in his grandson's invention. Sir James Pitman's alphabet has a different aim from that of his grandfather. It is an introduction to reading traditional print; his grandfather's was an alphabet for a reformed spelling. Hence the later alphabet could be devised to permit more compromises with existing tradition. The preservation of word-forms likely to prove acceptable and approximating within broad phonetic limits to ordinary spelling had been suggested by Professor Zachrisson in his Anglic; the coalescence of digraphs into one sign was used by Isaac Pitman in his Phonotypy. Nue Speling used the former: the Initial Teaching Alphabet uses the latter.

The general principles underlying the system are, therefore, mainly those set by the groups which constructed Simplified Spelling and later Nue Speling. The happy choice of type and the forms of the new letters and their highly ingenious upper half approximation to ordinary print and the combination of the virtues of all are due to the genius of Sir James Pitman. The Monotype Corporation produced the new type and its inventor has given away freely the copyright in the design to anyone who cares to use it. The only obligation is to conform in printed matter to what is becoming the conventional standard to be applied to English as the language of the English-speaking world and as a possible language for international communication.

Sir Isaac Pitman has been called the Father of English Phonetic Spelling. It would be equally just to call his grandson, the present Sir James Pitman, the father of the Initial Teaching Medium. His particular genius shown in the improvement, and modification for its particular educational use, of his grandfather's alphabet has been noted. It is true to say that since his entry on this scene in 1935, no one has done more to bring into being this experiment in schools of the 1960s. In Parliament, where he has been indispensable, and in private, he has devoted a considerable part of his life to advocating in an altruistic way, reminiscent of his grandfather, this certainty in his mind that children could be helped by simplification of the spelling in their first school books. In long-term strategic concept and in day-to-day tactics and persuasiveness, with the assistance of

those upon whom he has very timely called, he has achieved what it would be fair to describe as an educational miracle—the putting to the test of the grand idea through two great educational research bodies of Britain (the University of London and the National Foundation for Educational Research) with the active support of all three parties in education: teachers, local education authorities and —particularly—the Ministry of Education. A publisher of books himself, Sir James Pitman has given the copyright in his alphabet to the world and actively carried into effect the policy that as large a number of other publishers as possible should be brought into the publication of the children's books which are being used in the classrooms. Indeed the complete reading scheme of some hundred titles of another publisher was transliterated and printed and one or more titles from many other English and American publishers were commissioned and paid for. His firm's and his own personal monetary contributions to the work have been very large. In every way Sir James Pitman deserves the regard and esteem of educationists throughout the English-speaking world. Those of us who have been fortunate enough to be associated with him in this work know well the careful study, the devotion and the selflessness which have underlain his great efforts.

The 45 characters[1] of the alphabet are given below. There are 27 consonants, and 17 vowels in addition to y, which may be classified as either and is used as it is in traditional spelling.

Each character is shown with its name traditionally spelt[2] followed by a sample word showing its use, followed in turn by the same word in traditional orthography (t.o.).

b	bee	bat	bat
c	kee	cut	cut
d	dee	det	debt
f	ef	fit	fit
g	gay	got	got
h	hay	hunt	hunt
j	jay	jest	jest
k	kay	aks	axe
l	ell	lip	lip
m	em	mous	mouse
n	en	nævy	navy

[1] There were originally 43, but two have been added in the light of experience.
[2] The names of characters are for printers' use rather than teachers'.

p	pee	pens	pence
r	ray	rist	wrist
ɹ	er	first	first
s	ess	sorɗ	sword
t	tee	tiet	tight
v	vee	velvet	velvet
w	way	wun	one
z	zed (or zee)	zɛebra	zebra
ʂ	zess	horsɛʂ	horses
ᴄh	chay	ᴄhurᴄh	church
ŋ	ing	briŋiŋ	bringing
ʃh	ish	ʃhaft	shaft
ᴛh	ith	ᴛhaut	thought
ᴊh	thee	ᴊhis	this
wh	whay	whær	where
ʒ	zhee	meʒuer	measure
y	yay	yot, sity	yacht, city
æ	aid	cæs	case
a	at	caʃh	cash
ɑ	ahd	cɑm	calm
a	ask	casl	castle
e	et	net	net
ɛɛ	eed	nɛɛt	neat
i	it	nit	knit
ie	ide	niet	night
o	ot	not	knot
œ	ode	nœt	note
u	ut	tuf	tough
ue	ued	tuen	tune
ω	oot	tωk	took
ꞷ	ood	tꞷᴛh	tooth
au	aud	taut	taught
oi	oid	toi	toy
ou	owd	toun	town

Note that ɗ has an extended downstroke to distinguish it from b in reverse. Young children often confuse these two letters.

The rules for use are quite simple and any teacher will master them in a few minutes. Then a little practice in reading and writing is all that is necessary. In writing the letters are easily formed. Since

the alphabet is for use only with learners, the letters should not be joined as in ordinary writing.

1. y is used as vowel or consonant in accordance with normal practice: yet, pity, family (but note pitifcol, piteus, familiar); sylinꝺer, cylinder.

2. z, ᴣ. The former is used whenever it is normally used: the latter replaces the traditional s when it has the sound of z, e.g. zꝏᴣ (zoos), horseᴣ.

3. æ, ɑ, ɑ, a,

    æ is the diphthong or long vowel in *hate*—hæt

    ɑ is the long open vowel in *calm*—cɑm

    ɑ is the long (or short—as may be so pronounced) vowel

      in *grass*—grɑss

    a is the short vowel in *hat*—hat.

The character ɑ is used in print for the vowel sound in paꞇh, grɑss etc., which differs according to regional pronunciation. The children and their teachers will relate this deliberately ambiguous character printed ɑ to the a or ɑ of their pronunciation and will write whichever they use in speech.

4. c, k. Both represent the same sound. Use the one which occurs in t.o. kick, acsept (accept), cꝏk (cook).

5. ꭑ. ꝺiꭑh is not wrong, but ꝺitꭑh, being nearer to t.o. and quite unambiguous, is preferred.

6. j, ᴣ. The former is the consonant in jau (jaw) and the second is the middle consonant in viᴣon (vision). If a dg occurs in t.o. the i.t.a. form is ꝺᴣ (which gives the same sound as j) in order to retain the d and maintain a visual similarity to t.o.: thus rɑja (rajah), but heꝺᴣ. A child who writes hej is phonetically correct.

7. Alternative pronunciations are largely a matter of personal choice. Dr. Daniel Jones's *English Pronouncing Dictionary* and Dr. John S. Kenyon and Thomas A. Knott's *A Pronouncing Dictionary of American English* are the recommended guides, and, where they give alternatives, the spelling is preferred which corresponds most closely with normal spelling—often rather than aufen, sœlꝺier rather than sœljer.

8. ue. Some spellings must be arbitrary and, following the *English Pronouncing Dictionary*, ue is used in words such as postuer (posture), pictuer (picture), feetuer (feature). Again picꭑer is unambiguous, but is better avoided. Many people sound ꭑ for t in front of ue, e.g. in tueb (tube). Most of us do this in ritueal

(ritual). pictuer fits into a common pattern of writing where variety of pronunciation exists.

Initially ue begins such words as uenion (union) but y begins such words as yœr (your), yœth (youth), yuŋ (young). Traditional orthography is the guide.

9. au, or. It should be noted that while w (qu) is often followed by a in English, a hardly ever has its normal vowel sound in that position. Usually the character au is needed. waull (wall), wauter (water), waurm (warm), kwaurter (quarter), waurn (warn), but worn (worn)—as normally spelt, and born (born-e).

Also fault (fault), sault (salt), pau (paw)—cf. por (pore).

But note woʂ (was), whot (what), skwonḍer (squander). As with all English spelling rules, there are exceptions, e.g. wag, wax, quagmire, swam.

10. The neutral vowel common in English unstressed syllables is generally represented by the vowel found normally. It is usually, possibly always, a good test, if in doubt, to sound the word deliberately as one does when dictating slowly or pronouncing a word as a name, e.g. in the sentence: "The pronoun that is pronounced differently from the conjunction that." The two words that may, oddly enough, be sounded alike in this example for we use them as substantives, but in general use they sound differently. Compare them in "That man said that he would come." We spell both, however, with the vowel a for, sounded deliberately or as a name, we give to a its full value. Similarly we write ḍelicæt (delicate), for, if we carefully enunciate or slowly sing (as in "The lass with the delicate air") the last syllable, this is the sound we should give to it. Thus—

forward	forward	important	important
uven	oven	noledʒ	knowledge
select	select	lafter	laughter
ʃheateɾ	theatre	probabl	probable
evolv	evolve	arieʂ	arise

11. r ɾ. The second symbol is written when r is combined with any of the four vowels e i u y to represent the vowel sound in her fir fur myrrh: heɾ fiɾ fuɾ myɾr. It is used with no other vowels.

Examples: muʃher tæpiɾ ɑrʃhuɾ mɑrtyɾ peɾmit iɾksum buɾn wuɾḍ (word) myɾtl

but onor (honour) hɑrt (heart) fær (fair) fier (fire) yorkʃhier (Yorkshire) sorḍ (sword)

N.B. ᴇrriŋ (erring). The first consonant is vestigial if heard at all and is part of the vowel sound: the second consonant is a trilled **r** and clearly heard. As with ɑ in paragraph 3 the use of ɼ is optional for writing in school. With many Scottish speakers **r** after a vowel is rarely vestigial only. Printing in books will make the distinction. Similarly fuɼry, but note ferry, very, herriŋ, turret, furɶ, tyrrany, where the **r**s are always trilled.

12. Double letters are used when found traditionally, e.g. ill (ill), rollickiŋ (rollicking); ck is, of course, a double letter in this context.

13. The vestigial first vowel is retained in the final syllable of words like speʃhial, judiʃhial, ɶʃhean, sɶldiɼ. The form is readily accepted and leads easily into traditional spelling. But the i is not retained in -ʃhon, -jon, -ɖhon, -ʒon endings, e.g. stæʃhon, crɷsifiksʃhon, relijon, stanɖhon, televiʒon.

These are the spelling rules. Almost half of our traditional spellings do not change in any basic way and more than a quarter do not change at all. The following estimates are generally accepted—

(a) Words unchanged—26·5 per cent, e.g. anɖ, not, ɖiɖ, went, given, fitteɖ.

(b) Words with minor modification—23·75 per cent, e.g. riɖh, our, bᴇᴇn, gɷd, iꭥ, ʃhat.

(c) Words changed but still familiar in form and presenting no change of moment—10·5 per cent, e.g. hav, littl, mor, tiem. (Very often the only change is the omission of a final unsounded **e**.)

(d) words radically changed—39·25 per cent, e.g.

aut (ought)	cof (cough)	thrɷ (through)
wuns (once)	ɖun (done)	hɶl (whole)

XIII

Planning the Present Experiment

Few people would challenge the statement that reading is the most important subject in the curriculum of the elementary school; success in this subject conditions, to a large extent, progress in most other subjects and, as recent studies show, influences the whole attitude of the pupil towards school life. Thus progress in reading in infant and junior classes becomes a basic intellectual and emotional problem—failure in the subject resulting not infrequently in general scholastic backwardness or emotional maladjustment.

Professor F. J. Schonell, *Backwardness in the Basic Subjects* (1942)[1]

I N JUNE 1960 the Institute of Education in association with the National Foundation for Education Research published a pamphlet: "Some reasons why we are initiating an investigation into the early stages of learning to read, when the matter to be read is printed in a special form alleged to be easy to learn and leading easily to a full reading skill." The pamphlet points out that written language is indispensable to human progress but that learning to read is "one of the more difficult educational problems." Inquiry into the use of a special alphabet had never been investigated in a scientific fashion and only thorough trial under controlled conditions could answer all the objections raised by opponents in the past. The research would be planned under the guidance "of scientific experts, educational, psychological, statistical, typographical, phonetic, etc." The pamphlet was sent to many people, education officers, teachers and others to ensure an informed body of support—

It may be predicted from experience that the project will be specially vulnerable to fears and strong emotions. It is therefore desirable to have achieved, long before any research is launched on its classroom stages, wide acceptance and approval of the decision to undertake such an investigation—as a protection for those who will participate, and particularly for the children and their parents.

[1] Dr. M. D. Vernon (*Backwardness in Reading*, Cambridge University Press, Britain) and Dr. A. I. Gates ("The Role of Personality Maladjustment in Reading Disability", *Journal of Genetic Psychology*, 59) in U.S.A. have also related reading failure and personality disorders.

The statement was accompanied by letters supporting an investigation from the Minister of Education, the Secretary of the Association of Education Committees and the General Secretary of the National Union of Teachers. There was a form to be signed and returned to the Institute stating: "I agree that the proposed investigation ought to be undertaken, and commend the decision of those who will be collaborating therein in its conduct." All this is an indication of the fears which still existed that strong emotional opposition would arise against the scheme. These fears were not surprising when one thinks of an incident which George Bernard Shaw recalled in a letter to Professor Daniel Jones written in January 1949.

> As to teaching children I urged a Minister of Education to allow and encourage them to spell phonetically just as they speak, thus enabling the teacher to detect their mispronunciations and correct them. He replied that the least hint at such a heresy would banish him from public life. It is safer nowadays to be anti-Christ than anti-Johnson.

One or two newspapers talked of the children who were to learn the new alphabet as "guinea pigs" as though they were to risk sacrifice in the name of scientific research. One columnist pitied the children who were now to have to learn forty-three letters instead of the normal twenty-six! This lady clearly had not counted. (See page 106.) Some papers would no doubt have happily joined the pack if any responsible educationists had been willing to attack. In point of fact any who came like Balaam to curse were so impressed with the case for such experiments that they "altogether blessed them." There was thus far less newspaper criticism than had been feared. It was difficult to attack an educational inquiry into the efficacy of a teaching method whereas it would have been only too easy and popular to attack spelling simplification as such. Timely contributions to professional and other papers and television interviews had all emphasized the teaching research aspect. Also, the two well-supported Bills in the House of Commons in recent years had seemingly done much to clear the critics of our spelling of the charge of being cranks. Presumably too, those who were so certain that the end result would support their adverse opinions were content to allow the supposedly inevitable failure to prove their point.

It is surely true that never before had such precautions been taken in respect of pure educational research. Usually, when a school tries out a new method the teachers concerned simply put their ideas to

the test, and do not ask for public support and parental approval. This time parents' meetings were called to give approval of the method to be used. Apart from allaying any fears that antagonistic publicity might arouse, there was a good reason, of course, for informing parents in order that they might show understanding when the children read or wrote in the new way at home. Fortunately, parents in my experience were easily convinced that their children would not suffer and might gain. In my own area the education committee, having sponsored the original suggestions for an investigation eight years earlier, was only anxious to make a start. The local press was cautious but agreed that nobody could object to impartial investigation, provided that care was taken that no child should suffer as a result. Generally, education committees were cautious. Five others besides Oldham, grouped geographically for ease of administration, Burton-on-Trent, Staffordshire, Stoke-on-Trent, Wolverhampton and Walsall, were persuaded to join in the scheme (Walsall in respect only of remedial work), and the head-teachers of two schools, in Grimsby and Harrow, asked to participate. Training courses for the teacher volunteers were established in Stoke for the teachers in the Midlands and in Oldham for the local teachers and those from Grimsby and Harrow.

The experiment began in September 1961 with the infant entrants of that year. Generally speaking, schools were found as follows. The infant headteachers in the area were circularized and asked if they were prepared to do the work and schools were accepted only where the headteacher and the class teacher directly involved were willing volunteers. The parents of the children attending the school then had the new method explained to them and their assent secured. All these things were not easy. There were, for instance, cases where a headteacher was willing but the class teacher not as willing. Some felt that they were achieving results with t.o. which could not be improved and that they would be risking the children entrusted to their care. Many were just sceptical of the whole business. Possibly some were not ready to abandon schemes of work which had proved themselves over the years and to which they had become accustomed.

The experiment was organized and is being very carefully continued on a scientific basis. The infant schools chosen were themselves very varied. For instance, in Oldham, two were new county schools on housing estates, one of them temporarily organized as part of a junior school but soon to start a separate existence; three

others were very old denominational schools, two due for closure under the schools development plan. Alongside the experimental schools, a number of control schools were chosen. Every type of experimental school was matched by a control school which used the same series of infant primers: the books differed only in the alphabet and in the spelling. This latter point is important, for progress through the series of readers is being carefully recorded in both sets of schools for later comparison. These records are being kept in respect of all the children in the experimental and in the control schools, together with information showing the intelligence quotients and the reading ages recorded from time to time by objective testing as well as social background and so forth.

In 1964, that is, when the children who entered school in September 1961 complete their infant school education, the research team will begin to prepare a report on the comparative achievement in the experimental and control schools in reading and writing (i.e. spelling) in the traditional alphabet with traditional spelling. The research is intended ultimately to cover a total of 2,500 children.

Every foreseeable precaution has been taken to ensure that conditions in the two sets of schools are strictly comparable. In an attempt to ensure that special zeal in the experimental schools shall not affect the results, and that equal zeal shall be stimulated in the control schools, the Institute has provided special lectures for the teachers in the control schools on teaching methods. To some observers, the advantages seem to have lain with the control schools. The experimental schools had to start at a disadvantage since the supply of reading material available to their children at school, at home and in their general surroundings could never match that available to children in the control schools. Moreover what material there was had been oriented to teaching in t.o. and could not take deliberate advantage of the features of consistency in look-and-say and of reliability in phonic learning and syllabic extensions of which the new medium was capable, since the latter had been conceived and designed to afford these very features. At the beginning the teachers in the experimental schools had a particularly difficult job. Not only were they starting something new, without knowledge or experience to guide them in their first approach but there was for some months a shortage of books. This arose in some degree from the success of the work. The books of the reading scheme (James Nisbet and Co. Ltd.'s *Janet and John* series) were in supply, but

there was a dearth of books for the library corner and some children within a few weeks were searching the library corner for new books to read. There was also little printed apparatus for those teachers who felt a need for it nor were there classroom posters and printed cards, so common in infant classrooms.

The first teachers were pioneers of great courage and foresight, who moreover had a heavy task, and they deserve the gratitude of all educationists. Books were transcribed into the Initial Teaching Alphabet by hand and the handwritten pages were pasted over the printed pages. Books from many other countries were translated and gummed pages printed in the new alphabet were supplied with the books, shaped to fit between the illustrations of the original books. Many of these were very attractive books indeed. The shortage of books had one interesting result. Most of the early cases of children making the transition to normal print came to light because children, in their search for new books to read, marauded other classrooms in the school. In the first months, however, the work falling on the volunteers was really demanding. Their experimental work, not only in methods of starting the new teaching, but in such apparently routine matters as finding out the best way of writing the new characters, has benefited all their successors. Not only had they to find their way to a new approach and to transcribe books, but all classroom notices had to be printed by hand. There were some fifty books besides the readers at first; by the summer of 1962 there were some 250 titles and the number has grown since. The choice is, nevertheless, limited in comparison with the thousands of books which publishers offer to schools.

One school in Oldham, Fitton Hill Infants' School, is running what is in effect a controlled experiment of its own. The headmistress, Miss P. O. Bennett, when in charge of another school in 1947, had used *Dhe Litl Red Hen* to teach backward infant readers.[1] Of all the headteachers experimenting, Miss Bennett was the only one who was not completely a volunteer. I persuaded her against her inclination to undertake the work. My reason for this was that she was, so far as was known, the only serving teacher who had ever used the simplified spelling approach and, if she did not join in, what would others have to say? Miss Bennett and her staff had already had exceptional success in teaching reading and the school's work had gained publicity on television for its success. She was naturally

[1] See p. 90.

unwilling to put aside methods that had been proved empirically for experimental methods. The school had a two-stream entry, and finally Miss Bennett agreed that, while the older half of the 1961 entrants should continue to be taught traditionally, the younger half of the children should be taught in the experimental way. As she put it: "They are on average six months younger and will have time to catch up with the rest, if the method does not work." The result of this splitting of the 1961 entrants has provided some very interesting comparisons.[1]

Though the *Janet and John* reading scheme was based on a look-and-say rather than on a phonic approach, the reason for its choice was two-fold. The series was shown as a result of inquiry to be used in more British schools than any other, and James Nisbet & Co. Ltd., very kindly agreed to allow the whole series, including all the supplementary books with the teaching and individual apparatus, to be produced in the new alphabet.[2]

It had been intended that the experiment should apply only to infant schools but through the initiative of three men there evolved alongside the main experiment another and equally interesting one. These three men were Mr. K. W. Gardner of the Walsall Remedial Education Service, Mr. A. M. Harrison, headmaster of Northmoor Junior School, Oldham, and Mr. J. Kilgannon, teacher of a special class for retarded children at Beever Junior School, Oldham. They asked if they might use the new approach in trying to teach reading to children of junior age (eight to eleven years) who had so far failed to learn. The Institute of Education was interested in this proposal and allowed the specially printed books (the sale of which was carefully regulated) to be supplied to the three teachers. Their work could not be experimentally controlled as in the case of the work with infant children, but their results could be noted and subjectively compared with the former effects of their teaching and with work of a similar nature elsewhere.

Certain limitations on the experimental conditions affect the whole. Even in the classroom a position cannot be fully maintained where only print in the Initial Teaching Alphabet is on view, for the time comes when some children are using normal print, while others are still reading i.t.a. Children must clearly be allowed to transfer to normal print when they are ready to do so. We know that

[1] See p. 142.
[2] As did Messrs. Harper & Row of Evanston, Illinois, U.S.A.

some are ready in a very short time; other children take a much longer time. Outside school all the children see ordinary print and spelling around them everywhere. So far as possible, their attention is drawn to their special alphabet. Children are permitted to take books home (it is surprising how many four-year-old children want to take them home) and their parents are enabled to purchase books as presents, if they so wish. As the supply of i.t.a. books has expanded the control formerly placed on their sale has been withdrawn and the books can now be purchased generally.

The Initial Teaching Alphabet Foundation has been established at 9 Southampton Place, London, W.C.1. Its purpose is to promote and publicize i.t.a. Lists of all i.t.a. publications, wherever published, can be obtained there and panels of lecturers on all aspects of the work are maintained.

XIV

The Experiment Enters School

Dimidium facti qui coepit habet : sapere aude.

Horace, Epistles. I. ii. 40[1]

MY ACCOUNT of what has happened during the period of the experiment must of necessity refer in the main to my own area, the county borough of Oldham. For only in Oldham have I complete and direct knowledge. This by no means suggests that the work is any less successful elsewhere. Indeed, I know that it is equally successful in other areas. The work done in Oldham has one unique feature. In the other three areas, where infant entrants of 1961 have been taught by the new method, children first go to school at the beginning of the *term* in which they will become five years old. In Oldham they were admitted to school at the beginning of the school *year* in which their fifth birthday fell. This inclusion of a whole year's intake at the beginning of the year means, of course, that Oldham's children predominate in the total of those with longest experience of the experimental conditions. It was only in Oldham that virtually all the children in the experimental classes (there were a few late enrolments) began school together in September 1961. Thus, fortuitously, Oldham alone can show a complete year's work in August 1962, and two complete years' results in August 1963.[2]

The Research Officer to the Reading Research Unit of the London Institute of Education is Mr. John Downing, who was an industrial research officer. Mr. Downing was highly qualified for the work, being a graduate in psychology with teaching experience. He armed himself with a comprehensive knowledge of the various educational

---

[1] "He who makes a start has half finished the job: have the courage to be wise." The last two words of the Latin are the motto of the County Borough of Oldham.

[2] In 1963 this happy arrangement was ended by instruction of the Ministry of Education because of the national teacher shortage. A few of the youngest four-year-olds do not from 1963 enter school until after Easter.

researches in the related fields. Consideration of the many factors which affect learners in reading required immense patience on his part as well as on the part of many teachers, who wondered why all the many details of information which he has sought were necessary. The approach to schools needed great tact. Mr. Downing's tact and patience, combined with a natural courtesy, facilitated the progress of the work.

Mr. Downing was entirely free of any association with spelling reform or teaching method and approached his job as an entirely neutral inquirer. He would probably today confess to some acquired enthusiasm for the new approach to teaching reading but when he began he knew nothing of any prospective outcome from the inquiry and when interviewed for the position protested that he was as innocent of knowledge as he was devoid of opinions. As he then put it, his job was to find out the facts and to let them form his opinions.

Mr. Downing's first task, apart from the routine of organizing his research unit, ordering the required books and so forth, was to make known to the volunteer authorities his method of approach. Lectures were given to gatherings of teachers in the selected areas, after which they were asked to let their education officers know whether they wished to adopt the experimental method. Pamphlets were published for informing both teachers and parents. The teacher volunteers, besides being instructed in the use of the new alphabet, were instructed in the maintenance of their children's record cards, as were the teachers in the control schools. Lists of available books and apparatus were supplied to the schools.

The Oldham children began school life in the first week of September 1961, and their ages ranged from four years one month to five years exactly. All the children in both experimental and control schools were tested, their intelligence quotients at the time of admission were established, and records were made of their general background, father's employment, and so forth. This information was recorded apart from the class records. Individual Progress Cards were distributed to the class teachers and these have spaces on one side for date of birth, dates of admission to and of leaving the school. On the reverse side the books of the *Janet and John* Reading Scheme are set out, with spaces opposite each title for writing in the date when each book was begun and when successfully completed. There are also columns for showing periods of absence from school and for the teachers' general remarks.

Progress Cards—Janet and John Reading Scheme

	Date Started	Date Successfully Completed	No. of Days Absent	Remarks
Here We Go				
Off To Play				
Janet and John Book I				
Out and About				
Janet and John Book II				
I Went Walking				
Janet and John Book III				
Through the Garden Gate				
Janet and John Book IV				
I Know a Story				
Once Upon a Time				

The Oldham schools which undertook the experiment were of different types. Generally it can be said that all the children have a working-class background and the homes of very few would harbour books to any extent. Several of the children had very poor backgrounds, financially, intellectually, socially and linguistically. Two county schools were newly built on housing estates.[1] One of these, Fitton Hill Infants School, is the school where the older half of the 1961 entrants worked in one class on traditional lines and the younger half in another class with the new alphabet. A new class teacher took charge after the first three terms, a second teacher had the class for the fourth and fifth terms and a third teacher took over for the sixth term. This school alone of the five had modern buildings and also a life uninterrupted by building changes. Its special problem arose from this last fact: it has tended to become the centre for most of our visitors. During the first two years more than 4,000 visitors went

---

[1] A county school is a school provided by a county borough or county local education authority as opposed to a voluntary school which is provided usually by church authorities, although maintained in all respects, equipment, furnishing, staff salaries, and buildings (subject to certain reservations) by the local education authority.

there and the dislocation of normal working can be imagined.[1] The headmistress and class teachers bore this very cheerfully and accepted the role of "exhibition centre." The children became so accustomed to visitors in their classroom that they took intrusion as a normal part of the school day. Nevertheless, because of this impact their normal routine was affected and their school life was anything but peaceful and orderly. The second county school, Alt Infant School, was temporarily organized as part of a junior school while its own premises were being built and the children moved across the playground to their new infant school at the end of one year to a new headteacher but with the same class teacher. The three other schools were denominational schools in very old buildings. St. Mary's Roman Catholic Infant School is due for reconstruction: the same class teacher has been in charge throughout. The Parish Church Infant School buildings are very out of date and must be replaced in the near future: the class passed to a new teacher after the third term. St. Paul's Infant School offered the greatest problem of all. It began the school year 1961 with an i.t.a. class consisting of eleven infant entrants, and five second-year problem children who were taught with the eleven newcomers, all using i.t.a. The same teacher had in her class, but using traditionally spelt books, fifteen second-year and third-year children, making a total number of thirty-one. This mixed age class with its group of special problem children presented an exceptionally difficult task and the class teacher introduced the new system because of her conviction that there were possible advantages which ought to be tested and that her problem children needed something quite new, if they were ever to learn to read. At the end of the year eight of the sixteen children (six of the 1961 entrants and two of the problem children) transferred to the new St. Martin's C. of E. School, where they form a second-year group in a class of thirty-six children. It has therefore been possible to include these six in the records which follow concerning the 1961 entrants.

It will be seen from this description that the experimental schools were facing possibly more than the usual vicissitudes that can affect school work. They were certainly not in any way privileged or cosseted: rather is the reverse true.

---

[1] These visitors have come from all over the United Kingdom and from many different parts of the world. Most had read or heard about the experiment but some were teachers who had been amazed by the reading standards of infants who had migrated to their areas.

Numbers have varied from time to time with leavers and new-comers. I would like to put on record the names of the headteachers and the class teachers who volunteered. Theirs was no easy task with so much to be done and so many things to be improvised in the early days. With their colleagues in other areas they merit the gratitude of educationists everywhere for entering upon this experiment in the interest of educational research and in the face of much scepticism about the outcome.

Infant Schools

Alt School		42 children
Headmaster	Mr. R. Craig	
Class Teacher	Mrs. M. E. Boon	

Fitton Hill School		29 children
Headmistress	Miss P. O. Bennett	
Class Teacher	Mrs. M. Dyson	

Parish Church School		28 children
Headmaster	Mr. J. N. Sharrocks	
Class Teacher	Mrs. A. Dalzell	

St. Mary's School		40 children
Headmistress	Sister Mary Finbarr	
Class Teacher	Mrs. T. Leigh	

St. Paul's School		11 children
Headmaster	Mr. G. Taylor	
Class Teacher	Mrs. M. R. Kelly	

Remedial Classes in Junior Schools

Beever School	Mr. J. Kilgannon
Northmoor School	Mr. A. M. Harrison

XV

Results in Infant Schools

"What shall I find for them to read when they come to me?"
Junior School Headmistress after visiting an experimental school, 1962

THE SPEED OF the Oldham children's progress through the *Janet and John* reading scheme has been quite remarkable. There are 11 books in the series but the authors advise alternative ways of using them, either as a seven-book or a six-book series. Some schools use one group of books, some another: some use all. Therefore, in order to show comparative progress I have made a nine-stage scale as follows—

Stage
0. Non-starters. This stage comprehends all children who have not begun to read one of the following books of the Reading Scheme;
1. Children reading *Here We Go*;
2. Children reading *Janet and John, Book I* or *Off to Play*;
3. Children reading *Out and About*;
4. Children reading *Janet and John, Book II* or *I Went Walking*;
5. Children reading *Janet and John, Book III* or *Through the Garden Gate*;
6. Children reading *Janet and John, Book IV* or *I Know a Story*;
7. Children reading *Once Upon a Time*;
8. Scheme completed. This stage includes those children who have read all the six or seven books of the series as required in their school. At this stage virtually all are reading conventional print.[1]

The number of children reading the series in the new alphabet fluctuated throughout the two-year period under review (September 1961 to July 1963) between 135 and 163 for normal reasons such as change of address. The number reading the series in traditional spelling varied from 241 to 273. The stage from 0 to 8 in which each child fell was noted at the end of each term. The percentages of the total in each stage at each term is shown below.

[1] The percentage who had completed the scheme but had not actually read a conventionally printed book was at the end of the sixth terms 6·7 per cent of the 1961 group and 1·1 per cent of the 1962 group.

EXPERIMENTAL AND CONTROL GROUPS

TABLE I

December 1961—end of First Term

Stage	Initial Teaching Alphabet 150 children		Traditional Orthography 273 children	
	percentage at stage	percentage having reached or passed stage	percentage at stage	percentage having reached or passed stage
0	77·3	100·0	68·5	100·0
1	22·7	22·7	29·2	31·5
2	—	—	2·3	2·3

TABLE 2

April 1962—end of Second Term

	152 children		272 children	
0	17·1	100·0	21·2	100·0
1	19·1	82·9	50·5	78·8
2	22·4	63·8	25·3	28·3
3	12·5	41·4	3·0	3·0
4	15·8	28·9	—	—
5	9·9	13·1	—	—
6	2·0	3·2	—	—
7	0·6	1·2	—	—
8	0·6	0·6	—	—

TABLE 3

July 1962—end of Third Term

	150 children		273 children	
0	4·7	100·0	11·9	100·0
1	13·3	95·3	38·3	88·1
2	14·7	82·0	36·1	49·8
3	15·4	67·3	10·8	13·7
4	18·0	51·9	1·9	2·9
5	15·3	33·9	1·0	1·0
6	6·0	18·6	—	—
7	5·3	12·6	—	—
8	7·3	7·3	—	—

TABLE 4
December 1962—end of Fourth Term

Stage	Initial Teaching Alphabet 139 children		Traditional Orthography 253 children	
	percentage at stage	percentage having reached or passed stage	percentage at stage	percentage having reached or passed stage
0	2·1	100·0	5·2	100·0
1	3·6	97·9	25·0	94·8
2	3·6	94·3	29·0	69·8
3	7·2	90·7	17·6	40·8
4	13·6	83·5	18·0	23·2
5	17·3	69·9	4·0	5·2
6	20·2	52·6	1·2	1·2
7	5·0	32·4	—	—
8	27·4	27·4	—	—

TABLE 5
April 1963—end of Fifth Term

Stage	139 children		259 children	
0	1·4	100·0	1·9	100·0
1	1·4	98·6	10·4	98·1
2	2·2	97·2	25·1	87·7
3	2·2	95·0	17·0	62·6
4	7·9	92·8	20·8	45·6
5	14·4	84·9	16·6	24·8
6	9·3	70·5	4·3	8·2
7	3·6	61·2	3·1	3·9
8	57·6	57·6	0·8	0·8

TABLE 6
July 1963—end of Sixth Term

Stage	135 children		241 children	
0	—	100·0	0·4	100·0
1	0·7	100·0	2·1	99·6
2	1·5	99·3	17·9	97·5
3	2·8	97·8	17·4	79·6
4	7·5	95·0	22·0	62·2
5	6·0	87·5	19·5	40·2
6	12·6	81·5	14·5	20·7
7	3·0	68·9	1·2	6·2
8	65·9	65·9	5·0	5·0

The comparatively rapid rate of progress of the experimental children is evident from a glance at those figures. After three terms a significant proportion, 7·3 per cent, had completed the scheme, while only 3·9 per cent of their brothers and sisters learning with traditional orthography were even half-way through. By the end of the fourth term more than a quarter of the experimental children had completed the course and less than one in twenty of the t.o.

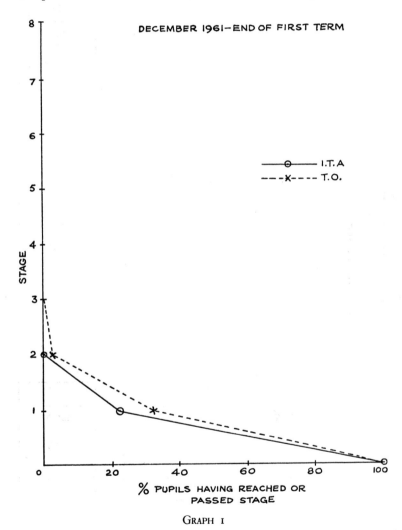

GRAPH I

children had passed the fifth stage. This means that one in four of
the former were reading in ordinary spelling any books that they found
interesting while the latter were still struggling with very simple
sentences. By the end of the fifth term more than half of the experimental children were reading widely in ordinary print and of the
traditionally taught children two only out of 259 were in the same
position. After two complete school years, more than 90 per cent
of the t.o. children had not reached Stage 7 (*Once upon a time*), while

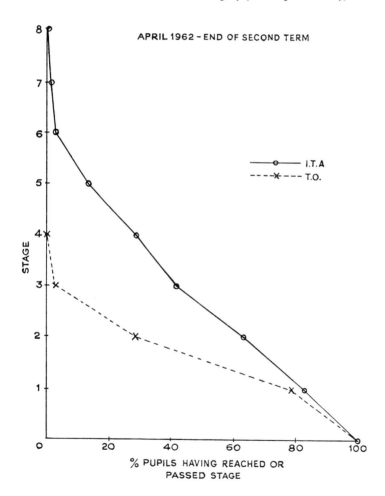

GRAPH 2

more than two-thirds of the i.t.a. children had done so and almost two-thirds had completed the whole scheme.

This can be expressed graphically as shown on pages 130–36. In these graphs the progress of the experimental children is indicated by solid lines, that of the traditionally taught "control" group by broken lines. When the children first entered school, assuming that none could read, the progress line would have been perfectly

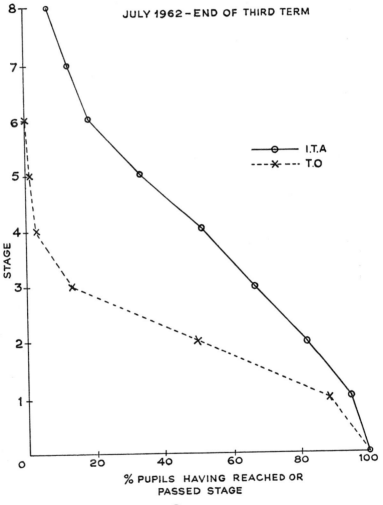

JULY 1962 – END OF THIRD TERM

I.T.A
T.O

STAGE

% PUPILS HAVING REACHED OR PASSED STAGE

GRAPH 3

horizontal at the bottom of the graph. At an imaginary point in the future, assuming that all children have successfully completed the scheme, the line will be vertical along the right-hand side of the graph. The lines, sloping from right to left, show actual achievement at various dates, and the nearer they approach the right-hand vertical position the more complete is the achievement of the group.

It will be noted (Graph 1) that only in the first term are the lines

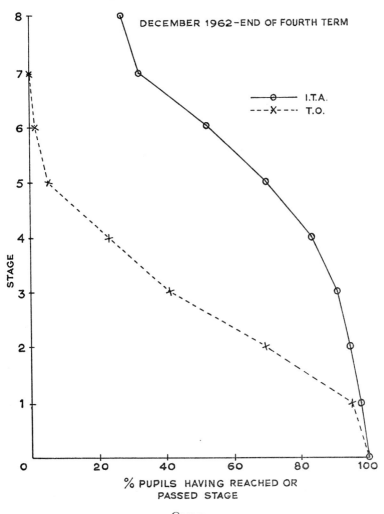

DECEMBER 1962–END OF FOURTH TERM

——⊖—— I.T.A.
---X---- T.O.

STAGE

% PUPILS HAVING REACHED OR
PASSED STAGE

GRAPH 4

even close together and then the t.o. children are slightly ahead. This means that the teachers of the i.t.a. classes were feeling their way with a new project and some did not begin methodical reading at all. By the end of the second term (Graph 2) the i.t.a. children are well ahead and thereafter comparison becomes meaningless: there is none.

The third-term curve of the i.t.a. children (Graph 3) approximates

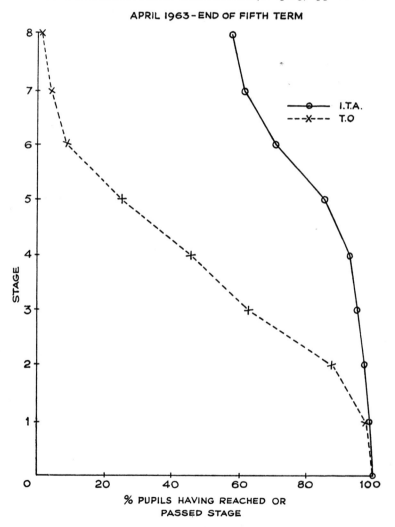

APRIL 1963 - END OF FIFTH TERM

GRAPH 5

to that of the t.o. children after six terms (Graph 6), suggesting
that the i.t.a. children are, as many teachers estimated, a year ahead
at the end of the first year. The curves of the i.t.a. children for the
fourth, fifth and sixth terms (Graphs 4, 5 and 6) are never at any
time in the two years approached by the t.o. children. This is shown
in the composite graph (Graph 7).

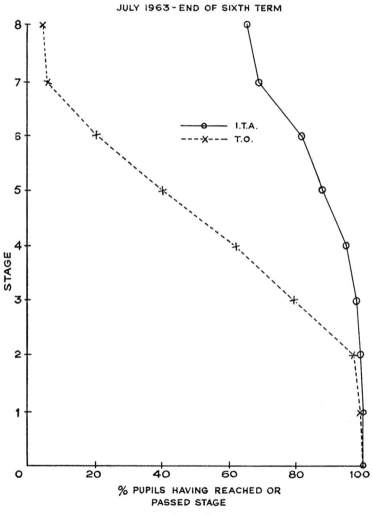

JULY 1963 - END OF SIXTH TERM

GRAPH 6

As is to be expected, both groups have for a long time their residue of non-starters. Once started, however, the gains of the i.t.a. children are continuous and accelerate in momentum: their graphed lines rapidly steepen and approach the upright position throughout, whereas there is a long period spent over the earlier stages by the t.o. children.

Progress through the lower reaches of the graph is made by the experimental group in simplified spelling but their arrival at stage 8 means that they are reading in ordinary spelling. Further, not only

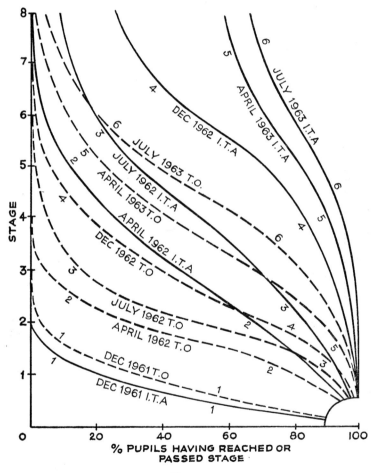

STAGE

% PUPILS HAVING REACHED OR PASSED STAGE

GRAPH 7

have they on the way up read scores and scores of books in simplified spelling, for extensive supplementary reading is an essential part of the work, but their earlier completion of the reading scheme means that a very large proportion (the great majority) will have read very many books (to say hundreds is not to exaggerate) in ordinary spelling before the control children have completed the reading scheme. It is a fact that many of these children in the experimental classes could have completed the scheme and turned over to normal spelling even earlier but emphasis is put on the desirability of abundant practice in reading before the transition to t.o.

The two graphs, 8 and 9, show the percentage of children at each stage of the Reading Scheme at the ends of the first year and of the second year respectively. The immensely swifter progress of the i.t.a. children is clear in both graphs. The much longer periods spent on the earlier books of the scheme by the majority of t.o. children is apparent: the t.o. bulge moves slowly across the graph. At the end of the first year it is very steep on stages 1 and 2 and only slowly flattens out and is still pronounced from stage 2 to stage 6 at the end of the second year. By contrast the i.t.a. children make a steady progress. Their curve at the end of Year 1 is comparable with that of the t.o. children at the end of Year 2, and is more even. In fact, one can scarcely evade the conclusion that English traditional spelling is a serious obstacle to learning to read.

One interpretation of these graphs could be that the advancing books of the Reading Scheme offer no progressive difficulty of note in i.t.a. When the books are printed in a consistent spelling, since ability is evenly spread over any age group, the i.t.a. children make their way through the Reading Scheme comfortably, taking the books in their stride, simply according to their ability to tackle this or any other task. On the other hand, some obstacle causes a blockage in the progress of the t.o. children. The only apparent obstacle faced by them, which the i.t.a. children do not face, is the spelling inconsistency of t.o.

This next consideration is worth pondering. When these children are eleven years old, some 20 per cent to 25 per cent of them by the present standards of our educational system in Britain will be designated the abler group, able to study by the methods and curricula of the grammar schools, capable of abstract thinking, of reasoning from the general to the particular, and of advanced specialist work. Of this 20 to 25 per cent of the abler children, less

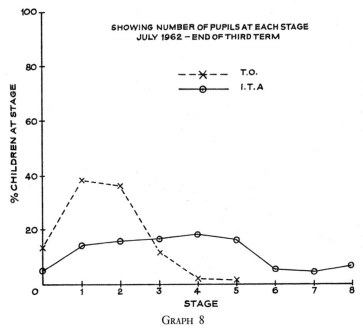

GRAPH 8

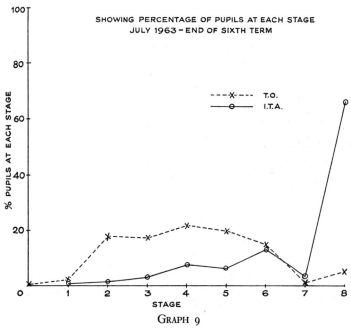

GRAPH 9

than a quarter (5 per cent) when using t.o. completed the Reading Scheme in two years, but using i.t.a., two and a half times as many as the prospective university entrants (65 per cent) completed the scheme.

The results achieved by the 1961 infant entrants were no flash in the pan. In 1962 the original five infant schools using i.t.a. had grown to thirteen and it was possible to compare the achievement of the first 150 or so children with the achievement of some 500–550 children who entered school in September 1962. The following terminal figures show that progress is similar and that what happened in the first year is being repeated in the second year with almost four times the number of children in many more schools.

EXPERIMENTAL GROUPS

TABLE 7
First Term Results

| | Beginners of 1961 | | Beginners of 1962 | |
| | December 1961 150 children | | December 1962 509 children | |
Stage	percentage at stage	percentage having reached or passed stage	percentage at stage	percentage having reached or passed stage
0	77·3	100·0	65·4	100·0
1	22·7	22·7	17·3	34·6
2	—	—	13·0	17·3
3	—	—	2·9	4·3
4	—	—	1·4	1·4

TABLE 8
Second Term Results

	April 1962 152 children		April 1963 547 children	
0	17·1	100·0	20·8	100·0
1	19·1	82·9	16·8	79·2
2	22·4	63·8	26·3	62·4
3	12·5	41·4	11·2	36·1
4	15·8	28·9	12·6	24·9
5	9·9	13·1	8·0	12·3
6	2·0	3·2	2·4	4·3
7	0·6	1·2	1·7	1·9
8	0·6	0·6	0·2	0·2

TABLE 9

Third Term Results

	July 1962 150 children		July 1963 538 children	
0	4·7	100·0	9·8	100·0
1	13·3	95·3	10·4	90·2
2	14·7	82·0	18·6	79·8
3	15·4	67·3	15·8	61·2
4	18·0	51·9	19·7	45·4
5	15·3	33·9	9·5	25·7
6	6·0	18·6	6·3	16·2
7	5·3	12·6	3·2	9·9
8	7·3	7·3	6·7	6·7

Graph 10 shows how closely the achievement of the 1962 entrants runs parallel with that of the 1961 entrants. The broken line refers to the 17·3 per cent of 1962 who outran the first entrants. The second-term curves are almost identical and there is very close approximation in the third term. The pattern of progress, indicated by the solid lines, is the same throughout.

The quicker start with the second group of children almost certainly springs from the growing experience of teachers with the new medium. The teachers who began in 1961 passed on their knowledge and ideas to those who began in 1962. Some, who had never given books to children in the first term at school, did not hesitate to do so in 1962. Some saw no point in 1962 in taking the quickest readers through the whole set of books and supplementary books: such children soon become ready for interesting story books and find the reading scheme tedious and boring before they come to the end. Still longer experience may bring still swifter progress and a quick beginning is good in that it heightens early interest. Swifter progress seems more than likely when lengthening experience brings books and methods devised to take advantage of the consistency characteristic of i.t.a. spelling.

Oldham has thirty-seven infant schools. In July 1963, thirty-five infant headteachers had requisitioned books printed in the Initial Teaching Alphabet for the school year 1963–4. Oldham's headteachers had outstanding opportunity to judge these results and to visit the schools producing them. The decision of these headteachers and their staffs is not surprising when all these facts are studied.

The original nineteen infant schools using i.t.a. in 1961 had

increased by 1962 to seventy-eight schools in the areas of eighteen education authorities in England, Ireland, Scotland and Wales. The two schools and one clinic using i.t.a. remedially had increased to fifty-seven schools and clinics in twenty-three areas. The school year 1963–4 will see these numbers greatly expanded and it seems that well over half of the education authorities in Britain will have teachers somewhere in their areas using i.t.a.

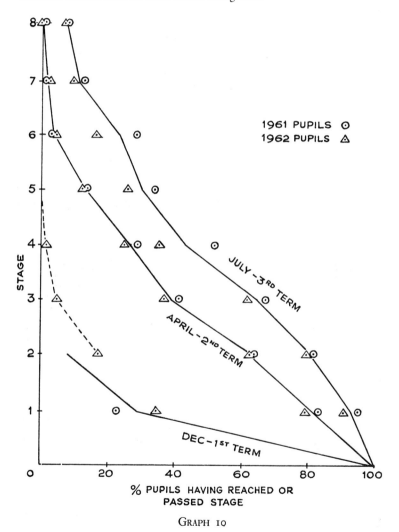

GRAPH 10

Several objective tests have been set during the two years under review. In July 1962 Mrs. V. Southgate of the Institute of Education in Manchester University visited Fitton Hill School to give a Reading Age Test to the two classes of 1961 entrants, both the traditionally taught and the experimental class. She used a normal standardized test, traditionally spelt, the Southgate Group Reading Test 1B. The headmistress at first demurred to the giving of a test printed in t.o. to the children in the experimental class because in July 1962 no child in that class had completed the Reading Scheme in i.t.a., and in school at least none had been allowed to see matter printed in t.o. With much misgiving, she finally agreed to give the test to these children with the warning that they must not be expected to read it at all. Mrs. Southgate says, "Before encountering the children in the present class, I should have been horrified at the thought of this test being used with children barely five years old." The test asked a great deal of the older t.o. children for it had been standardized on six-year-old children and was not recommended for general use with five-year-olds. Every child present in each class was included in the test: there were thirty-five traditionally taught children and twenty-seven experimentally taught children.

The t.o. children were a very good group. Their mean reading age was six years one month, compared with their mean chronological age of five years six months. Any teacher could be very pleased with such a result. The mean chronological age of the experimental class was five years one month and their mean reading age was six years three months! In other words, while the older traditionally taught group were seven months ahead of normal expectation, the younger experimental group were fourteen months ahead on the very same test, printed with an alphabet and in a spelling which they had never studied. Naturally the visitor was amazed.[1]

A term later, in December 1962, Mrs. Southgate returned to the school with the Southgate Group Reading Test 1C (Word Selection) for the experimental class. Six only of the thirty children in this class had by this time completed the Reading Scheme and were reading normal print. This second test, also in t.o., was intended as a check on the July test, to see whether the incredible could be true. The average chronological age had now, of course, advanced

[1] These tests were reported in the *Educational Review*, Vol. 16, No. 1. (Birmingham University Institute of Education. November 1963).

to five years six months. The test showed the average reading age to be six years eight months. The gain was still fourteen months: there was no doubt about it. In fact, there was an increase in the gain for the top children ran out of the test: it did not go far enough for them. The norms of the test did not go higher than seven years nine months! The children who had registered a gain in reading age of eighteen months or more over their chronological age were re-tested with the Southgate Group Reading Test 2A (Sentence Completion). The scores of these nine children in the two tests were as follows—

TABLE 10

Child	Chronological Age	Reading Age	
		Test 1C	Test 2A
1	5.7	7.9	8.3
2	5.4	7.9	7.10
3	5.7	7.9	7.9
4	5.7	7.7	7.9
5	5.5	7.7	8.4
6	5.5	7.3	7.2
7	5.6	7.0	absent
8	5.6	7.0	7.2
9	5.5	6.11	7.3

Maybe these were the nine brightest children, but nine were a third of the class and 33⅓ per cent is a highly significant proportion in any context.

This class of children was again tested by Mrs. Southgate in July 1963 when the Southgate Group Reading Tests 1B and 2B were used. Twenty-nine of the thirty children were present on the day of the test, and of these nineteen had made the transition to normal print. The results are shown in Table 11.

In March 1963 a Reading Accuracy and Comprehension Test was given to all the 1961 entrants in both experimental and control schools. This was the *Neale Analysis of Reading Ability*.[1]

In accordance with instructions to the Test, the Comprehension Test was given only to children with a minimum R.A. of six years. The results were as follows—

[1] These tests are formulated by Dr. Marie D. Neale of the University of Sydney. Published by Macmillan & Co.

TABLE II

Fitton Hill Infants School—Children on i.t.a. since September, 1961
Age and scores in years and months.
Average C.A. = 6 years 1 month.
Average R.A. on Test 1 = 7 years 0 months.

Date of Test, July 1963
Children scoring an R.A. of 7.0 took the second test.
The first nineteen children had made the transition.

Child	Chronological age	Test 1B (top score assessable 7.9)	Test 2B (top score assessable 9.7)	Gain by lower R.A. scored
1	6.2	↑	9.7 plus	3.5 plus
2	5.11		8.4	2.5
3	6.2		8.5	2.3
4	6.2	7.9 plus	8.4	2.2
5	6.1		8.1	2.0
6	6.0		8.1	2.1
7	6.0		8.9	2.9
8	6.0	↓	absent	1.9 plus
9	6.2	7.7	7.3	1.1
10	6.0	7.7	7.2	1.2
11	6.1	7.6	7.8	1.5
12	6.1	7.6	7.6	1.5
13	6.2	7.6	7.1	0.11
14	5.11	7.6	7.0	1.1
15	5.11	7.5	7.2	1.3
16	6.2	7.3	7.0	0.10
17	6.2	7.1	7.0	0.10
18	5.10	6.9	—	0.11
19	6.1	6.7	—	0.6
20	6.2	7.5	7.1	0.11
21	5.11	6.10	—	0.11
22	6.0	6.10	—	0.10
23	6.2	6.9	—	0.7
24	6.5	6.6	—	0.1
25	6.3	6.5	—	0.2
26	6.0	6.4	—	0.4
27	6.1	6.4	—	0.3
28	6.0	6.3	—	0.3
29[1]	5.11		below normal	
30	5.11		absent	

[1] Educationally sub-normal child.

(a) Children taught through traditional orthography—

    Mean Chronological Age   6.0

    Mean Reading Age   6.6   Children tested: 219

    Mean Comprehension Age 6.11   Children tested: 142

                                (64·7 per cent)

(b) Children taught through i.t.a.—

    Mean Chronological Age   5.11

    Mean Reading Age   7.5   Children tested: 128

    Mean Comprehension Age 7.4   Children tested: 116

                                (90·6 per cent)

Owing to the lower achievement of the t.o. children only 64·7 per cent of that class took the comprehension test compared with 90·6 per cent of the i.t.a. children. It happened that eighty-two of these latter children scored Reading Ages of six years eleven months or more. This is 64·1 per cent of the whole i.t.a. group and it may be that a fairer comparison can be made between the t.o. and i.t.a. groups if one takes the scores of the same proportion of children in each, who presumably comprise the more progressive children. The results for this 64·1 per cent of the i.t.a. children are—

(c) Mean Chronological Age   5.10

    Mean Reading Age   8.3

    Mean Comprehension Age 7.11

The tests show average scores exceeding normal expectation for both t.o. and i.t.a. children but the comparison is enormously favourable to the latter. The comparative gains after eighteen months in school shown by tables (a), (b) and (c) are—

under Traditional Orthography approach—

Reading Age for all the children   +6 months

Comprehension Age for 64·7 per cent of

    the abler children   +11 months

under Initial Teaching Alphabet approach—

Reading Age for all the children   +1 year 6 months

Comprehension Age for 64·1 per cent of

    the abler children   +2 years 1 month

XVI

Appraisals of the Infant Experiment

"It makes me cry but I keep on reading it."
—A literary appreciation of *Black Beauty* by a five-year-old

IN 1964 the Institute of Education will begin to assess its findings and statistics and figures galore will indicate the comparable achievements of children, but objective tests and statistics are not necessarily the most convincing arguments to the world at large. The average infant teacher is perhaps more likely to be impressed by the subjective assessments of her colleagues, by their reports of what they have found compared with their recollections of what used to occur. Some things cannot be assessed objectively: such are the sense of purpose in the classroom and of pleasure in the daily round, confidence in work, general conduct. One has to depend for judgment on what those in the centre of things say. Anecdotes can be very revealing.

In June 1962 (after nine months' work including the Christmas and Easter holidays), headteachers were asked to write their considered views on the effects of the experiment as then apparent. Their views are as follows—

(1) Concerning reading standards, there was general agreement that they had significantly improved: "There is a higher reading standard all through the class" and "Reading standards this year are far higher than previously."

(2) Learning was more rapid everywhere: "Children seem to progress at a quicker rate and are eager to find out words for themselves."

> The rate of progress is faster. The slower children are showing a small gain in this field, the average child is showing a considerable gain, whilst the top 25 per cent are showing phenomenal gains not only in the fact that they have read more basic readers but that they have also read—and read for pleasure—some fifty to one hundred other little

books. .... Some bright children are almost equal to children twelve months ahead . . . and in general are reading more difficult books except that they are in a.r. The written work compares favourably with that of the third year except that it is in a.r. The slower children are equally as good as the children at the lower end of Infant 2; they have more confidence and more interest. I would therefore say that the overall gain, taking into account bright and slow children, is approximately one year's schooling.

(3) The five headteachers were unanimous in their agreement that the new method had substantially reduced the number of children failing to begin reading.

(4) Greater confidence in dealing with books was noted: "the children know that they can do it." The children had no fear of a new word. In one school the headmistress very conscientiously decided that the look-and-say method used in earlier years would be strictly maintained. Apart from the stressing of individual sounds when pointing to words during blackboard reading, phonics were not taught at all. Before the end of the first term, the head-mistress told me that the children had beaten her. The brighter ones had detected the sound values of letters and were happily word-building. In the class teacher's words, "The children had extracted the phonics through the visual consistency without any definite lead." "We did not want to use phonics but by Christmas 1961 we had to have a reappraisal of method and to follow a phonic programme side by side with look-and-say. A few children still needed look-and-say."[1]

(5) Enthusiasm for reading and heightened interest in books was abundantly clear. One headmistress was worried that she might be rearing a brood of bluestockings and forbade reading in the after-noons. Children in some schools had to be ushered out to play and their books taken from them: "Their enthusiasm for reading has to be seen to be believed . . . Some children have to be urged to do something else for a change." "I have been concerned because these children preferred to sit with their noses in books rather than play with the many and varied toys in the classroom." The book corner was the busy part of the classroom in free activity periods and when parcels of new books arrived there was a rush for them: "Books are

---

[1] Many educationists have laid it down that children are not "ready" for phonic word-building until they attain a mental age of six and a half years. These children were hardly five years old. They certainly insisted on building words *in a consistent spelling*. I doubt very much whether all who did this had an I.Q. of 130 (i.e. a mental age of $6\frac{1}{2}$).

read at any odd moment and greatly loved by the children." The children have made reading a game which they love to play: "Often they can be found happily engaged not only reading to themselves but reading to other children in small groups."

(6) The teacher's work was different and happier. The increased independence of the bright children, because the consistent spelling made it possible for them to read new books without help, left the class teacher free to devote much more time to the duller children. "The top group children can work alone and leave the class teacher free to work with the bottom group." One teacher said: "Never have I taught so little reading and heard so much."

(7) Spontaneous writing was discovered. "Discovered" is the right word since creative writing, not limited to words already learnt, was unknown among children of this age. The first example occurred when a class was invited to copy the weekend news, a simple sentence, ſhe sun woſ ſhieniŋ on ſundæ, from the blackboard. One little boy to the consternation and delight of his teacher wrote a composition of some thirty words describing clearly and legibly his own weekend. Very quickly the news spread and, given pencil, paper and an initial suggestion, in no time at all large numbers of these tiny tots were regularly producing compositions, relating facts or invented tales, of fifty to one hundred words, all interesting and meaningful. The language is their own, including baby talk, slang, and words sandwiched together for they have not always learned to analyse phrases into word units, e.g. kumfort (come for t'— come for the). Vocabulary is unrestricted: what they can speak they can write: "Creative writing in the first class of the Infants' School usually consists of two or three short sentences at best. These children write freely. The better ones write stories like Cinderella, Brer Fox, retold in their own words, or inventions of their own, or reports of topical events, which may vary from thirty to one hundred words, with an excellent degree of continuity and relatively few mistakes. In my experience this is unheard of in 'Reception' class." It is true to say that, whereas formerly little children expressed themselves in drawing and painting, these children as often express themselves in writing.[1]

---

[1] One little boy of four years six months was given boards and crayon for drawing. He had not written before, but instead of drawing he covered the four sides of two boards with the following: tωdæ is mie dadiſ birfdæ. hee is twenty seven. hee has haɖ twelv birfdæ cardſ anɖ wεε ar haviŋ jelly for uſ tεε. No teacher taught him to write "birfday" nor "us tea": that is how he spoke.

8. EXAMPLES OF CHILDREN'S WRITING

The examples of children's writing shown below and in the following pages illustrate the remarkable fluency which is achieved at a very early age by children who have been taught to read by the i.t.a. method. These illustrations are from the following schools:

Alt Infants' School—"The Selfish Crocodile"
—"One day there was a fire . . ."
Fitton Hill Infants' School—"A little bird . . ."
—"Last week I went on a coach . . ."
Holy Rosary Infants' School—"Today is Wednesday . . ."
Limeside Infants' School—"I had a little nut tree . . ."
St. Anne's Infants' School—"When I grow up . . ."

last week te went on a
cæch and ie rravelld on mie
woe ru graet yarmuen, ie
travelld aul hiet ril ren æ
clock nekst morniŋ thæ let
us oul tov the cæch in the miul
ov the niet for sumthiŋ tu ea
and tu gæ tu the toi.let

"Last week I went on a coach and I travelled on my way to Great Yarmouth. I travelled all night till ten o'clock next morning. They let us out of the coach in the middle of the night for something to eat and to go to the toilet."

Written by a little girl of five years and one month.

"A little bird was dying I saw it lying there head down so I took it to the doctor's and he stroked its little head."

> Written by a little boy of five years and three months. Note the sentiment, remarkable in so young a child.

The story shown opposite is the composition of a child just six years old. This child first went to school in September 1961. He made the transition from i.t.a. books to t.o. books in June 1962. The composition was written in October 1962, and there had been a six weeks' holiday since June.

It will be noted that the child already uses traditional spelling to a great extent, even trying to do so when the traditional spelling is not known as in "mite" (might). The complete lack of any inhibition in expressing himself in writing is typical of these children. As they talk they write. The attempted and often successful punctuation is noteworthy.

The whole story runs in t.o. as follows:

One day there was a fire and I saw some fire engines. I heard the bells ring and I heard police with their sirens and I saw ambulances in an emergency. So there must be a big fire and I saw them going down Holts. I think there will be an explosion and there might be some people injured. If they got trapped in the building it would be serious. The building might collapse. I could see flames in the distance flying high over the roofs of the houses. I hurried to tell my mummy and she said she would take me to see the fire. When we arrived at the fire, all the road was (wer) flooded. It looked like a river. The water was running down the street and the people will have to go in hospital and stay there for a few weeks. Probably they will have an operation if they have been badly burned. It would be serious. The people who were badly burned will have a serious operation. When the people are better they will go home and then they will buy a new house and live in it.

One day there was a fire
and I saw sum fire enjins. I
herd the bells ring and I herd
polces with there sirens
and I saw ambulanses in an
emerjansy sœ there must
be a big fire and I saw them
gœing daun helts. I think
ther will be an eksplœzon and
ther mift be sum peepl injerd
if thœ got trapt in the
billding it wud bee seerius.
the billding mite colaps.
I cud see fleems in the distens
flieing hie œver the rwfs
or the houses. I herid to tell
my mumy and she sed she
wud take me tw sœ the fire
wen we arivd at the fire
aul the road wer fluded.
it lookt like a river. the
wawter was running daun the
street and the peepl will hav
tw go in hospital and stae
there for a fue weeks. probibily
thœ will hav an opereashon if
thœ hav been badly berhd
it wud be seerius, the peepl hœ
wer badly bernd will hav a
seerius operœshon wen the peepl or
beter thœ will gœ home and then thœ will
bie a nue hous, and liv in it.

the selfish crocerdiel

once upon a time ther was a selrish
crocerdiel hw lived in a fish
pond and every fish he
saw
he æt it and soon he grw stroger and soon he grw biger than
the pond and he had to stik is
head out ov the pond and all the

people hw saw his teeth were afræd.
wun day a little girl thaut it was
a house so she opend its mouth
and went in and the crocerdiel
shut its mouth and the little girl
seid it is dark in here just
whot can I do she mermerd and
she cried until its mouth
sudenly it opend and the little
girl went out verry unhappy
sæying iel never go in thær eny
more.

THE SELFISH CROCODILE

This imaginative writing is the work of a girl of five years and nine months old. She had made the transition to traditional reading three months before. The spelling would be very good indeed for a child traditionally taught and the language and literary confidence far exceed that expected at this age.

THE SELFISH CROCODILE

Once upon a time there was a selfish crocodile who lived in a fishpond and every fish he saw he ate it and soon he grew stronger and soon he grew bigger than the pond and he had to stick his nose out of the pond and all the people who saw his teeth were afraid.

One day a little girl thought it was a house so she opened its mouth and went in and the crocodile shut its mouth and the little girl said, It is dark in here. Just what can I do, she murmured. And she cried until its mouth opened. Suddenly it opened and the little girl went out very unhappy, saying, I'll never go in there any more.

when e gre u p e
am goeig tw bee a
fer man and fer
men hav tw slak
fers out wiv
walter and the
hav tw swich the
walter on and
yo hav tw klem
up the lader and
fer men/hav
helmits

This boy from a Polish-speaking home first went to school at the age of five years one month. He was then far from fluent in English. At six years one month he could not read at all and was started afresh on i.t.a. His reading ability leapt ahead and eight months later he wrote this. The headmistress has said: "This boy was a C child: he will be an A child."

"When I grow up I am going to be a fire man and fire men have to slak(e) fires out with water and they have to switch the water on and you have to climb up the ladder and fire men have helmets."

ie had a liTTl n uT
rree nuthing weud it
ber but a silver
n u r meg and a golden
per the cing ov
Spæings dur doura caem
too visir mæ me and
al for tho se sæ k
ov mie litrl hut
tree

This was written three days from his fifth birthday by a boy who had just learnt the song "The Little Nut Tree." He had never seen any other print than i.t.a. print at school. Apparently he had already noticed that ŋ was the combination of n and g which adults used and he preferred the latter.

> "I had a little nut tree and nothing would it bear
> But a silver nut meg and a golden pear.
> The King of Spain's daughter came to visit me
> And all for the sake of my little nut tree."

twdae is Wensdae
Wee hav anuther hot sunny dae
Soon it will bee tiem for
the holidaes Sumovus
ar goeing tw the See
Wee shall dw eksSie ting
things bie the See.
mee and me nana ar
goeing tw blakpool
tw seeClif Richad
at the See thee ater
I'm Staeing at a
laedy hw me nana
noes ie caleranty
Jois ie thinkme
baebycusan
is cumming
with us He is
aulwaes in
miSchee f

This composition was written by a girl of five years and seven months. She was still reading i.t.a. as the spelling shows. The spontaneity of this writing is remarkable: the child put the account on paper exactly as she would have rendered it in speech. Cliff Richard is a popular stage artiste. The writing of A.B.C. Theatre is to be noted: it was a name heard in speech not a sequence of letters. The child did not know the letter C by that name.

"Today is Wednesday. We have another hot sunny day. Soon it will be time for the holidays. Some of us are going to the seaside. We shall do exciting things by the sea. Me and my nana [grandmother] are going to Blackpool to see Cliff Richard at A.B.C. Theatre. I'm staying at a lady who my nana knows. I call her Auntie Joyce. I think my baby cousin is coming with us. He is always in mischief."

(8) Some headteachers already felt that the children were benefiting in more personal ways in behaviour and that they possessed a greater maturity, a greater steadiness of application: "They seem slightly more mature in outlook and more settled in behaviour. This is possibly due to the increased interest in books, writing and drawing, all quiet occupations." "Their behaviour would appear to be a little more mature in consequence of their command over reading and writing. They want to do things more and play less. I think that they all really like to come to school."

The views of headteachers were sought by the Institute of Education from all the schools using i.t.a. The replies sent in from the other fifteen schools in other areas agreed with all that the Oldham teachers reported, although, as has been said above, their experience was more limited because only one third of their five-year-olds had begun school in the previous September, one third in January and the last third in April. *After nine months at most in school* this is à remarkable consensus of opinions. It is difficult to keep in mind that the average age of the children at the time was five years three months, and much of what is described, e.g. their writing and reading ability, was already established before most of them were five years old.

There is an "Initial Teaching Alphabet" section in the Juvenile Department of the Oldham Central Library. It was in April 1962 that the Public Librarian rang me up and asked if I knew that every Saturday some fifty children under five years of age visited the library to borrow books. It was one of these children who first to our knowledge in Oldham made the transition to reading ordinary print.[1] This little boy of four years five months mischievously wandered from "his" i.t.a. section and took home Anna Sewell's *Black Beauty*. Parents had been asked to co-operate with us and not to give the children books in normal spelling. The specially printed books could be borrowed from public library or school for home reading. This boy's father told his little son that he could not read *Black Beauty*, to be told in reply, "I have read it." Father unbelievingly gave the boy his paper to read and it was read. Recently this little boy, then five years five months old, was asked by his headteacher what books he liked best. He replied, "*Peter Pan, Winnie the Pooh, Treasure Island*" (and after a thoughtful pause)

[1] A five-year-old girl in Stoke-on-Trent is recorded as making the transition after only one term.

"and *Black Beauty*. It makes me cry but I keep on rea(
that is the most youthful example of literary apprec
ever heard.

The next case of transition was noted in St. Mary's l
olic School about March 1962. One little girl of fo
months had returned to the classroom after playtime
teacher. On the teacher's desk was an edition of *The*
Saints, from which the teacher intended to read to the cl
child was busily reading "The Life of St. Christopl
quickly found that several children were well able to read ordinary
print. It was, however, deemed undesirable to encourage them to do
so, but better that they should strengthen and extend their skill and
confidence by reading widely in the new alphabet.

It would have been easy to point to many children who had
"transitioned," if we had wished to press this aspect. It was a
temptation to teachers to do this, for the sceptics still asked, What
will they do with ordinary spelling and type? The temptation was
conscientiously withstood. The answer is known today. There is
no problem whatever: in fact there is no noticeable step from the
simplified alphabet to the traditional. Once it was thought by many
that special teaching would be needed and apparatus and special
books were being planned for the transition. All the books and the
plans have been jettisoned. One minute the children may be reading
i.t.a. and their next book can be traditionally printed and they pick
it up and read and seem unaware that there has been any change.
In one school yellow chalk is used when writing t.o. on the blackboard to distinguish the print from i.t.a. which is in white chalk.
The children who have not yet made the transition know by the
colour which part of the writing is for them. One child of five years
was asked at home by his eight-year-old (!) brother how to spell
"Saturday." The answer, reported by his parents, was: "I can spell
it in white and I can spell it in yellow, but I don't know how it is
done in real spelling." The class had not been told that the "yellow"
spelling was "grown-up" spelling, lest they imagine that it have
strange difficulties.

It was apparent from the second term that many children, once
they begin to read, can read anything in i.t.a. Book VI is almost as
easy as Book I. There is accordingly no point in going from book to
book to supposedly more difficult spelling forms. There are no more
difficult spellings. The only material point is to widen vocabulary

in order to understand, to attain fluency in order to take in phrases and sentences rather than syllables or single words, to gain confidence and interest, to realize that books are fun and not drudgery. After that it seems that we could use any alphabet, italic or black letter. Show the children the sounds indicated by the letters and they will read. The facility with which they accept spelling anomalies is even more surprising. By the fifth term more than half of the children had made the complete transition including the anomalies. Every week the numbers who still had to make the transition dwindled. For the vast majority time alone was needed and by comparison with their traditionally taught brothers and sisters the time was remarkably short. Whether there will be a residue who do not ultimately make the transition, time alone can show. By May 1963 the last of the 1961 beginners had read *a book* after nineteen months in school. Of one thing we can be sure: that residue of unfortunate children (if there is a residue) would never have read at all by any other system. The success in teaching remedial classes gives us hope that the residue, if residue there be, will be infinitesimal.

The effect of their wider reading on the children's vocabulary and speech is remarkable. The effect on enunciation is not measurable but teachers are sure it exists: clarity and clearer speech are generally believed to be evident. The widening of vocabulary is easier to judge: these children's choice of words is certainly wider, more varied, more expressive. One often recalls with surprise a child's age after hearing him speak or after reading what he has written. This startled realization that it is a baby that is speaking or writing is proof of the novelty. One little six-year-old describing a fire wrote: "I could see flames in the distance flying high over the roofs of the houses." No child, I am sure, would ever have written such a sentence without a never-before-achieved wealth of general reading in very impressionable years. One little boy under five years old, on being told by his mother that his older brother had been sent early to bed, did not ask "What for?" but said to his amazed mother: "I should be interested to know why." Mother's consternation was such that she brought him to school next day to ask his teacher: "What are you doing to him? He talks like the b—— television." Then she added with shrewd foresight: "But won't he get a good job some day?" The achievement made possible at school had a tangible value and that is an immensely useful association of ideas in the parent's mind. Maybe such thoughts are going to make

education and schools appear worth while in homes where that has never before happened.

Another mother brought her infant son to school to tell the teacher how the child had ended a family argument by changing his parents' quarrel to laughter when he looked up from his book to say: "I cannot do with all this fighting and disputing." Many teachers know the school book in which tiger cubs are fighting and disputing. Until i.t.a. made that book readable by a child under five years old, no teacher will have known any instance where such a child read the book for himself and then unconsciously made the phrase part of his everyday vocabulary. Children use many variants for a simple phrase such as "He said." We hear or read instead, heε anserd, or cæm ſhe replie, or ſheε mermerd, and so on. These are actual examples and this is literary achievement which would do credit to children twice as old.

The extensive reading is naturally extending comprehension and general knowledge. A five-year-old asked one of Her Majesty's Inspectors the meaning of "evaporation." The inspector took him to the school kitchen and demonstrated with boiling water. Another child of similar age confounded his teacher by asking the meaning of "seismic."

By the summer of 1963 the headteachers of the infant schools which began to use i.t.a. in 1962 had sent in their reports on the first year's work. Everything they said tallied with what was reported by the headteachers who began in 1961. None of them regretted the new departure. There had been swifter progress, more confidence, less teaching, more reading: "It is impossible for a teacher of a class of forty to hear the children read as often as they desire." One headmistress said of her first-year infants, "My main problem is keeping them supplied with sufficient reading matter. Many children have already read most of the books belonging to the third-year classes." "Children get pleasure from the stories and are less concerned with the pictures." In 1962 the newcomers to i.t.a. were prepared by the experiences of 1961 for the early beginning of writing, unlike the teachers in 1961 who discovered it by chance and unexpectedly. It is understandable therefore that the 1962 children were given earlier opportunity to use their pencils and the 1962 headteachers marvelled at the results. This is typical—

In this school we usually had only an odd child who could "write" (i.e. without the teacher first writing the sentence for him). Now many

of the children sit down and write freely either stories or accounts of their activities. It is this that delights us most: the children can sit down and write without any help at all from the teacher. Some words are not written correctly but this does not worry the child or impede his flow of thought. From my observations the children do this more freely than the class who are due to be transferred to the junior school in a few weeks' time.

That is, the first year i.t.a. children are better than the third year t.o. children. Another headteacher said that "it is difficult for the teacher to find time to keep pace with the children's rapid progress," and: "Children can write at will. Some sent postcards in i.t.a. from their holiday centres. We were delighted." (These children were then just five years old.)

Another instance may be cited—Sister Mary Finbarr, the head-mistress of St. Mary's R.C. Infant School, used i.t.a. in 1961–2 and was delighted with the result. Nevertheless, she wished to be certain beyond the remotest doubt that she was acting rightly, so in 1962–3 she reverted to t.o. to test once more the traditional approach. She must be the only headteacher who has used i.t.a. and then tried t.o. again. It seemed indeed that she intended to use t.o. until the Institute of Education published its report. After one year's rever-sion to t.o. she wrote—

One can safely say that these children [the second year i.t.a. class] are really a year in advance of the normal standard achieved by this age group. The amount of reading accomplished per week is noticeably far greater. The mechanics of reading being over at a much earlier stage, the children are now reading for comprehension and enjoyment. Reading is for them a pleasurable occupation, not a task to be endured. In this second year the quality and quantity of creative writing has increased immensely. The children express themselves with greater freedom and fluency than ever before. Vocabulary and flow of sentence has been greatly developed. This power of being quite free to put their ideas on paper, has given great satisfaction even to the youngest. . . . The general attitude of the children in the i.t.a. group is most striking. They show more aptitude towards work, they appear to have an unin-hibited proficiency about them, to be more purposeful in the way they go about all activities and they display a great confidence and inde-pendence. We are all now quite convinced of the great benefits derived from teaching with the new method. Those directly concerned would have no other.

St. Mary's Infant School took up i.t.a. again in 1963–4.

XVII

Remedial Work

"I have good reason to be content, for thank God I can read."

John Keats to John Taylor (1818)

I HAVE MADE mention earlier of the special experiment (at first an unanticipated and certainly an unplanned sideline) in using i.t.a. remedially which was started by Mr. K. W. Gardner of Walsall, and Mr. A. M. Harrison and Mr. J. Kilgannon of Oldham. This "side issue" is now as important as the main infant work.

The first report came from Mr. Gardner, who is Head of the Walsall Remedial Education Service, in December 1961 after one term's work. Mr. Gardner said that he had tried to subject i.t.a. to a very searching test and that he had not been very generous in the time given to Remedial Teaching; four thirty-minute sessions per week were less than he would normally allocate. He had also insisted that there should be no supporting work, on the part of the class teachers who had the children, outside their remedial reading periods "in order to approximate to a very common situation."

Fifteen children, who had transferred from infant to junior schools, had been selected as those most likely to have difficulty in learning to read out of twenty-six children unable to read more than three words on the Schonell scale. The children were divided into two groups, those with an I.Q. of more than 90, and those with an I.Q. of less than 90. "At the end of four weeks the first group were able to read all the infant series with reasonable fluency. After eight weeks' teaching it was clear that the children using a.r. could reach a more mature standard quicker than in t.o. and there was an encouraging atmosphere of confidence and interest."

These judgments were the result of observation only, but the Remedial Service records provided comparable progress figures for similar groups. As a result, Mr. Gardner was able to draw three main conclusions—

1. There has been a growth of confidence and interest in the pupils, which has activated reading and has resulted in a positive attitude to school work as a whole;
2. Good reading habits have been established very early;
3. The use of a reading text devoid of "exceptions" has encouraged the pupils to use their own resources in attacking reading material.

There was no confusion through the use of two kinds of print, one in the reading lesson and the other in other classes: the pupils accepted the two forms "quite naturally." The group with a 90+ I.Q. (Mean I.Q. 99) were transferred to reading books in traditional print after sixteen hours' reading with i.t.a.: "This transfer had been the subject of much thought, and a careful scheme was prepared, backed up by a mass of apparatus. In fact, the scheme has been jettisoned and the preliminary apparatus discarded, for fluency in a.r. was transferred immediately to fluency in t.o." Mr. Gardner noted that "some very dull children were reading and enjoying mature junior material."[1]

The second report came from Mr. A. M. Harrison, the headmaster of Northmoor Junior School, Oldham. His special class contained eighteen children of the second, third and fourth junior years: "All the children were backward, some of them severely so, to the point of not even knowing their letters or being able to do the simplest numerical calculations."

One boy with a severe speech disability was in the care of the speech therapist, four had been referred for special education but were given a further trial in the school, two were receiving psychiatric treatment. Much of the backwardness was "due to innate dullness" but there was in respect of several of the children a background of unfortunate home circumstances, frequent change of school, illness or the magistrates' court and probation. Self-confidence and sense of purpose were lacking: "Almost without exception it was true to say that the children in this class were completely lack-lustre." *At the end of the first term* the headmaster could write—

It could be that some of the apparent progress will be due to the normal process of maturing and to the special interest being shown in

---

[1] Mr. Gardner's experiment, the beginnings of which only are noted here, is described in *Educational Research*, Vol. V, No. 1, published for the National Foundation of Educational Research in November 1962, by George Newnes Ltd.

Further work has shown that the superiority of the i.t.a. taught children persists and extends to later reading of t.o. books.

the selected group. The obvious question which must spring to mind is, would the same progress have been made with a t.o. scheme and the same degree of attention? I think it fair to answer in the negative. I feel that the incentive of something which the children had never seen before and the feeling of "our" alphabet have been powerful spurs. There has obviously been a growth of self-confidence and there is much more liveliness generally. Most of the children were persistent absentees before. Now there has been no significant absence . . . Children who could not literally read a word before are now reading the first three books of *Janet and John* and the associated supplementaries. The majority, who at the end of *last* term could not successfully get beyond the first five words of the Schonell Graded Spelling Test, can now cope with twenty or thirty and in some cases even more. There have been two cases in which there has been little if any progress.

These early reports were very encouraging. Mr. Harrison compiled the following list of test results made during the year. All the testing was done with Schonell Graded Word Tests, normally printed. In almost every case there had been frequent change of school. The individuals marked H had in addition disturbed home backgrounds: those marked L could not when they began i.t.a.,

TABLE 12

Northmoor Junior School—Special Class of Backward Readers, 1961–2

Child		Chronological Age	Reading Age		
		September 1961	September 1961	April 1962	June 1962
1		10.0	↑	7.7	8.4
2		10.4		7.1	7.7
3	H.	10.7		6.9	9.2
4	H.L.	10.0		6.0	6.2
5	L.	9.0		7.0	7.9
6	H.L.	9.8	less than 6.0	6.0	6.7
7	H.	9.9		7.0	7.11
8	L.	8.5		7.1	7.6
9	H.	8.7		10.3	14.0
10	H.L.	8.8		6.5	6.10
11		8.10		5.7	6.7
12	H.L.	8.11		6.10	7.7
13	L.	8.0		8.3	9.6
14		8.7		6.10	8.2
15	H.	8.10	↓	6.7	6.10

Note: Ages are given in years and months.

recognize letters with any degree of consistency. "There was a general apathy towards school work and an almost complete resignation to failure."

The other three children of the eighteen originally in the class were reading adequately before the end of the first term and returned to the normal classes. When one views this progress in ten months from a nadir of achievement or even hope, the story is striking.

Mr. Harrison was asked whether he had noted any changes in the atmosphere of the classroom. He could not say that discipline was different. In the junior school children of this type are not "difficult": that description may be appropriate at the senior stage. The children are apathetic and too young to be rebellious. In his view the children certainly became more animated. Children who would never have been expected to take any initiative were wont to ask: "Can we get our books out?" This was a great step forward in display of initiative and in confidence. Furthermore, it was evident that for the first time in the lives of these children a book was seen as potentially pleasurable. Within the bounds which home and clothing made possible the children appeared to want to be tidier and cleaner: most of them had a new self-respect.

Mr. Harrison began his experiment in a very sceptical frame of mind. Indeed, his first reaction to the invention of the Initial Teaching Alphabet had been to write to the press about the confusion which would be caused to children. He felt in particular that confusion would arise in the transfer from the special print to normal print. He began to use the new method since these deprived and retarded children could at least come to no harm, for no achievement could reasonably be expected, and it seemed possible that the new books would make them aware that somebody had a special interest in them. He used with the children a mixture of books, sometimes i.t.a., sometimes t.o. This was because he feared the anticipated break at transition and the effect if children reading only i.t.a. left his school for another—a not uncommon happening with these children. In fact not a single child transferred to another school during the year. Today he would not worry about transition: he has learnt that there is nothing to cause worry. In future he proposes to use i.t.a. with any child in his school whose reading age is two years or more behind his chronological age.

All fifteen of the eighteen children still in the school in the year

1962-3 were in normal classes and all played their part adequately to the degree permitted by their general intelligence, limited experience and home background. Their experience was extremely limited and this was very apparent when they were taken from the streets in which they lived on school excursions. Their astonishment on seeing the commonplace beyond their normal narrow daily environment was moving. The part which they later played in school would in the headmaster's view quite definitely never have been realized with formal methods of reading. While still in need of frequent help, they did not give up when confronted with a book: "Instead of just looking at pictures, they will now come and ask for help with the reading. They know the print has meaning and value."

Staffing difficulties forced the headmaster to take on responsibility for a normal class in the year 1962-3 and the formation of another special class was not practicable. So sure, however, was he by now of the value of the new approach to reading that in February 1963 he used it again with four particularly backward children who received special reading instruction in i.t.a. for approximately fifteen to twenty minutes morning and afternoon, and class teachers intermittently during group reading lessons heard these children read from their i.t.a. books. The children could not read at all when they entered the school in September 1962. All read less than five words on the Schonell Graded Word Test and failed to score at all on the Kelvin Test of Verbal Ability: "They were completely uninterested in anybody or anything." One told a newcomer, "Pretend to be daft like me and you can go to special reading." Special reading was a refuge from work. This was interesting, for each child, whether he thought that he was escaping work or not, was now making an effort which before was lacking and could read, two of them well. Here is the test record of their progress—

TABLE 13

Child	Chronological Age at end of February 1963	Retardation in Years and Months by Schonell Word Recognition Test			
		End of March 1963	Mid-June	Late June	Mid-July
1	8.10	− 3.9	− 1.5	− 0.9	− 0.2
2	8.6	− 2.11	− 0.7	− 0.3	− 0.2
3	8.7	− 3.6	− 3.3	− 2.9	− 2.4
4	8.7	− 2.11	− 2.4	− 1.10	− 1.8

Mr. Harrison summarized the work thus—

> The overwhelming problem was one of establishing self-confidence, and in some cases self-respect as well, and removing the general attitude of resignation to failure and incapacity. I can only repeat what I have said several times before, that the i.t.a. has provided a unique instrument for this purpose, and has thus had effects far beyond the immediate one of teaching reading, either more expeditiously in the initial context, or in the remedial situation.

Mr. J. Kilgannon of Beever Junior School relates how for some fifteen years he had tried to teach non-readers to read with but limited success. He had used numerous schemes and methods and still found that he was fighting a losing battle with many children. In November 1961 he began to use i.t.a. with three boys between ten and eleven years old—three reading failures who also presented behaviour problems. Their Reading Ages were less than five-and-a-half years. One responded to no test and his referral card simply carried the word "Hopeless." *Within a fortnight* all three had read *My Little Books*, Nos. 1 to 32, *Here We Go* and *Off to Play*.

> They were delighted and their enthusiasm knew no bounds. By February these three boys had completed the basic readers of the *Janet and John* scheme and were working through the various supplementaries. Indeed they had become such avid readers that at times I was obliged to stop them and re-direct their energy. . . . As their confidence grew, the behaviour problem disappeared.

Mr. Kilgannon has said: "The introduction of i.t.a. was met with scepticism by many. I was in the 'fortunate' position of knowing that my children had nothing to lose and everything to gain." Nevertheless he was very cautious in his use of i.t.a. and initially involved only three boys. After this first success he gradually introduced the remainder of his class of twenty children to the alphabet. By April 1962 there was not a single non-reader in the class. By May the first three children had read in i.t.a. every book in the classroom and he re-introduced books in traditional orthography. The first three children began to read the *Adventures* and *More Adventures in Reading* series by Gertrude Keir. By October 1962 they had read the twenty-two-book series. By Christmas they had read the Griffin *Pirates* series and were given free access to the class library. The other seventeen children were meanwhile making excellent progress. In April 1963 Mr. Kilgannon could report that of all the twenty

children, eighteen had made the transition to traditional print and that everyone could read. Never in sixteen years of this special work had he had to purchase new books because everything had been read: now he had for that reason to add to the class library: "My once ample stocks had to be substantially increased." Mr. Kilgannon noted with some surprise that the transition to t.o. presented no problems whatever: "It just happened." He was particularly impressed by the way in which the logical consistency of i.t.a. instilled self-reliance: "Instead of asking the teacher to pronounce a difficult word the child now re-phrases his question: 'This word says —, doesn't it?' " Success in writing has accompanied success in reading.

> Before i.t.a. the backward reader was very reluctant to commit his thoughts and ideas to paper because of spelling difficulties and limited literary background. Now he is able to express himself with clarity in the new medium. In the past I have often asked children to read their book to me because of my inability to decipher it. There have been times when they have been unable to do this. Since using i.t.a. this position has never arisen. The writing transition develops shortly after the reading transition. . . . Spelling problems are bound to arise but my children, when confronted with such difficulties, write the word in i.t.a. spelling. I praise them for their ingenuity and at the same time point out the t.o. spelling.

His final remark was: "Never in my teaching experience have children such as these derived so much pleasure from books. Never before have I enjoyed the teaching of reading so much."

The interest of parents in the school work of their children has grown. As can be surmised, the parents of these children are not likely to be those most interested in the doings of their children in school, but their attention has been attracted now. About half of these children's parents have remarked to the teacher on the improvement in their children's work and conduct. One mother said (and she is not alone in this by any means) that she wished her child had been taught in i.t.a. in his first school—these children were gathered together in this special class from several schools.

Mr. Kilgannon has also taught three adult non-readers. In all three cases transition to t.o. took place after ten weekly one-hour lessons. The three adults were then able to read stories in magazines.[1]

---

[1] Since this was written the number has grown. One man living 200 miles away was, with the aid of his wife, taught by post. In seven weeks he wrote a letter in i.t.a. asking for more books.

TABLE 14

Beever Junior School Remedial Class

| Child | C.A. July 1963 | Beginning of i.t.a. instruction | | R.A. July 1963 (by Schonell test) | Time on i.t.a. (in months) | Advance in R.A. in months | I.Q. (by Terman-Merrill test) | | R.Q. | |
		Date	R.A. (5.0 indicates 5 years or less)				On entry	July 1963	On entry	July 1963
1	12.7	November 1961	5.0	12.0	20	84	68	80	50	96
2	12.5	November 1961	5.0	10.2	20	63	97	95	50	83
3	13.3	November 1961	5.0	10.4	20	65	93	93	45	79
4	11.0	February 1962	5.0	13.0	17	96	78	91	50	118
5	11.5	February 1962	5.0	10.2	17	63	65	74	48	92
6	11.1	March 1962	6.6	12.0	16	66	87	85	65	108
7	11.1	March 1962	6.6	9.0	16	30	84	77	65	82
8	12.6	March 1962	6.9	14.1	16	88	85	74	64	117
9	12.9	March 1962	5.6	10.5	16	60	71	85	50	82
10	11.1	April 1962	5.0	9.2	15	50	69	73	50	83
11	11.1	April 1962	5.0	10.3	15	64	85	86	50	92
12	11.5	April 1962	5.0	7.3	15	28	83	85	48	65
13	10.7	April 1962	5.0	10.0	15	60	87	88	55	95
14	9.2	September 1962	5.0	9.0	10	48	82	84	62	97
15	11.9	October 1962	5.0	10.2	10	64	96	100	50	87
16	9.9	September 1962	5.0	11.0	9	72	63	63	57	112
17	11.1	February 1963	6.1	9.0	6	36	79	75	57	83
18	8.10	February 1963	6.6	8.5	6	24	78	79	77	98
19	8.0	March 1963	5.0	7.1	5	25	82	—	67	88
20	10.3	April 1963	5.0	8.0	4	36	—	—	50	78
21	8.0	May 1963	9.0	12.0	3	36	—	—	118	133

Note: Ages shown are given in years and months.

In 1962 an interesting innovation was tried in St. Anne's Roman Catholic Infant School. The headmistress, Miss A. Walsh, had decided to adopt i.t.a. in her reception class. Alongside this she used i.t.a. with a backward infant group. Twenty-five children were in the class: twenty-two of them had already spent two years on normal spelling without making any progress; three had been in the school for one year. Five could recognize some letters; the rest had not begun to read anything at all. This is the terminal record of their progress through the *Janet and John* Reading Scheme. They began in September 1962, when their average age was six years three months. The progress is better than that of a normal class using traditional books.

TABLE 15

St. Anne's Infant School—Remedial Class of Six-Year-Olds

Stage reached	December 1962	April 1963	July 1963
0. Non-starters	1	1	1
1. Here We Go	1	1	—
2. Book I	5	—	—
3. Out and About	14	1	1
4, Book II	4	5	4
5. Book III	—	10	6
6. Book IV	—	4	5
7. Once Upon a Time	—	3	5
8. Completed Scheme	—	—	3

Mrs. K. MacHardy, the class teacher, said that apart from reading ability, behaviour generally had improved remarkably. The headmistress reported: "For a C class, the children are very enthusiastic and full of self-confidence. Their reactions are quite different from those of any dull children whom I have ever seen before. They are like A stream children in their general manners, the only difference is in achievement."

Without i.t.a. the headmistress is sure that this story could never have been told. A little boy of five arrived at the school, his second school, with a deplorable record of bad conduct. His mother was in despair. Although the headmistress was assured that the boy could talk at home, he was never heard to speak in class. He grew tense when spoken to and refused to touch book or pencil. He seized every opportunity to destroy and to steal. He would bedevil any child's activity by breaking toys, squandering building bricks, tearing books,

and all without uttering a sound. The Principal School Medical Officer was in touch with the case and had already written that official ascertainment as educationally subnormal was possible but further trial at school was desirable in view of the boy's age. After many weeks, when his teacher was despairing of him, he picked up a crayon and scribbled meaninglessly. But he was proud of his form-less scribbling. When his teacher commended it, he blushed and he took lots of it home several times to show to his mother. Then a whispered "Yes" or "No" was sometimes heard. The first time that he spoke in school in a normal voice was when he shouted out while another child was reading, "Hear me read." And he could. It was halting but it was his first apparent effort. His teacher thought that the wish to read was a near-miracle. That happened when he was seven years old. At seven years ten months he was reading Book III of the *Janet and John* series and his conduct was normal.

In the neighbouring junior school, St. Anne's Roman Catholic Junior School, the headmaster, Mr. T. H. McGreal, made a special third stream class of the twenty weakest children coming into his school from the infant department in September 1961. The class was in the charge of Mrs. J. Nolan, who kept careful objective records throughout the year.

The average chronological age at entry was seven years four months and the average reading age five years three months, the average deficiency being two years one month. The best child was one year eight months retarded. At the end of the school year all the children had made tremendous recovery. Four children only were retarded by a complete year or more and eight (40 per cent) showed reading ages exceeding their years! All the tests were ordinary traditionally spelt Schonell tests and so the children (apart from three who made the transition to t.o.) were being tested in a medium different from the print in their school books.

The class teacher says that reading in September 1962 was almost non-existent and that there was not a single child who could write spontaneously. The best of them could copy a couple of sentences from the blackboard. By the end of the second term, compositions of two or more pages were commonplace. Reading was at first so weak that the class started with the large *Janet and John* first books. Tackling the first reader, *Here We Go*, was out of the question. The children's general attitudes developed; their speech improved noticeably. The headmaster says: "This is not a C stream class

socially: the children within six months were socially transformed. They are friendly and talkative."

This is the record of this class's progress at the end of each month through the *Janet and John* Reading Scheme. It far exceeds the initial performance of normal children.

TABLE 16

St. Anne's Junior School—Remedial Class of Seven-Year-Olds 1962–3

	Number of children on the following stages[1]							
	1	2	3	4	5	6	7	8
September 1962	7	6	5	2	—	—	—	—
October	—	—	6	9	5	—	—	—
November	—	—	4	5	6	5	—	—
December	—	—	2	3	4	6	5	—
January 1963	—	—	—	2	3	7	5	3
February	—	—	—	1	2	5	6	6
March	—	—	—	1	2	5	—	12
April	—	—	—	—	1	4	—	15
May	—	—	—	—	1	4	—	15
June	—	—	—	—	1	1	2	16
July	—	—	—	—	—	2	2	16

Table 17 is taken from the class record and shows the reading ages of each child at different points in the year. All the children were first-year juniors and their chronological ages in September 1962 ranged from seven years one month to seven years eleven months.

The Reading Ages were established by the Schonell Graded Reading Vocabulary Test. The degree of retardation or advancement is shown in years and months.

It should be noted that this class pursued throughout the year a

[1] The numbers refer to the same stages as on page 127. Reaching Stage 8 indicates completion of the scheme and that the children are reading ordinary print well.

TABLE 17

*St. Anne's Junior School—Remedial Class of Seven-Year-Olds, 1962–3
Reading Accuracy Tests*

	Extent of Retardation or Advancement in years and months				Total Gain[1] from September to June
	September 1962	December 1962	April 1963	June 1963	
1	− 2.5	− 1.0	+0.8	+0.10	4.4
2	− 2.2	− 1.1	− 0.9	− 0.10	2.1
3	− 1.11	− 1.1	− 0.7	− 0.6	2.2
4	− 1.11	− 1.1	− 0.1	+0.3	2.11
5	− 2.2	− 1.2	− 0.4	+0.1	3.0
6	− 2.1	− 1.0	− 0.5	− 0.4	2.6
7	− 2.2	− 1.0	− 1.0	− 1.2	1.9
8	− 1.10	− 0.5	− 0.5	− 0.5	2.2
9	− 2.1	− 1.0	+0.3	+0.3	3.1
10	− 2.1	− 0.9	− 0.7	− 0.3	2.7
11	− 1.9	− 0.5	− 0.1	+0.3	2.9
12	− 2.3	absent	− 0.5	0.0	3.0
13	− 2.0	− 0.2	− 0.5	− 0.6	2.3
14	− 2.2	absent	− 0.10	− 1.4	1.7
15	− 2.6	− 0.7	− 0.8	− 1.0	2.3
16	− 1.11	0.0	− 0.3	− 0.2	2.6
17	− 1.8	+1.3	+1.7	+2.3	4.8
18	− 1.11	+1.1	+0.10	+0.9	3.5
19	− 2.0	− 1.0	− 1.4	− 1.1	1.8
20	− 2.8	− 0.6	+0.6	+0.5	3.10

timetable and curriculum which was quite normal for a backward
group: the children took part in all the usual school activities. They
were under one very able class teacher and their reading and writing
were in i.t.a. They were tested, however, for record purposes in t.o.,
although many of them at the time of the earlier tests were reading
i.t.a.

When the value of i.t.a. in improving reading standards in junior
schools became known, a number of secondary school headteachers
became interested in its possibilities with older children. Such
remedial work among children of eleven and more years of age had
not been anticipated and books with content suitable for senior
children had not been prepared: only infant books had been published in the new alphabet. That deficiency of reading material still
exists but some has now been prepared: more is needed. The joy

[1] That is, the improvement in the extent of retardation from September 1962 to June
1963, including the nine months by which each child's chronological age had increased.

of these children on finding that they can read, when all hope of equalling their fellows had gone, is thrilling. Some months after his secondary school had begun to use i.t.a., I rang up one headteacher to ask if any of the new "senior" books had yet arrived. Infant readers only had been available at first. The answer which I received has been repeated by other secondary headmasters. "The children are so delighted to find that reading is within their scope that they are devouring infant books with avidity for the sheer pleasure of knowing and showing that they can read after all." Children in one school informed visitors that they were "studying Augmented Roman" as proudly as though they were announcing that they had been selected to study Ancient Greek or some other recondite subject. The story is very similar to that of the junior schools. Apathy gives way to initiative; conduct improves considerably. It was a thirteen-year-old boy who had been taught to read after years of failure who told an American visitor he wanted to be a cook. The visitor (a bishop from one of America's very big cities) told him of the high earnings in the United States of good hotel chefs. The boy's eyes widened. Then he asked eagerly, "Do you think I could get a job like that, sir? I can read now." There is pathos in such a remark and joy. It is sad that until his thirteenth year this child could not read clearly because of needless difficulties which foiled his attempts to learn. The power to read lay latent. Now it has been aroused and that child can read and his joy on realizing that the impossible is possible and that he can do as others do is the sort of thing that makes a teacher's job rewarding. Besides, for the first time in his life he saw a point in coming to school, an end product which made learning worth while.

Mr. J. F. Horrocks, the headmaster of Clarksfield Secondary School, was the first to establish a senior remedial class. A group of children aged between eleven years one month and twelve years two months was put in the charge of Mrs. M. Young, an able teacher with a vocation for helping these less fortunate children, who had seen the possibilities of i.t.a. when she undertook some intelligence testing of infants on behalf of the London Institute of Education at the beginning of the Infant Reading experiment. The children in this class varied widely in general intelligence.

Intelligence testing was carried out in April 1963 by the Education Committee's psychologist, a trained and experienced tester using a special non-verbal test battery derived from the Wechsler Intelligence Scale for Children. The children had then been learning to

read through i.t.a. for seven months. Two of the children showed an I.Q. greatly exceeding the normal. Why they had not been able to read is a mystery. Some blockage, the cause of which is baffling, had apparently impeded their learning. (Several such cases have been brought to light by this work.) Most of the children were of average or near average intelligence. Some were not bad readers but were not confident readers and not interested in books. Yet, without special effort these children would have left school to be classed as illiterate.[1]

The headmaster writes—

For five years a class for backward readers has operated in this school, taught by enthusiastic and capable teachers using traditional methods, and progress was certainly made. But the fact remains that one could still find non-readers in the upper classes. . . . What worried me most was the existence of cases of non-reading in children who in every other respect were obviously intelligent and capable, yet who would never obtain a post suitable to their abilities since we judge ability, rightly or wrongly, by a child's ability to read and his ability to express his ideas and knowledge in writing.

Of the 1962 i.t.a. class he writes—

Since their level of reading was such that it would have been farcical to give them a normal timetable of academic subjects relying on the use of text books and the library reference system, it was decided to sacrifice such subjects in favour of twelve periods a week of i.t.a. It was felt that the material available for reading, designed for four- and five-year-olds, would create an immediate revulsion in eleven-year-olds, and in consequence most of the summer holiday was spent in trans-literating and over-printing books of more mature subject matter, a task borne by Mrs. Young, who has had complete control of the scheme from its inception. In fact, we were to discover that the children were so delighted to be able to read at last that, at least in the initial stages, they were quite happy to read the material provided for infants.

Mr. Horrocks then discusses the figures in Table 18. In conclusion he writes—

The scheme has achieved its objectives with all but two of the original members of the class and will be continued with each 11+ intake as long as is necessary. I assume that, as the contributing schools adopt i.t.a., the need for remedial work in secondary schools will diminish. Having comparative results at hand from previous intakes, all of whom were tested on the same test, I am in no doubt whatever that i.t.a. has given the children much more rapid progress by a much less painful

[1] See page 177. Table 18.

process. The enthusiasm engendered has been abundant; children who were ashamed of their inability to read at the outset have openly asked me to come to their classroom to listen to their reading—to listen to their new-found ability. I am not alone in believing that a considerable proportion of cases of delinquency have their origins in academic failure, the basis of which is backwardness in reading. Consequently, it is not surprising to be able to report that at least one "hard" case of delinquency appears to have been cured by success in i.t.a. From one who slunk about the school wearing a furtive expression he has become a changed personality. He is now a happy, confident lad, proud of his achievement.

Twelve periods of reading weekly was a large assignment and such intensive effort would doubtless have attained results by any system. The headmaster is certain from his past experience that the gains would neither have been so great, so widespread nor so rapid. They were made "pleasantly and with enthusiasm, . . . rather than at the pistol point." As the year proceeded, with co-operation from the History and Geography teachers the children were able to take these subjects in the normal way based on the task sheets normally employed, but written in i.t.a. It is an achievement indeed to have a backward class working with large individual independence from written task sheets, consulting their own reference books and so forth.

The gains shown in the fifth column were made in eight months, seven of which, allowing for holidays, were spent in school. They would be remarkable in any circumstances. When it is recalled that these children were in general included in the class because of personal maladjustments and overall failure, the gains are still more remarkable—and valuable.

I.t.a. was introduced into Hollinwood Secondary Modern School in September 1962. Part of the school is housed in an annexe, a quarter of a mile from the main building. The headmaster, Mr. A. Tate, organized the remedial work in two quite distinct systems. The younger senior children were under the direction of Mr. F. Smeeton in the annexe and the older under Mr. M. G. Brown in the main school.

There were twenty children in Mr. Smeeton's class. After determination of their reading ages by various tests, they were chosen as those of the first senior year with the lowest reading ages. These children after five or six years in school had achieved little. The

timetable was so arranged that the children took part in normal lessons but had on average through the week one period per day in English. In the other subjects of the curriculum, some of the work was done in i.t.a. *but not all*. Mr. Smeeton reports that a willingness

TABLE 18

Clarksfield Secondary School

Mean Chronological Age	11.5
Mean Intelligence Quotient	96
Mean Reading Age	9.8
Mean Reading Age deficiency	1.10

(*Ten children had made such excellent progress by April that they were moved to other classes of the school and replaced by eight children whose achievement, originally superior, was now inferior.*)

Child	Chrono- logical Age	Reading Age by Schonell Word Recognition Test		Gain in years and months	Intelligence Quotient
	September 1962	September 1962	May 1963	September to May	April 1963
1	11.1	− 2.5	+ 1.8	4.1	135
2	11.4	− 3.4	+ 1.6	4.10	121
3	11.5	− 2.3	− 1.2	1.1	104
4	11.3	− 0.1	+ 1.2	1.3	104
5	11.6	− 1.6	+ 1.4	2.10	103
6	11.8	− 0.9	+ 3.0	3.9	100
7	12.0	− 4.6	− 0.5	4.1	97
8	11.5	+ 2.8	+ 3.7	0.11	97
9	11.6	+ 0.4	+ 3.4	3.0	97
10	12.0	− 3.7	− 3.9	− 0.2	93
11	12.0	nil	− 4.4	2.8?	90
12	11.7	+ 0.10	+ 3.1	2.3	89
13	11.7	− 3.8	− 0.4	3.4	87
14	11.5	− 2.9	− 2.0	0.9	86
15	11.10	− 1.3	+ 2.5	3.8	86
16	11.6	− 2.2	− 0.6	1.8	86
17	11.11	− 4.10	+ 0.6	5.4	83
18	11.8	− 2.4	− 1.8	0.8	83
19	11.11	− 0.4	+ 2.0	2.4	79
20	11.9	− 3.9	− 1.7	2.2	These children were not present for the intelligence testing. Some had already been moved to other classes.
21	11.2	− 5.0	− 2.11	2.1	
22	11.9	− 2.7	+ 0.5	3.0	
23	12.2	− 4.5	− 0.7	3.10	
24	11.5	− 2.9	− 2.0	0.9	
25	11.6	− 2.8	+ 1.2	3.10	
26	11.9	− 5.4	− 2.6	2.10	
27	11.6	− 1.6	+ 1.4	2.10	
28	11.9	− 4.7	− 3.2	1.5	

to learn and a keenness to do well have been shown which exceed any he has known in fourteen years' teaching of this type of backward child. Reticence and hiding away from reading gave place to volunteering to read. Mr. Smeeton thought that at first they found the change from what they had striven so long to learn a little disconcerting, but this only lasted for a short time and was quickly replaced by enthusiasm.

It is noteworthy that any advance at all can be recorded among these senior children whose reading skill was negligible. The force of the figures in Table 19 lies in the last two columns. All these children had read a substantial number of i.t.a. books in the course of the year. More and more i.t.a. books suitable for older children are needed. These weak readers want a library and a great field for practice in the spelling medium in which they have confidence—

TABLE 19

Hollinwood County Secondary School—1st Year Remedial Class

Child	Chrono-logical Age September 1962	Reading Age			Number of i.t.a. Library Books read by June 1963	Stage[2] reached on *Janet and John* Scheme (i.t.a.)
		September 1962	June 1963	Increase[1]		
1	11.11	6.5	7.7	1.2	21	7
2	11.6	6.8	8.0	1.2	28	5
3	11.2	6.6	9.0	2.4	35	7
4	11.3	6.5	8.0	1.5	20	7
5	11.6	8.0	10.4	2.4	48	8
6	11.11	6.7	7.9	1.2	32	7
7	11.9	6.9	7.9	1.0	23	7
8	11.9	5.2	5.8	0.6	6	4
9	11.8	5.5	6.7	1.2	14	5
10	11.11	6.8	7.6	0.8	15	4
11	11.8	6.8	7.9	1.1	26	7
12	11.3	6.1	7.2	1.1	28	5
13	11.9	6.1	7.3	1.2	26	5
14	11.11	6.8	7.9	1.1	25	5
15	11.11	8.1	10.8	2.7	54	8
16	11.9	7.1	8.3	1.2	23	3
17	11.5	7.0	7.8	0.8	19	7
18	11.2	6.6	7.5	0.9	13	5
19	11.4	5.5	7.1	1.6	13	4
20	11.5	6.9	7.9	1.0	24	5

[1] This is the total gain, including the nine months by which the chronological age had increased.   [2] See page 127.

confidence both in their own ability and confidence in the reliability of the spelling.

Mr. Brown, teaching the older backward children in the second- and third-year senior classes, tried to find out—

(1) If it were possible to use i.t.a. in secondary modern schools with backward readers in a group where the range of retardation is very wide;

(2) How best to work with such a group;

(3) What is the effect of instruction spread over both i.t.a. and t.o. in use at the same time.

With reference to the first point, this was a remarkably backward group and the range of retardation very wide and grave, from three years five months to eight years one month. On the second point, it is to be noted that there were twenty-one children in the group, a large number for a class of this type and normal treatment would have required their division into four or five approximately homo- geneous groups. In connection with the third point, not only were the eight least retarded taught wholly in t.o. but the thirteen most retarded children, outside two daily forty-minute periods in i.t.a., spent the rest of their time under other teachers receiving instruction where t.o. was used.

The work of the whole class was planned to fit into the normal secondary modern school[1] timetable so that the children covered the usual curriculum. Their timetable was arranged so that the first two periods each morning were General English and Reading lessons. The less able group, using i.t.a., had a reading age less than approximately seven years five months and those with higher reading ages were taught wholly by traditional remedial methods. The basis of selection was the R.A. of the child concerned in September 1962, and the test used was the Schonell Graded Word Scale. There was a slight overlap at the borderline between the two groups where behaviour problems influenced the class allocation. Mr. Brown was well aware that a comparison of the results from these two imper- fectly matched groups (lower and upper retardation age groups) could not be statistically significant and could be criticized as un- desirable since varying external factors invalidate direct comparison,

---

[1] A secondary modern school is a school for senior pupils over eleven years of age which, unlike the grammar school, does not ordinarily lead to advanced specialist study with transfer to university and other forms of higher education.

e.g. the starting points of the children are very different. Yet he deemed the results likely to be of interest in respect to the three questions stated and also in relation to the respective achievements of the two groups.

It could be expected that the children who started with the greatest degrees of retardation would be those likely to achieve least and those likely to be slowest in making any initial progress. Their previous history of itself indicates these things. Further, it was Mr. Brown's experience (as also that of others) that some children receiving remedial treatment for reading often make initial progress and then reach a plateau where progress is negligible or ceases and some regression may even set in. This "saturation point", when it occurs, appears to be related directly to lack of ability and to be reached earliest by the most backward children.

The number of children involved was small but the experiment seemed to show that—

(1) The poorest readers in the group using i.t.a. were able to maintain "progress pace" with the better readers. Usually the near non-readers would have been left behind by those of more ability.

(2) Many children are backward readers because of inability to cope with spelling inconsistencies and i.t.a. shows very positive results when used with these children.

(3) I.t.a. leads to a generally steadier and more consolidating progress with backward readers of the 13+ age groups.

The two groups of children, upper and lower grades, were taught together throughout the year 1962–3; books in the class library were in both alphabets, i.t.a. and t.o. The i.t.a. children were free at any time to take a t.o. book. All the children began to read books in ordinary print before the end of 1962 with the exception of three, so that for the greater part of the school year all but three were reading t.o. One of these three transferred to ordinary books in April 1963. The two children with the lowest reading ages (Nos. 13 and 19) still preferred at the end of the school year to read books printed in i.t.a. (Table 21).

The ultimate overall gains related to their advancing ages are slight, but this group of children were as backward as one would find anywhere outside a special school for the educationally subnormal. With such a group the important thing is the number of months gained in the school year rather than the relationship between the

reading and the chronological ages: reading ratios are a secondary issue. The absolute gains in reading skill in the course of the school year, in Table 20, averaged 10·5 months for the t.o. group and 10·77 months for the i.t.a. group. That was in both cases an achievement by children and teacher.

This backward class of 12- and 13-year-old children is set up in the school at intervals as the children needing special attention gather. The last similar class was organized in the school year 1960–1. There were 15 backward readers in that year. The figures below are the basis of Graph 11. They refer to the "upper" group (wholly t.o. taught) of 1962–3, the "lower" group (begun on i.t.a. but fairly soon on t.o.) of 1962–3 and the wholly traditionally taught group of 1960–1. They show clearly that the more backward group's achievement is close to that of the t.o. group, instead of being far behind and is indeed throughout the period under review slightly ahead. Their progress is generally constant.

TABLE 20

Hollinwood County Secondary School—Second- and Third-Year Remedial Class

Retardation and Progress figures are in Months

	Average Retardation September 1962	PROGRESS			
		November 1962	January 1963	March 1963	June 1963
t.o.	– 57·87	2·62	4·25	5·77	10·50
i.t.a.	– 70·46	4·46	6·31	8·10	10·77
	Average Retardation September 1960	November 1960	January 1961	March 1961	June 1961
t.o.	– 66·25	2·66	3·58	6·81	10·18

The graph indicates—

(1) The more rapid improvement which is common to every group in the first two months because of the special remedial instruction.

(2) The slowing up of progress that comes with traditional instruction but leads later to a more rapid advance. In Mr. Brown's experience this is a customary development. The increasing tempo

begins as he puts it "when things begin to click." The child seems to establish a relationship between symbol and spoken language and at last can go ahead.

(3) That with a beginning on i.t.a. the earliest progress is far more impressive, *even though these children are the most backward of the backward.* This first surge is similar in length of time to that of the t.o. children although much greater in degree. This last is remarkable. The upper group could be expected not only to associate symbol with sound earlier but to associate and blend together earlier sounds in syllables, syllables in words, words in sentences.

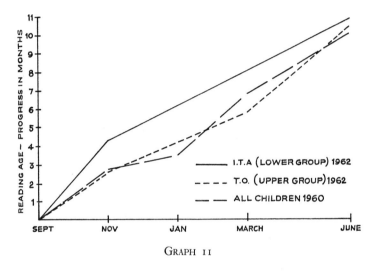

GRAPH 11

(4) That after the first surge the progress of the i.t.a. group is absolutely steady and continues equally steadily after their change-over to t.o.

(5) That all arrive at the year end at the same point in terms of progress. Again it must not be overlooked that the poorest in quality are always ahead in terms of relative progress.

One is forced to ask oneself what the i.t.a. group would have done if they had not reverted so early to t.o., when one recalls the progress of the higher quality younger (and therefore not comparable) group at Clarksfield Secondary School. Those children who were backward readers started with an average deficiency of 31·92 months and gained in a year an average 30·62 months. (See page 177.)

TABLE 21

Hollinwood Secondary Modern School—Progress of Children more than 3 Years Retarded

The children were tested throughout on three tests, the Schonell Graded Word Scale, the Holborn Reading Scale (a Sentence Method basis), the Daniels and Diack Standard Reading Tests. There was a close correlation between all the test results but where they differed the lowest score was accepted. The figures refer to years and months.

Children Using Traditional Orthography

Child	C.A.	September 1962		November 1962		January 1963		June 1963		
		R.A.	Retardation	R.A.	Progress since September	R.A.	Progress since September	R.A.	Progress since September	Retardation
1	13.3	8.0	−5.3	8.3	+0.3	8.7	+0.7	9.3	+1.3	−4.9
2	13.3	8.4	−4.11	9.0	+0.8	9.6	+1.2	9.7	+1.3	−4.5
3	13.11	8.1	−5.10	8.6	+0.5	8.7	+0.6	9.2	+1.1	−5.6
4	13.3	9.7	−3.8	9.7	0.0	9.5	−0.2	10.1	+0.6	−3.11
5	13.2	8.3	−4.11	8.7	+0.4	8.8	+0.5	9.2	+0.11	−4.9
6	13.1	7.5	−5.8	7.5	0.0	7.3	−0.2	7.6	+0.1	−6.4
7	13.2	9.9	−3.5	10.1	+0.4	10.3	+0.6	11.3	+1.6	−2.8
8	13.2	8.3	−4.11	8.0	−0.3	8.3	0.0	8.8	+0.5	−5.3

Children Using Initial Teaching Alphabet

Child	C.A.	September 1962		November 1962		January 1963		June 1963		
		R.A.	Retardation	R.A.	Progress since September	R.A.	Progress since September	R.A.	Progress since September	Retardation
9	13.1	7.3	−5.10	7.8	+0.5	7.2	−0.1	8.4	+1.1	−5.6
10	14.1	8.5	−5.8	8.7	+0.2	8.7	+0.2	9.5	+1.0	−5.5
11	14.1	8.5	−5.8	8.8	+0.3	9.0	+0.7	9.5	+1.0	−5.5
12	13.2	7.5	−5.9	7.6	+0.1	7.8	+0.3	7.8	+0.3	−6.3
13	13.6	5.6	−8.0	6.6	+1.0	6.6	+1.0	6.9	+1.3	−7.6
14	12.5	5.8	−6.9	6.3	+0.7	6.8	+1.0	7.6	+1.10	−5.8
15	12.10	6.5	−6.5	7.3	+0.10	7.4	+0.11	7.5	+1.0	−6.2
16	12.6	6.8	−5.10	7.0	+0.4	7.2	+0.6	7.4	+0.8	−5.11
17	12.6	7.8	−4.10	8.0	+0.4	8.1	+0.5	8.7	+0.11	−4.8
18	12.8	8.4	−4.4	8.6	+0.2	9.1	+0.9	9.4	+1.0	−4.1
19	13.1	5.0	−8.1	5.0	0.0	5.3	+0.3	5.2	+0.2	−8.8
20	12.5	7.7	−4.10	8.3	+0.8	8.4	+0.9	8.7	+1.0	−4.7
21	12.5	8.1	−4.4	8.1	0.0	8.5	+0.4	8.7	+0.6	−4.7

Some children seem to suffer from what has been called "word-blindness," complete inability to make the associations stated in paragraph (3) above. The question arises whether some cases of suspected "word-blindness" are not rather attributable to a combination of emotional or mental defect with inconsistent spelling.

It can be contended that these records and these stories of achievement in remedial classes are not controlled experimentally. The teachers who have reported them have their own long experience to compare with the results they see today. Most of these teachers had no early interest in i.t.a.; some were openly sceptical. The achievements recorded and the tales about individual children told here are, in the view of the teachers who provided them, things that have not happened before, things which they could not hope for, much less expect. Only teachers with their hearts in their work and a calling for helping the most helpless undertake experiments of this nature in their efforts to find a means somehow of rescuing the handicapped and the emotionally bereft. Their satisfaction in the outcome, their sureness that they have made another step forward in combating the psychological and mental afflictions which beset some of their charges, is as compelling to me as a host of statistics and more reassuring.

XVIII

Conclusion

Tolle lege, tolle lege (Take up and read)
St. Augustine. *Confessiones*, VIII, 12

IN PARLIAMENT on the eleventh of July 1963, the Minister of
Education (Sir Edward Boyle) referred to ". . . these exciting and
interesting experiments." And the Ministry of Education has
as a result made financial contributions towards the cost of the
inquiry. The wheel has surely turned full cycle since the days of Sir
Isaac Pitman.

What I have said in the foregoing chapters is by past standards
quite incredible. If I had been told these things I should have been
incredulous. One must see for oneself. This is not a mere improvement in method bringing small easily measurable gains: this is a
revolution. One eminent visitor from an American university called
it "the biggest breakthrough in English education since the invention
of the printing press," and still another said that we had opened
the door of the intellectual slum. He was not referring to streets and
buildings but meant that the wealth of English literature and learning
had been made accessible to vaster numbers. As the results accrue,
one begins to wonder whether indeed the importance of the new
approach to reading can be exaggerated. Clearly none but a fool
would claim to have found a panacea for all educational ills: there is
no sovereign remedy for everything. Equally clearly we have demonstrated a means of alleviating a host of difficulties and troubles, to an
extent which no other teaching approach has ever achieved, and
this in the teaching of reading which is the key to all educational
progress in every sphere of knowledge. It is a basic skill, perhaps
second only to speech, which distinguishes man from beast. Without
the skill to read, so little can be achieved that he who lacks this skill
suffers from feelings of inferiority and from frustrations that lead
in many ways to loss of personal qualities and values.

The Central Advisory Council for Education has pointed out[1] that as the life of our society becomes more complex, the demands made upon us grow: "One of the reasons why there is a quite proper anxiety over the general standards of literacy today is not that fewer and fewer people can read and write, but that more and more people need to do so with greater competence" (Chapter 1), and "Literacy is not . . . the power to translate written symbols into sounds. It involves the power to invest words with meaning" (Chapter 15). Reading power opens the doors to understanding of human culture and achievement. The earlier that power is conferred, the earlier reading selectivity will begin and the greater the progress made possible to the best intellects. Others can by the acquisition of reading skill be saved from psychological strains and attendant social problems. It is possible, and indeed already seems proved, that some persons possessing potentially high intelligence have been hindered from personal development by early reading difficulties which the new approach can often overcome.

The new approach is not a teaching method: it is merely a simplification of the medium, of the early material with which the child is required to deal. He learns and puts to use 45 characters instead of more than 2,000 characterizations and he has to learn to decode only these 45 signs in the greatly simplified code. That is the sum and the substance of the i.t.a. approach. Only when he has learnt to do that simpler task does he tackle the complexities of normal spelling. Methods of using this simplified medium will vary and different teachers will find themselves apter with some methods than with others. Teaching quality will always vary and we already know that some teachers are more successful than others with the new medium. The fact remains that the least successful teachers are more successful than they used to be—and apparently more successful in this particular job of teaching reading than the very best teachers using the old medium.

There has been much reference in these pages to tests of reading achievement and of comprehension. These are of value only in comparing the relative achievement of these children taught by the new medium with what used to be expected of children of their age. The tests are now meaningless when applied to the children themselves. It is silly to say that these six-year-olds read like children of eight or nine or twelve: they read as children of eight or nine or

---

[1] *Half Our Future*; The Newsom Report, 1963.

twelve used to read. The truth is that the standard has utterly changed and new objective tests need to be evolved to find the standards to be expected when the new system is applied. Not only must the reading accuracy tests and the reading comprehension tests be re-made; so must the general intelligence tests. One of the children referred to in this book as an outstanding child had an intelligence quotient determined at 95 when he first went to school. It is a pity that that assessment was not checked and counterchecked. It was accepted at the time along with all the other assessments of the entrants to school made for the London Institute of Education and nobody saw any reason to doubt it. This boy's achievement in reading prompted a special request to the School Medical Officer that the I.Q. be again assessed in July 1963. This is the Medical Officer's report—

This is the boy who was said to have an I.Q. of only 95 about the time of school entry but has acquired an extraordinary reading ability. We have no record of his previous test, do not know what scale was used and have not had access to his score sheet on that occasion. At this examination he was given the Stanford Binet Intelligence Scale in its most recent form (Form L–M). [The boy] applied himself very well indeed to the test and finished with a mental age of seven years ten months which, with his chronological age of six years two months, corresponds to an I.Q. of 130. None of the twenty or so sub-tests given in this test required reading ability as such and, except in one respect, his performance on different test items was very even. The exception was in the vocabulary part of this scale where words have to be defined and in this test he passed at a ten-year-old level. Even if this vocabulary test was completely ignored, however, the I.Q. on this scale would be somewhere in the order of 125. This test result in itself suggests that [the boy] is of good or even superior intelligence and it is difficult to correlate this finding with the earlier figure of 95. While reading ability would certainly help in the vocabulary scale and may be of some slight assistance in other test items it is not felt that this alone could have caused this difference. [The boy's] reading on the Schonell word recognition scale confirmed previous assessments that his reading age is about thirteen to fourteen years.

It seems possible that verbal skill and the great extension of interest and general knowledge through wide reading have great effect upon ability potentials.

This need to look again at all the accepted normal standards applies too to the theories and the ideas of educationists. It was a

member of the staff of one of our biggest teacher training colleges who said to me rather sadly that he must now go back to his college and re-write all his lecture notes. Professors of education must think again about theories of reading readiness, about the mental ages when children are ready to begin reading, and of how early in life differences in symbols can be distinguished to the extent necessary for reading. When a child is interested, he can do much that is beyond him when interest is lacking.

Some teachers find it very difficult to accept the evidence of their own eyes, when things happen which through long experience they have regarded as impossible. Thus for example I have been told that—

(1) The experimental schools must be spending an excessive amount of time on reading. We have shown that this was not true and that the children were as good as ever, and even better, in other school activities.

(2) The children would not be able to read ordinary spelling. We have, however, clearly proved that no difficulty at all is found.

(3) The children read without understanding. Objective tests have shown this to be entirely false (as if a child would willingly read what he did not understand and enjoy).[1]

(4) The children would not spell properly. One must wait some years before one can say categorically of these particular children that their spelling is better. There are, however, at least three reasons why I feel sure that they will be better spellers. First, the reports of the 1870s and 1920s have been proved correct in every detail that could so far be paralleled. Those reports always say that spelling was better: it is unlikely that they will be wrong in this one respect. My second reason is based on purely *a priori* reasoning. If a child learns to spell according to rule, he is likely to remember exceptions to the rule; when he learns amid chaos without any rules he has no guide to what is right or wrong. My third reason is purely practical: most of us remember spellings because we have seen them often; generally the more we read the better we spell. (I asked a group of typists to write for me the two words "referring" and "reference." I then asked why they put two r's in the first and one

---

[1] One visitor turned up with a book on higher physics and asked whether the six-year-olds could read it. Parts were duly read faultlessly. Said the visitor triumphantly: "But they can't understand it." The headmistress properly replied: "I do not know whether you can understand it. I certainly can't, but I can read it."

in the second word. None knew the rule about the effect of the stressed syllable but all spelt the words correctly because they had read and written them often.) Most of these children are going to read hundreds, maybe thousands, more books than they would once have done and this in very impressionable years. The few who may not have learnt to read before they leave the infant school would never learn to spell by any method.[1]

Finally it has even been said that the children should not be reading the books they read and be writing as readily as they do: "It is not good for them." Surely if a child of infant age wants to read, enjoys reading, loves books, is happy reading them, wants to write without any external pressures at all—what is wrong in that, and how can it be harmful? It would be harmful to deny him the opportunity. The critics would boast joyfully if their own children were doing these things—even under pressure. It is unrealistic to complain for a hundred years that many children cannot be taught to read well and then, when the means to teach them is found, to complain that they are learning far too fast and far too readily.

The truth is that infants in these i.t.a. classes have often to be made to do other things than read. They have often to be told to close their books and go out to play in the fresh air. "Please, Miss, I want to finish the story," is a common plea at playtime. Permission to get a book from the Book Corner is the prize for doing other things. In these early years with too many visitors, timetables have often had to be revised to enable the visitors to see reading and writing. In some schools so affected physical education and number work and free activities have been moved for the day to unusual places in the timetable for the convenience of the visitors and to the disadvantage of the children. Then some visitors, unable to believe their eyes and ears, have accused us of doing reading at all times. In fact all the other activities of school have been carefully given their full allocation of time and care, despite the difficulties of accommodating visitors and often despite the children's wishes. In a class of thirty the children were asked individually what lesson each preferred. Not one replied that he liked Reading best. All the other activities of school were chosen by one or other of the children, but in a class where they cannot be kept away from books, not one single child gave as his preference Reading. Equally no child mentioned Playtime. The inference is clear. To these children Reading

[1] Cf. pp. 206–7.

is not a lesson: the idea of work is not in any way associated with it. Reading is second nature, a game, and books are toys, things to give pleasure and effortless enjoyment.

Much, of course, remains to be done. The ultimate effects of this new venture will not be revealed for a very long time. All sorts of things have to be inquired into and investigated; and the effects on personality development will occupy research workers for years. Psychologists have now to distinguish the maladjustments which have their origin in reading inability (and they are evidently many) from other maladjustments, behind which lie other and varied causes.

In the immediate future we must investigate the value of i.t.a. in special schools for children suffering under different handicaps. One of the most interesting innovations in Oldham in the school year 1963-4 is the introduction of i.t.a. into the Oldham School for the Deaf and Hard-of-Hearing. I.t.a. has seemed in the last two years particularly beneficial for children who experience little verbal communication at home, who are little listened to when they seek to communicate, and consequently have slight experience with words. It is here that we have noted an unprecedented expansion of verbal dexterity, which has roused the attention of parents apart from exciting the interest of teachers more prone to awareness of such development. It is in this very sphere that deaf and near-deaf children are handicapped by nature. For them any background of meaningful sound which can be linked with printed and written forms is entirely lacking. Language can come to them only through the senses of sight and touch. Are not therefore rationalizations of the visual forms of language likely to be even more profitable to them than to physically normal children? Blind and partially-sighted children who learn to read through the sense of touch may also be expected to find help in simplified spelling, at least in the degree to which their handicap makes the already difficult task of learning to read more difficult still. I.t.a. has been introduced this year into Oldham's School for Part-Sighted Children. Other types of handicapped children in special schools for the physically handicapped, the delicate and the educationally subnormal will be using the new medium. In various ways the potential experience of these children is limited and their communication problems accordingly greater. This work will be watched with great interest.

We have a number of immediate problems in the infant schools. The most pressing are—

(1) What sort of introductory readers are needed? Many of these children refuse very early to use reading apparatus: they want books. Obviously, the old type of reading scheme graded for word difficulty is out-of-date.

(2) How long need an introductory reading scheme be graded for progressive, for average and for slow children? Do they indeed require the same sorts of reading schemes?

(3) What books shall we give to the infants who have made the transition from i.t.a. to t.o.? At the moment we are providing books previously supplied in junior schools. It may be that these infants need the matter of these books but still need the abundant and colourful illustrations of their infant reading books. Such books are rare and may have yet to be devised. The final books of existing Reading Schemes are used by several headmistresses in their search for appropriate books. Many of these books suit the brighter children but even their stories are not "geared" to an average five-year-old's interest although he easily reads them.

(4) At what reading age is the child ready for transition? Glancing at the figures in this book, I get a general impression that children transfer themselves to t.o. naturally at a reading age of 7+. They could probably do it earlier but fluency and confidence seem by then to have been achieved by the normal child. Perhaps it does not matter. I am disposed to think that the longer the infants are reading i.t.a., in the first two years at least, the better; they are establishing great ease with and love of books.

(5) What reading material should we provide for seven- to eleven-year-olds in the junior schools? Many of these infants will already have read much (or most) of the present junior school library before they reach the junior school. Some are already reading children's classics and understanding and delighting in them.

(6) What method of selecting the appropriate secondary school course shall we use if we are confronted at the age of eleven years with a group of children who have read hundreds more books than another group, through no fault of the latter? (This could be a real headache for some educational administrators and parents.) Bright children, capable of grammar school and university performance, are obviously going to read no better when they reach their 'teens through learning by one system than through learning by another. Yet at eleven years of age the general reading of the early starters is going to be more extensive than the reading of later starters and

the background knowledge of these early starters will be potentially wider. At eleven years of age the width of knowledge of children of only average ability may clearly surpass that of very intelligent children who, learning through t.o., take much longer to become proficient readers.

Many, many slower children who would never have read with ease are going to read with enjoyment. The total of Oldham children remaining in the same schools who started this work in September 1961 may not have been large (139 in July 1962), but the fact remains that by May 1962—after less than twenty-one months—every single child could read a book. The last child began to read in May. At four to five years of age, we do not know who will be the bright ones and who the slow. If the bright ones cannot suffer, surely it is good to start all off on the new approach. The slowest would never read without it and it seems clear that the rest read more quickly with it. When I refer to quick learning, it is not that I think speed of learning of value for itself, but I am sure of its value in teaching language and in giving quick confidence and so strengthening the foundations of future success.

Even if all these gains had not been made, the new approach to reading would have been worth while in making their first months in school so much more enjoyable for little children. The brightest children might later read as well, write and spell as well, and reason as clearly whatever the system of teaching, but even for them, the favoured ones, the early months are made more interesting.

The early interest shown by young children in reading is paralleled by the interest developed in teachers. Striving to teach reading to children who find it difficult is sometimes a soul-killing job. Repetition with uninteresting books and the slow progress, often so slow as to be hard to perceive, is unrewarding and daunts many. The inability with big classes to give individual attention to weaker children accentuates the boredom. The speed with which children progress with the new spelling and the teacher's greater freedom to help the weaker while the stronger read their books, clearly increases the interest and zeal of teachers. As with the children in their classes, so with teachers, early progress promotes keenness and efficiency. Parents are often unaware of the phenomenal progress of their children by earlier standards and take the children's ability to read as a matter of course, except where there is an older child in the family or next door. Then we get comparisons and sometimes ex-

pressions of regret that the new medium was not in use earlier. Parents have often noticed their children's extraordinary vocabulary and in the case of backward children the sudden gain in skill and liking for school. One headteacher said that so unaccustomed to writing were many of her children's parents that they would rather take a day off work to visit the school than write a simple letter. It is particularly gratifying when one is able to catch the interest of parents, themselves largely illiterate, and to excite in them an enthusiasm for and confidence in the school.

While I have quoted figures, what I have had to say is not put in the main into columns of statistics. I am neither mathematician nor statistician. That presentation will be done in due course with all the caution of the research worker. I have tried to tell the story in a manner easily understood by anyone who has little regard for or little patience with figures. The reader may omit all the figures and the graphs and the story will still be complete.

I have tried to state factually what has happened in Oldham schools where the new alphabet has been in use. My facts, figures and stories have been supplied to me by the teachers doing the job or come from my personal experiences while visiting schools. Assessments may vary from one individual to another but all these teachers who gave me information can make a comparison with their own past experience, and however much individual judgments and standards vary, the universal approval which has been forthcoming is convincing. I shall probably be criticized for not mentioning the difficulties and the problems. I have, however, gone from school to school in Oldham and in many other areas where i.t.a. is used and asked to be told about misgivings and difficulties and nobody can tell me of any. Never have I seen educational theory so completely and so quickly realized in educational practice. Maybe difficulties have yet to be discovered: they will have to be great indeed to outweigh the gains.

APPENDIX I

The Writing of the i. t. a. Characters

Care must be taken to copy the printed i.t.a. forms when writing and the teacher should not lapse into script forms like *f* instead of f. Script *a* and the looped *l* seem particularly difficult to drop. It is important in the early stages to preserve a consistent form. The child will ordinarily be using the traditional alphabet by the time that he is joining letters in fast script writing.

The letters are all easily formed and teachers will readily evolve their own ways of writing them. Here are some suggestions which have been found effective:

a   One continuous stroke or two strokes adding the belly separately after completing the downstroke

æ   One continuous stroke

f   Two strokes (cf. crossing a t)

ɛɛ   Three strokes

k   Two strokes

ie   One unlifted stroke, down and return on the lower half of the i

œ   One continuous stroke, beginning at the mid-point of the O where the loop of the e begins

ʒ   Care and practice are needed. One stroke is possible and easy for some, but many find it simpler to make the top stroke twice, forward and back. This fixes the line and lends itself naturally to righthanded writing. Some make the top and bottom strokes in parallel first and then join the two either upwards or downwards.

ue   An unlifted stroke is easy, repeating the lower half of the straight stroke in the u

ȼh   Two strokes are needed

ʧh ʧh   Three strokes are used by most writers, the crossing being the last normal crossing of the t. Some use two strokes crossing the t and continuing with the h

ʃh   Opinions differ. Some start at the bottom of the s but most find two strokes easier

au   One stroke is easy but some prefer to add the loop of the a after completion of the whole

ŋ   Most people find the best outline comes by going up again from the end of the n to make the g. One stroke only is needed whether this is done or whether one continues the circle of the g in the same direction as the second downstroke of the n

APPENDIX II
Teaching Method

When I talk to teachers about i.t.a., I am often asked how to apply it in schools. My advice is the same as I gave when the first schools began to use i.t.a. in Oldham: do as you have always done.

Nobody has yet had time to explore the application of various teaching techniques to the use of the new alphabet and, judging from past history of classroom practice, there will arise many different ways of doing the job. Every teacher finds by practice what methods best suit her and at this early stage in the use of i.t.a. it would be arrogant on anybody's part to say this or that is the method for teaching it.

The important thing is not to be afraid of i.t.a. because it is new—be neither afraid to write it (you cannot be significantly wrong) nor to handle it (you will find that your accustomed methods bring better results than before). Watch yourself when you write the characters and copy the printed forms: these are the forms the child knows. Give the letters their correct sounds when you name them. One little boy of four after five weeks in school left his teacher a note with an article which he put on her desk. The note said, "Kepit." This phenomenal initiative in writing so early delighted his teacher but betrayed the fact that she had unthinkingly been calling e ee, which can be applied only to ee.

There is almost universally a settling-in period and sometimes preparatory speech work, chatting about things around the classroom and the school, or "preparing for reading," e.g. by familiarizing children with the characters in their primers. This rarely nowadays goes beyond the first few weeks. It used often to be longer but usually children are beginning to read by i.t.a. by the second half of their first term.

Many teachers first introduce children to print by showing them the sentence affixed to the large picture, of which there may be a dozen or so. The first real step in reading is usually "whole-word" recognition with flash cards, but almost all teachers agree that phonetics with a view to word-building comes much earlier than it used to come. Little difficulty is found in learning the initial teaching alphabet and children seem to like to start on the strong vowels æ ee ie œ ꟍ. They soon add consonants. The first letters in the chosen Reading Scheme are commonly the starting point.

"Progression" is now almost a meaningless word in relation to movement through a reading scheme. As one teacher put it: "You don't need a

scheme any more." She meant that the children did not need a scheme, of course. The teacher needs a scheme at first to see that the children get hold of the books that will help and not daunt them.

Many teachers hear each child read all the books of the Reading Scheme but the time comes early when some can have the run of the i.t.a. Library Corner and then they need only be heard from time to time and the teacher can concentrate on aiding the slower children. With the swifter it will be noted that their silent reading is far more efficient than their reading aloud and that, while simplified spelling does not get in the way of enunciation like the older spelling, it imposes a mild barrier. Reading aloud regularly is still necessary to test the child's ability, to reward his natural pride in his achievement and to hear his articulation, which itself may need correction.

Since teachers have begun to use i.t.a., they appear to have varied their older methods gradually but not all have followed the same lines of evolution. One teacher has almost discarded apparatus—the blackboard, the card and the book are sufficient: but not all by any means do this. Another teacher soon takes her bright children off the Reading Scheme, and encourages them to read story books. She says that when they have successfully dealt with polysyllables the Reading Scheme has little further value for them. It is important that children should not be bored and that their self-confidence and reading should both be increased. Teachers will at first be surprised by what these young children can understand. Early opportunity should be given to write. As soon as the child is reading easy sentences, most teachers provide this opportunity.

Do not rush into traditional print. The children are happy to know that theirs is an easier form and that some day they will read grown-ups' books. Many will do this surreptitiously but let them read some 300 or 350 i.t.a. books at least. The children must learn to "skim the tops" of lines of print. The old standards of reading with hesitations between words are not good enough. There must be speed and accuracy: the children must not be "seeing words." One little girl of five years expostulated, without pause between the words, as she looked at a well-known Reading Test: "Tree, little, milk, egg, book—it doesn't make sense." That is the attitude to be expected.

The vitally important thing is complete confidence and the realization that a book is enjoyable. Remember too that when a child makes the transition he can still read i.t.a. and will sometimes want to do so, for instance, when new attractive books arrive. I am sure most teachers will allow this without qualm. The time will come at a later age when i.t.a. books are no more and he sees only traditional spelling. Then he will learn to write and spell traditionally.

Traditional spelling will begin to appear more and more in written

work as more t.o. books are read. At first both spellings will appear mixed haphazardly—both are right so long as the correct pronunciation is known.

There will be a time when some children are reading traditionally while others are still using the initial teaching medium. Different blackboards or different coloured chalks and the children grouped appropriately near the writing intended for them is the usual answer to this situation.

You will not need to order a copy of each primer for every child in the class. The children will soon be on different books and a few of each of the earlier and very few of the later books in the Reading Scheme will be wanted. Many, many Library Corner books will be wanted—mainly one copy of each. A headmistress, requisitioning t.o. books for her second-year infants, told me how delightful it was not to be ordering sets of class books, just single copies of "joyous books."

I have said more than once that teachers need have no fears of i.t.a.: I repeat that. When the experiments in 1961 first began, two-day courses were provided for the first teachers. In 1962 we in Oldham reduced the length of the training to one day and in 1963 we trained our new teachers in half a day. In fact, training is scarcely needed: any teacher can teach herself in an hour or two. Courses for teachers are essentially confidence injectors.

APPENDIX III

The School Experiments of 1914–1921

NOTES TO CHAPTER VIII

The following extracts are from reports collected in Pamphlet No. 7 of the Simplified Spelling Society, *The Best Method of Teaching Children to Read and Write* (Pitman, 1924). Letters refer to Chapter VIII.

A. Clepington School, Dundee. Extract from a report by Mr. R. Jackson, Lecturer in Phonetics, Dundee Training College, 1915.

> On the day of my visit the Head Master and the Infant Mistress brought together the subjects of experiment. At this time they had been fourteen months at School, during the first ten months of which their instruction in reading had been given through Simplified Spelling. A book in the conventional spelling was put into their hands, and each child read a passage, after which he or she was given certain words to spell. No child was passed over in either reading or spelling.
>
> Next, about the same number of children, who had been nineteen months at school, and who had been taught in the usual way, were brought in and read the same passages from the same reading book, and were also given words to spell.
>
> On the whole, the reading of the two sections, as regards the naming of words, was very similar. Words of irregular spelling that gave trouble to the first section gave trouble to the second section also. The pupils who had had only four months' experience of the vagaries of the ordinary spelling were quite as good as those who had had nineteen months.
>
> Such difference between the two sets tested as revealed itself was found in the results of the speech-training. The pupils of the Simplified Spelling section had a freer, clearer, easier pronunciation, and a more distinct and clear-cut articulation, than those of the other section.
>
> To sum up: The Simplified Spelling pupils, taken at random from a group of new pupils, after ten months' instruction in Simplified Spelling and four months in the conventional spelling, could read the latter as well and spell as well as the pupils who had worked at it exclusively for nineteen months. The balance of advantage was altogether on the side of the children who had been taught on the new lines. They had had a better training in the relations of sound and symbol; they had acquired a better and a more natural utterance and expression, and had laid a more solid foundation for the subsequent cultivation of good, clear speech. This too, under conditions which the headmaster and the infant mistress responsible for the experiment did not consider altogether favourable.

B. Extract from a paper read by Miss McConochie, infant mistress at Clepington School, Dundee, to the meeting of the Simplified Spelling Society, January, 1916.

It (Simplified Spelling) has certainly great possibilities and advantages. In the first place, the saving of time is very considerable. The pupils learn the short vowel sounds, the consonants, and the nine combinations of vowels which make up the sum of the long vowel sounds. That preliminary work completed, and the initial difficulty of putting the sounds together to form words overcome, the work proceeds smoothly. The pupils have absolute confidence in their symbols, and this faith is not disturbed by the unexpected appearance of exceptional words, multiplicity of symbols for one sound or of sounds for one symbol. There is increased fluency in reading, as there is no hesitancy, and it is found that quite ambitious words can be introduced into the reading lesson. The advantage resulting from this is that the child is enabled to possess an enlarged vocabulary, an aid to self-expression both orally and in writing. As teachers in elementary schools know, pupils from poorer homes come to school with a very limited vocabulary indeed; and much of that even may have to be unlearned. In fact, they have almost to learn a new language, and any method which is helpful in this matter is very valuable. The system also admits of more time being spent on drill in phonic work, resulting in greater purity of sound and clearness of articulation.

C. Extract from a report by Mr. R. Loggie, headmaster, and Miss J. D. Paten, infant mistress at Dens Road School, Dundee.

In June, 1917, at the end of six months, children who had been in regular attendance were able to read in Simplified Spelling as difficult matter as is usually read by pupils at the end of the Infant School course. Children who returned to School after five or six weeks' absence—there had been an outbreak of measles—could take their part in class work almost as if they had not been absent at all. They had forgotten neither the symbols nor their values.

It would appear, therefore, from the present results, that the adoption of Simplified Spelling would lead, in reading and speech training, to a great saving of time in the first two years of school attendance.

D. Extract from a report by Miss Edith Law and Miss Edith Luke, teachers at Morgan Academy, Dundee, 1917.

All the children, about eighty in number, beginning school life in August, were made the subject of an experiment in teaching reading on the principles embodied in the First Reader in Simplified Spelling. By the end of the month the children knew the sounds and their symbols, and were putting them together in simple words. Very soon these words were used in the formation of easy sentences, which were eagerly read by the children. The advantage of the method was very apparent at this stage, for instead of sentences such as, "He is up," "Do I go so?" etc., the children were reading sentences which both interested and amused them, and at the same time afforded material for systematic speech training.

At the end of six months the first Reader had been read, and the transition stage was entered upon. A simple Fairy Tale Reader was put into the children's hands, and the ease with which they sounded unfamiliar and unphonetically spelt words was astonishing. In previous years this book has not been attempted till the children have been eight or nine months at school.

In teaching to read by this method, much of the drudgery and monotony of many of the pages of Infant Primers have been avoided. During the initial and most difficult stages of learning to read, each symbol has only one sound,

and the children have nothing to worry and confuse them in the way of irritating exceptions, so that reading very soon becomes a real pleasure to them. During this period their vocabulary rapidly increases, owing to the abundant practice they have in reading practically all words within their power to understand. To this is due their greatly increased fluency and ease of utterance, when they reach the stage of reading ordinary English spelling.

E. The report from which these extracts and information are taken was written by Mr. William Bennett, headmaster of the Bridge of Allan Intermediate School. The assistant teachers concerned with him in the work were Miss Mary Bain and Miss Elizabeth Bain, 1924.

F. The headmistress of Honeywell Road School, Battersea, whose work is reported was Miss Walsh. Her assistants were Miss Parker and Miss Renwick. See also Simplified Spelling Society Minutes, 17th October, 1918.

G. This headmistress was Miss McLeish. She reported in 1923:

> This reproduction has been of great value in enabling us to detect hitherto unsuspected speech defects and inaccuracies. The common use of v for th in mother, father, etc., the substitutions or omissions of sounds, as taiboo for taibl, hanz for hands, flourz for flouerz, cau for coal, widoe for windoe, have been revealed; also inaccuracies due to the yet undeveloped speech of little children as chesh ov drauz for chest ov drauerz, sisd for sister, fendh for fender, among others. Other interesting inaccuracies have appeared in jrum, for drum, chrumpet for trumpet, chrain for train. In all these cases the ability of the child to represent his own speech accurately has been demonstrated, even in the case of jrum and chrumpet, to an appreciation of the voiced j and the voiceless ch, which in his speech were substituted before r for voiced d and voiceless t.

Once having detected these inaccuracies, the correction is a comparatively easy matter.

H. Mr. E. Sykes was headmaster of York Road School, Leeds, in 1918.

J. The teacher at Hetton-le-Hole was Miss A. E. Thompson. Her report concluded:

> The results can be summed up as follows. The children can now read fluently, with the exception of two or three children, and a great number of the former read very fluently indeed, from books in the ordinary spelling, the transition stage having been more than successfully passed over. And these results, in spite of the fact that there have been many drawbacks on account of children's absence from diseases, more than ordinary. And another important side, not to be neglected, is the amount of time saved on the part of the children and teacher—less drudgery for the teacher, more interesting work for the children—who find they can read sooner; even if the reading seems different from the ordinary, this does not matter to them, as at this age the child is only concerned with wanting to read, not with how the words appeal to him. There is a real saving of time which can be much more profitably spent. In just over a month we have gone through the course, which by the other spelling takes at least a year. The average age of the class is six years.

K. Miss R. Lobel, headmistress of Ellerslea Private School, Victoria Park, Manchester, 1924.

L. Miss M. Brook, headmistress of the Thomas Stretton Infant School, Hull, 1924.

M. Mr. William Mellers, headmaster of Bodenham School, Hereford, 1924.

N. Miss M. Warrener, headmistress of Southall Street School, Manchester, 1924.

Explanatory Memorandum to the Simplified Spelling Bill of 1953.[1]

The Bill requires the Minister of Education and the Secretary of State for Scotland jointly to institute researches with a view to reducing and, if possible, eliminating the widespread inability of the children of Great Britain to read their own language. The recent report of the Minister of Education discloses that 30 per cent of the children who in 1948 were fifteen years old, were classed as "backward readers."

The research to be carried out may be general and must be particular. The Association or Associations designated for this purpose by the Ministers may examine in general any methods likely to improve the teaching of reading, and must in particular examine the assistance to children likely to result from the use (in the earlier stages of teaching reading) of matter printed in a spelling which uses the letters of the alphabet consistently and from a transfer, in due course, to the reading of matter printed in the existing orthography. The ability to read matter printed in the existing orthography with fluency and understanding will be the test for determining the efficacy of all the methods investigated by, and the recommendations, if any, of the designated body.

Safeguards are provided to protect the freedom of choice of parent and teacher and the well-being of the child.

A report on the investigations is to be submitted to the two Ministers. If favourable to a method using a new spelling the report would include a description of the particular new system of spelling recommended. The report, including any recommendations, is to be laid before Parliament.

The Ministers may adopt the system of spelling recommended, either as it stands, or subject to any alterations they consider necessary, or, alternatively, may substitute some other new system of spelling. In either case the system finally adopted is to be embodied in a scheme which will be subject to affirmative resolution by both Houses of Parliament. The scheme will also cover the methods for facilitating the teaching of reading using that new system.

The long-standing freedom to adopt such methods of teaching as they consider best is, however, additionally reserved to Education Authorities.

[1] See p. 84.

The money required for the investigation will have to be found by the designated Association. There is, however, at least one Association in receipt of a grant from the Minister of Education for educational research and the Bill provides that in the event of such a body being designated by the Ministers the payment of the grant would be subject to the condition that the research was carried out.

APPENDIX V

Note on Spelling

The two letters that follow seem to be an indication that we need have no qualms about the future spelling of these children. Susan and Gerald, who wrote these letters, were respectively six years two months and six years three months old. A visitor who had heard them read sent them books as a gift. Following the receipt of the books the two children asked their teacher for an envelope and only then did the letters come to light. Not only is the spelling noteworthy but also the language, for example, "I said in my mind", and, of course, the initiative and readiness of these children in writing letters of thanks.

Fitton Hill Infant School,
South Croft,
OLDHAM
November 18th

Dear Mr. and Mrs. Pogson,

Thank you very much for those beautiful books that you sent for me and Gerald they are so nice I have read some pages of one of them and one of the storys are about a family who went for a holiday on a house boat and some of the pages were coulord in with crayons and the uther book was very funny, and Gerald has read his story all the way thro it and I am surprised at Gerald he fineshed at dinner time, and he read it really quickly.

With X X X love from Susan.

Fitton Hill Infant School,
South Croft,
OLDHAM
November 18th

Dear Mrs. Pogson,

Thank you very very much for the book that you sent me I like it very much I read it through and I thouht about it and said in my mind the people who sent it must have been very kind to send me this book.

With love from Gerald.

Susan's spelling "coulord" for "coloured" is especially interesting. Clearly she remembered that the vowel sounds were spelt with "o" and "ou." This could be an indication of what I have suggested on page 188, that, when they have learnt according to rule, children are likely to be alert to exceptions. The fact that Susan put "ou" in the first syllable and "o" in the second shows how completely upsetting is the chaos of English spelling. Given that "o" and "ou" should be used, Susan's reversal of the usual order quite logically accords with the sound. She remembered the strange spelling and was, even so, misled by the second stage of spelling inconsistency.

The two children who wrote these letters had made the transition to the reading of traditional print just twelve months earlier. Six months after writing these letters in 1963 their punctuation as well as their spelling had become wellnigh perfect.

ADDENDUM, April, 1964

While I have been reading the proofs of this book, several headteachers have told me that the third year of this experiment has produced clear indications that the spelling of the children who started on i.t.a. in 1961 excels any hitherto known. For instance, in one class of 35 unstreamed children, the *average* number of words correctly spelt on the Schonell Graded Worded Spelling Test A was 54·5 out of 100. The smallest number of words correctly spelt by any child was 31, the highest 94. The average age of the children was 6 years 7 months. Teachers who know the test must marvel.

The average Spelling Age is 10 years 9 months and half the class coped unhesitatingly with words like "through, cough, daughter, search" and very many of the children with words such as "affectionately, anxious, mechanical, courteous," etc.

INDEX